Between Sovereignty and Integration

Jonathan P. G. Bach

A publication of the Center on Transatlantic Foreign
and Security Policy Studies,
Freie Universität Berlin, Department of Political Science

Between Sovereignty and Integration

German Foreign Policy and National Identity after 1989

Jonathan P. G. Bach

LIT VERLAG

St. Martin's Press, New York

First published in Germany by

LIT VERLAG

Dieckstr. 73 D-48145 Münster

Die Deutsche Bibliothek – CIP-Einheitsaufnahme

Between sovereignty and integration : German foreigns policy and national identity / Jonathan Paul Gregory Bach. – Hamburg : LIT, 1999
  (Forschungsberichte internationale Politik; 23.)
  ISBN 3-8258-3869-2

NE: GT

First published in the United States of America 1999 by

ST. MARTIN'S PRESS, INC.
Scholary and Reference Division,
175 Fifth Avenue,
New York,N.Y. 10010

ISBN: 0-312-21922-9

Library of Congress Cataloging-in-Publication Data

Bach, Jonathan P. G.
  Between sovereignty and integration : German foreign policy and national identity after 1989. / Jonathan Paul Gregory Bach.
    p. cm.
  Includes bilbliographical references and index.
  ISBN: 0-312-21922-9
  1. Germany–Foreign relations–1990- 2. Germany–History-
-Unification, 1990. 3. Nationalism–Germany. 4. Liberalism-
-Germany. 5. Sovereignty. I. Title.
  DD290.3.B33   1999
  327.43–dc21   98-29183
                                                            CIP

© 1999 LIT VERLAG

Printed in Germany

Foreword and Acknowledgments

This book fuses diverse interests in international relations theory and modern German intellectual history and politics, especially foreign policy. As a student during the Cold War, I wondered how political processes made situations "normal" which could otherwise be considered quite absurd— from the Berlin Wall to the nuclear weapons policy of "mutually assured destruction." The sudden end of the East-West conflict dislodged decades of rigid assumptions, and offered a unique historical opportunity to observe the recreation of political foundations in both parts of Europe. Within these larger events, German unification brought with it disorientation about its newly found, yet ill-defined, national identity. The wars in the Gulf and in Yugoslavia made coming to terms with Germany's new incarnation all the more difficult by raising the question of the appropriate use of the German military. The 1995 parliamentary debates on the first use of German troops in a combat situation since 1945—to the former Yugoslavia, which Germany had occupied fifty years earlier—presented an excellent locus for examining the interplay of history, identity, language, and politics in the new Germany and beyond.

The following investigation began as a dissertation in the Department of Political Science at the Maxwell School of Citizenship and Public Affairs at Syracuse University. Prior to commencing my studies at Syracuse, I spent the fascinating unification year of 1990/91 at the Center on Transatlantic Foreign and Security Policy at the Free University of Berlin. The Center has generously included this book in their series on international politics, edited by Ingo Peters, for which I remain deeply obliged. I also extend gracious thanks to Lit Verlag, especially Veit Hopf, and to St. Martin's Press for publishing this work.

It is with pleasure that I gratefully acknowledge the people and institutions whose manifold forms of support enabled the completion of this work. I had the good fortune to carry out empirical research as a visiting fellow at the Institute for Peace Research and Security Studies at the University of Hamburg (IFSH) during 1995. The entire staff of the Institute was benevolent, considerate, and made me sad to leave; they have my heartfelt gratitude and appreciation. Hans-Joachim Giessmann was particularly magnanimous in helping me take advantage of this opportunity. Jacek Rulkowski, then of the German Society for Foreign Policy (DGAP), offered indispensable assistance and friendship. Also in Germany, Kati Bahn, Thomas Bauer, Andreas Eickelkamp, Hans-Arthur Falkenrath, Burkhard Freitag, Hajo and Petra Giessmann, Joanna Haiduk, Magarditsch Hatschikjan, Veit Hopf, Matthias Karadi, Ingo Peters, Susanne Peters, Franzis Stich, and Heinz Gärtner in Vienna, among many others, provided succor of myriad kinds. Very special thanks are due all the persons in Bonn who took the time to talk with me about this project. The Center for European Studies at Harvard University has kindly provided an eminently hospitable environment in which to revise the manuscript, and to think beyond it.

Any errors or faults in the work are, of course, mine alone. Any insights are the product of fruitful interaction with many persons. I owe Katalin Fábián more than I can express. To my professors at Syracuse I remain indebted, especially to G. Matthew Bonham, Fred Frohock, John Nagle, Naeem Inayatullah, Mark Rupert, John Agnew, Linda Alcoff, Mehrzad Bourejerdi and Lily Ling. Special thanks to Michael Shapiro. My friends deserve gratitude for their intellectual, moral and immoral support, especially Jim Josefson, Scott Solomon, Judith Poxon, Lakshmi Srinivasan, Marian Paules, and Katerina Galacatos. Yukiko Koga encouraged, assisted and suffered through the preparation of this manuscript in ways too multitudinous to enumerate. Finally, Robert and Suzanne Bach, my parents, deserve the richest thanks for their unflagging dedication and confidence throughout this academic endeavor. This book is dedicated to my grandmother, Eveline Gordon, whose courage, compassion, and gentle confidence provides a model for us all. In einer guten Stunde...!

Table of Contents

8

Introduction

The catchwords "national identity" and "international security" increased in caché following the end of the Cold War in 1989/90 as "identities" began to be rediscovered and recreated across Europe in the wake of the Soviet Bloc's demise. For the major schools of thought in the study of International Relations, "identity" and "security" tend to be approached as variables in a complex causal relationship. Yet viewing identities and policies as variables tends to shift attention away from the *processes* of symbiotic interaction. Through the prism of foreign policy, this book explores how the concepts of "national identity" and "international security" shed light on each other as mutually constitutive processes. Foreign policy, as the locus for defining and implementing international security, plays a significant role in the interpretation and maintenance of a nation's identity. Conversely, different understandings of national identity create different possibilities for the conceptualization and implementation of foreign policy.

My vehicle for this exploration is the united Germany of the early 1990s. Since its formal entry into the era of nation-states barely one and a quarter centuries ago, Germany has been a tumultuous example of the tension between state and nation, running the gamut of violently opposing political configurations. Defined by its division for the first forty postwar years, the abrupt re-unification of 1990 resurrected the German state while simultaneously unsettling interpretations of the German nation. The state found itself challenged with (re)creating the nation, which it represents. In this context foreign policy came to play an important identity-defining role in the search for a "normal" Germany.

The question of whether Germany, now united, is "normal" is often accompanied by an unspoken modifier: "normal enough to...." Is Germany "normal enough" to bring its laws on asylum, or immigration, into accordance with the West European "norm?" Is Germany "normal enough" to send troops to UN or NATO peacekeeping missions? Is Germany "normal enough" to have a permanent seat in the UN Security Council, or possess nuclear weapons? Two aspects of these formulations should be immediately noticeable: First, these questions assume an international standard of normalcy to which Germany can aspire. Yet the international standard of normalcy is also in flux, which automatically begs larger questions about the international system. Second, most of the issues where Germany can prove it is "normal enough" to participate are security related. This is not by chance, for the sovereign nation-state system remains the model for national identity even in an age of uncertain globalization. This model too, however, is in flux, raising at least the possibility that seekers of "normalization" might be asking the wrong questions.

They are not the wrong questions, however, in the sense that they go precisely to the raw nerve of German self-identification and its image of itself in the world: does the German past proscribe or prescribe the present, and how? Does the present make the past past? Which past are we talking about? Do we have a responsibility to the past, or for the past, or does responsibility consist of "drawing a line" under the past? What is this responsibility? From a historical, policy analysis, or general reader perspective, coming to a fuller portrait of these issues is a task of considerable importance. The post-unification debates on foreign policy in Germany allows students, scholars and other interested readers to observe firsthand the interplay of foreign policy and the search for national identity in one of the late twentieth-century's most important industrialized states.

The methodological shift from a language of interacting variables to a language of mutually constitutive processes requires a somewhat different approach than traditionally found in the toolboxes of International Relations. This work is purposely not an exercise in policy analysis, although it analyzes central policy-making processes. By undertaking a form genealogy regarding seemingly "innocent" political concepts such as "normalcy" my analysis focuses on how certain policies come to be. The book is concerned with treating foreign policy as a practice rather than as the actions of a unitary, *a priori* actor. Viewing foreign policy this way allows it to be seen as part of the process of constituting national identity by setting the boundaries of the acceptable version of the nation's story and by creating the necessary continuity between eras. These "ordering" functions necessarily choose certain paths and preclude others. Which ones are chosen, and how, are the research questions inherent in this approach. Foreign-policy makers weave narratives which legitimize particular world-views, delineate the boundaries of sovereignty, and ultimately form the justifications for concrete policy, including the deployment of military forces.

This process occurs primarily discursively in response to events and demands, material and psychological. Accordingly, the focus is on the discursive realm, affording us the opportunity to observe the emergence of positions and remind ourselves of the ambiguity, which accompanies such a process. There may indeed be an elite consensus in Germany today regarding multilat eralism, the inclusion of conflict and crisis management in military doctrine and European integration, but it emerged out of a significant uncertainty about the nature of (German) power and "responsibility." The components that make up this uncertain approach to (German) power remain extant to influence future variations of consensus.

The first chapter introduces the quandaries of united Germany–to what extent does unification represent continuity and change, and from what? The notion that Germany represents something qualitatively new is often accompanied by a subtle fear that new beginnings hide new "special paths" behind which lurk specters of historical disaster. What are the origins and 'original sins' of the German nation-state, in particular the geopolitical "trap" of German history? The current state incarnation firmly locates itself in "the West." Yet, as the ongoing debate about the role of the national socialist legacy illustrates, can agreement can be reached on the geopolitical status of today's Germany? The chapter ends by showing how unification has produced a discursive disorder within which contending foundational myths about the German state and nation emerge and vie for influence.

The second chapter lays out methodological assumptions central to this work: how narratives influence social reality. I identify four main functions of narrative: ordering, the ontological function; delimiting, the epistemological function; perpetuating, the hegemonic function; and challenging, the counter-hegemonic function. From there I address national identity, sovereignty, and foreign policy, showing how the nation-state can be understood as a discursive community and foreign policy as one of its constitutive elements. The chapter concludes with a discussion of the paradoxes of sovereignty resulting from German unification. Readers interested solely in the recent foreign policy debates may wish to start directly with chapter three.

The third and fourth chapters articulate the two main narratives of German foreign policy, which I identify here as normalist and liberal. Normalism re-articulates classic political realism to incorporate a sense of responsibility, and ultimately rests on a re-affirmation of traditional views of the nation and state, skepticism of political integration and concern about the lack of positive national identity. The liberal discourse emerges from the neo-liberal tradition, working out its world-view through the twin concepts of the "societal world" and "world domestic policy."

Sentiments broached in both discourses take center stage in the major foreign policy debate of the early 1990s, the role of the German military. Known as the "out-of-area debate," referring to whether German forces were constitutionally permitted to partake in multilateral peacekeeping operations outside NATO territory, these debates demonstrate the centrality of German identity to foreign policy and provide examples of discourses "in action" on the floor of parliament. Chapters five and six focus on these debates. Chapter five situates the debates historically and maps out the way in which the key concepts of "responsibility" and "normalcy" become practical and moral imperatives. Chapter six is a discursive analysis of the particular parliamentary debates on sending German ground troops to participate in the peacekeeping mission to the former Yugoslavia sanctioned by the Dayton Peace Accord. The historic decision to send troops was the first deployment of German troops to a combat area since the end of World War Two. The final chapter reassesses the foreign policy narratives and the debates in light of the primary tension of universalism and particularism, heightened by the ambiguous role of the state caught between traditional views of sovereignty and uncertain trajectories of integration and globalization. The emerging discourse is ultimately caught in a structural paradox which restricts its encounters with others (the "foreign" in foreign policy) to versions of hierarchy or a mirror of the self.

The approach employed here embeds the practice of foreign policy in meta-theoretical questions. These questions – of identity, of self and other, of particularity and universality, and of the creation and resolution of such oppositions – lie at the core of the foreign policy debate. These questions connect our social selves, from individual actor to policy-maker to scholar. We cannot hope to come to terms with ourselves and others, and perhaps most importantly, the other in ourselves, without making room in our discussions of International Relations to include such considerations. In this spirit I hope this work is a small contribution to the study of International Relations theory, of national identity, foreign policy, and modern German politics.

1. The Eternal Return

United Germany: West Germany Writ Large?

In 1990 the Federal Republic of Germany achieved what the Hallstein doctrine of 1956 so brazenly pursued: the status of the sole representative of the German nation-state.[1] At the same time the notion of "Europe" expanded to encompass, at least rhetorically, its Eastern brethren. The rush of rhetoric from Eastern Europe about "joining Europe" left little doubt that the European Community, soon to be the European Union, assumed the *Alleinvertretungsanspruch* — the status of sole representative — of "Europe."

The revolutions of 1989 were supremely flattering to Western Europe. These were "safe" revolutions, reifying the mimetic process of modernization and democratization and long-established convictions of Northwest European innovation and Southern and Eastern imitation.[2] In the Western celebration of Eastern Europe's revolutions, Slovenian philosopher Slavoj Zizek wryly observes that, "it is as if democracy, which in the West shows more and more signs of decay and crisis and is lost in bureaucratic routine and publicity-style election campaigns, is being rediscovered in Eastern Europe in all its freshness and novelty...[Eastern Europe functions as] the point from which the West sees itself in a likable, idealized form...."[3] In the primitive dualism of the Cold War the implosion of "real existing socialism" appearing as a spontaneous wildfire consuming the dried wooden gerontocracies of Communist Europe, was *per se* a victory for capitalist Western Europe.

The feelings of validation which accompanied Western Europe's gaze toward the East were bolstered by a momentous awareness that the logic of 'an ever greater union' of Europe had been freed from the artificial barriers of ideological division. This historical opportunity, however, was tempered by the paradox that precisely the artificial division of Europe provided the impetus for unprecedented integration. Euphoria was mixed with consternation as the relative comfort of a community of 12 European states suddenly ceased to be the constellation for the future. Further economic and political integration (planned for 1992 and 1997) seemed suddenly endangered. The greatest immediate concern in 1989 was that West Germany, the pillar of European integration, would sacrifice European unity for national unity. Barely muted

---

1 For the essential text of the Hallstein doctrine see Chapter 5, Document 11 in Schweitzer et al., 1995: 127. On competing claims to be the sole representative of "Germany" see Lemke, 1992.

2 On democratization trends see Linz, 1996.

3 Zizek, 1993: 200.

resistance toward German unification from the highest offices in Britain and France, as well as Soviet fears of renewed German power, and American concerns that a united Germany remain in NATO made the unification of Germany within the context of European integration—were it to happen at all—inescapable.[4]

The Western "victory" over communism was briefly unsettled by the fear of a united Germany undoing European unity. It was therefore profoundly reassuring to see the merging of the German Democratic Republic into the constitutional structure of West Germany; a triumphal legitimization of the Bonn Republic's system as the legal and moral heir of "Germany." The literal incorporation of East Germany into the federal structure of West Germany (following Article 26 of the Basic Law) quite naturally implies an expanded Federal Republic rather than a fundamentally new Germany rising from the emptying Soviet military bases and vacant border installations. The comforting notion of an enlarged Federal Republic also allowed for a sense of orientation among the vertiginous events of 1989. A solid majority of Germans polled after unification wanted Germany in the year 2000 to be either "like Switzerland" (40%) or "like Sweden," (27%), the two countries whose economic success and neutral political profile mirrored many West German's understanding of the Bonn Republic absent the threat of Soviet intervention.[5] Yet unification's also contained a palpable, exciting, even seductive promise of the new. Ironically, unification simultaneously solidified West Germany's "old" Western identity while creating a new basis for resolving Germany's seemingly eternal identity crisis. From the moment of its inception re-unified Germany was caught in a tension between cementing its somewhat provincial postwar identity and the intangible promise of a new beginning.

Challenges to the Integration Narrative

To view united Germany as West Germany writ large maintains the continuity of the West European integration narrative of progress and prosperity.

---

4 There has been much written on the fear of a resurgent Germany. Two German edited books – Wickert, 1990 and Trautmann, 1991– provide a good overview of fears voiced in the first few years of unification in Germany and abroad. The most famous anti-German comments were probably made by British Minister Nicholas Ridley, who saw ghosts of Hitler in Germany's unification and plans for the EU. Ridley was echoing his superior, Margaret Thatcher, who convened the infamous "Chequers" meeting in late, 1989 to debate the dangers of German reunification. French President Francois Mitterand also aired serious reservations about Germany, going so far as to meet with Gorbachev in what was widely interpreted as a move to convince the Soviet Union not to allow unification. In English see James and Stone, 1992.

5 Original poll conducted by Infratest, cited in Merkl, 1995: 6.

Postwar West Germany, in the absence of a positive national identity, had largely made this narrative its own.[6] The image of a united Germany fitting seamlessly into the scheme of an expanding union is powerful, and its power partially rests on minimizing and concealing challenges to the integration narrative, including any posed by German unification itself. Yet these challenges do exist, complicating the notion that the united Germany is merely an enlarged West Germany.

The first challenge to the integration narrative lies firmly within the social codes, the discourses, which are employed to construct and reinforce identities. On the one hand restoring the German "fatherland" is a task that relies on the language of the nation. On the other the telos of European integration relies on a post-national vision positing the transcendence of the traditional European nation-state. The simultaneous need for national and supranational integration in Germany greatly exacerbates the already existing tension between national and European identity.

A second challenge is the translation of Germany's increased size into increased influence, especially in the European Parliament.[7] Unification has shifted demographics in favor of Germany, who with 80 million inhabitants (in 1992) far exceeds France, the next most populous country. The expansion of the European Union to include Austria and most of Scandinavia, and the likely future inclusion of at least Poland, the Czech Republic and Hungary, raises concerns that, given these countries' ties to Germany, Germany could exert decisive influence over a powerful block of states in the European Union.[8] This concern about a German block in Europe stems largely from virtual German domination of foreign investment in East Central Europe, and the gravitation of the Eastern region to an attractive regional hegemon: Germany acts as Eastern Europe's advocate for membership in the European Union and NATO, is the greatest financial power, and exerts a growing cultural presence.[9]

The third challenge concerns the role of the German military. While successfully integrated into NATO and German society, the German military still operated in 1989 within the broad constraints of Germany's legacy as an aggressor nation. German troops were constitutionally forbidden from participating in operations beyond self-defense and the defense of NATO allies. The combination of the end of the Cold War with the restoration of full legal sov-

---

6 See the collection of essays in Merkl, 1995.

7 See Markovits and Reich's discussion of the German role in the EU in Markovits and Reich, 1993: 277-82. See also Merkl and Glaessner, 1993: 390-94.

8 See Stares, 1992 and Smith, Paterson, and Padgett, 1996.

9 See Bach, 1996, also Verheyen and Soe, 1993. For a look at West German-East European relations see Haberl, 1989.

ereignty made special limits on the German military seem particularly anach-ronistic. From the Gulf War onwards the call for German troops to take part in multilateral peacekeeping operations outside of the traditional NATO area have gained momentum.

Questions about the German military reflect the fourth challenge, which is the definition and use of power vis-à-vis itself and other states. Economically, West Germany was used to thinking of itself as a "power." Politically, and especially militarily, however, "power" carries negative connotations. Now Germany can consider itself—and is considered by others—to "be" a power in all of those respects. But the *use* of power is not prescribed, and it was le-gally and morally proscribed. Coming to terms with power is also a process of defining identity: Germany is a "power," but exactly what kind, and exactly what that implies, is far from clear.

On what basis then can one view Germany as an enlarged version of its Western half, and to what end? This interpretive possibility remains important as a reassuring reminder of Germany's immutable commitment to the "Atlan-tic" culture of the "evening lands" (*Abendländer*). The postwar institutions symbolize the much-touted values of the "West": solidarity, cooperation, pro-gress, technology, democracy, and prosperity. If Germany is unquestionably bound to the West, then the rude excesses of the past remain anomalies of an unenlightened era whose quick-fix cruelty had temporarily overpowered the civilized impulses of a quiescent culture.

Politicians are, however, quick to admit that united Germany has funda-mentally new responsibilities which require abandoning postwar conceptions of a provincial pseudo-pacifism. This entails a double move: only by situating united Germany in the predictable paradigm of "Western values" can calls for new responsibilities and new roles avoid the penumbra of Germany's past. The assumption of new responsibilities in the context of "Atlantic civiliza-tion" defines the process of "normalization" at its most basic: "Normaliza-tion" is both the establishment of Germany as a great power (continuity with the past status) and Germany as an equal player (if not *primus inter pares*) among the leading Western powers at the beginning of the twenty-first cen-tury (the embodiment of something qualitatively new).

Westbindung: Antidote to the Fear of Eternal Return of the Same?

This desired synthesis—Germany as a great *Western* power—represents the hope that Germany can shake the shadow of the Nazi era. George Santayana's famous aphorism about the perils of forgetting the past is a motto of sorts for German political culture since World War II. The dream of Germany as an accepted and admired Western democracy contrasts with the nightmare of cultural determinism, the eternal return of the Nazis, themselves signifiers for a barbaric cultural Mr. Hyde lurking behind the enlightened Dr. Jeckyl of Goethe, Kant, and Beethoven.

The fear of an "unmasterable past" suffuses culture and politics, caught between the Scylla of repression and the Charibdis of recognition. From the 1979 controversy surrounding the US made-for-TV film "Holocaust, through Ronald Reagan's 1985 visit to the Bitburg Cemetery, where SS soldiers lay buried, to the 1996 reception of the American political scientist Daniel Goldhagen, the past remains present, despite repeated calls for the past to pass.[10] Goldhagen's controversial work on the allegedly unique nature of German anti-semitism among its European counterparts and its concomitant telos in the Holocaust committed by, as the title of his book states, "Hitler's Willing Executioners," is a prime example of how the nightmare of the eternal return to Nazism remains present. The reaction from the media and the public was overwhelmingly welcoming despite admonishments from established historians about the book's methodology, claims and assumptions.[11]

Fear of Germany falls under two broad categories: fear that there is an essentialized Germanic character prone to totalitarian tendencies, and fear that German history makes it geopolitically fickle, a power-in-the-middle whose alliances represent tactics, not values. Goldhagen's book evokes fears of the former (although he would decry such an over-simplistic summation). Fear of the latter is evidenced by the aforementioned resistance to German unification on the (unfounded) grounds that Germany might place national considerations above European integration, or might leave NATO in order to achieve unification. This fear of Germany mollifying the Soviet Union/Russia in pursuit of unification is not new. The Stalin Note of 1952, where Stalin sought German unification at the price of neutrality, fueled exactly such fears (although Germany had no intention of taking that offer seriously). Germany's efforts at *Ostpolitik* were always slightly suspicious for its allies, and the originally pejorative term "Genscherism" in the 1980s referred to fears that Genscher would pursue good relations with the East at the expense of the West.[12]

The two fears are complimentary: German national aspirations are feared because of the essentialized image of the German nation as fearsome if left alone. Germany's worst-case scenario is a "special path" (*sonderweg*) which leads it away from the values of the West (and presumable precludes any alli-

---

10 On cultural and political consequences of the unmasterable past see Postone, 1993. On Reagan's visit to Bitburg see Hartmann, 1986.

11 See Goldhagen, 1996. On his reception in Germany see, among others, the series in *Die Zeit* September 6, 12, 13, 21 and 24, 1996.

12 On *Ostpolitik* see Ash, 1993, and on Genscherism and its shift from anathema to laudable see Szabo, 1990.

ance except those based on self-interest) toward a rejuvenation of German nationalism, with its attendant specter of aggression and war. Fear of Germany treading down a "special path" is a guiding geopolitical element of modern German history.[13] Accordingly, there is a geopolitical solution: the key to a peaceful future is to overcome Germany's position in the middle of competing political and economic systems. This addresses both fears, absorbing specious arguments about a totalitarian German character and more serious arguments about the negative historical construction of German national identity based on its position in the middle. Binding Germany to a system of other powers is thought to prevent any dangerous elements (such as may be) from leading Germany down a special path. At the same time integration necessary for precisely such an act of binding can transform the collective identity of Germany away from its geopolitical problematic. This, in a sense, was the "task" of NATO and the European Economic Community—to bind Germany to the West as an answer to the "German Problem."[14]

Securing Germany in the West is an antidote to the fear of eternal return because it promises a solution to Germany's famed *Mittellage*, or position in the middle of Europe, its geopolitical "trap."[15] Although first articulated by nineteenth century geopoliticians, the geopolitical trap reflects more than the spatial ontologies of imperial geographers. It is an expression of the pre-war territorial ambiguity of the German nation, and the cultural ambiguity which accompanies it. "Germany?" no less than Goethe asks in his aphorism entitled *The German Empire* , "But where does it lie? I don't know how to find that land; where the scholarly begins, the political ends."[16]

Many tensions built into the ambiguous and often tumultuous transformation of Germany into a modern nation-state remain relevant today: was Germany a fundamentally Western culture, retarded in its development by the Thirty Years War and prodded into modernity by Napoleon's occupation, or was it fundamentally non-Western, its modern identity forged in dialectical resistance to Napoleon and through rejection of the French and English experiments with parliaments and fraternity?[17] This question about Germany's ontological orientation has a geopolitical correlate: did Germany's precarious

---

13 On the German "Special Path" see Grebing, 1986 and also Bracher, 1982. For a more recent overview in English see Kühnl, 1997.

14 Of course this is the focus of Lord Ismay's infamous quip about NATO keeping the Russians out, the Americans in, and the Germans down, in that order.

15 This term takes its cue from John Agnew's "territorial trap." See Agnew, 1994a. See also chapter 2 in Dijkink, 1996.

16 "Deutschland? Aber wo liegt es? Ich weiß das Land nicht zu finden; Wo das gelehrte beginnt, hört das politische auf." In Goethe, 1986: 179.

17 See Dann, 1994; Gruner, 1993. See also Mosher, 1998.

position between the Russian and French Empires condemn it to a buffer zone between East and West, or to a fickle player of allegiances, now Eastern, now Western in orientation? Is Germany a bulwark against the decadence of the West, or a purveyor of Western religion, technology and philosophy to the Eastern kingdoms? The 'geopolitical trap' of the German state laid the basis for its (in)famous primacy of foreign policy (*Primat der Aussenpolitik*), which in turn provided the framework for addressing and re-solving questions of identity. Let us therefore begin our exploration of German identity and foreign policy by interrogating the concept of the geopolitical trap.

Origins and Original Sins: The "Geopolitical Trap."

A CULTURE-NATION AT THE TABLE OF NATION-STATES

The concept of "trap" arose from the particular political constellation of Europe during the rise of the nation-state. As the Nineteenth Century became the apex of this phenomenon, the "dual revolution" of French political and English industrial transformation became the standard prerequisites for the nation-state emerging from aristocratic torpor.[18] New classes were sought as bearers of meaning for a new era of dark satanic mills and unprecedented popular protest. Adam Smith's entrepreneurs and Danton's masses, Hegel's bureaucrats and Marx's working classes illuminated new sources of political power as the old order eroded. Yet while Britain and France acquired the archetypal contours of the modern nation-state, Germany remained a jumble of three hundred fiefdoms and city states in a web of allegiances—running the gamut from Hapsburg Austria to East Prussian Königsberg—under the anomalous appellation of the Holy Roman Empire.[19]

The patchwork quilt of Holy Roman Empire encouraged the German states' deviation from the spatial development of its Western neighbors. Many principalities lacked projectable power, and those empires who amassed real power—the Hapsburgs and the Hohenzollern— had difficulty extending their grip exclusively over the diverse German-speaking territory. The vast flat fields of the East, North, and West made for difficult borders, and even on the far side of the Southern and Southeastern mountains lived German speaking peoples. The absence of strictly demarcated (or demarcatable) territory gave rise to the notion of Germany as a "culture-nation," where identity resides in

---

18 See Hobsbawm, 1962 on the concept of the dual revolution.

19 A parody of college exams once quite aptly asked a mock history question: 'the Holy Roman Empire was neither Holy, nor Roman, nor an Empire. Discuss.'

language and culture, not in the shape or nature of the state as a political institution.[20]

France and England touted their ability to recognize truly universal elements for governing—rational thinking, representation, constitutionalism (in France), and natural rights. Yet the enlightened insights of the French Revolution came to Germany via Napoleon's cavalry, and the German reaction to France's invasion is arguably the source of the continuing geographic-ideological identity crisis within Germany: Modern German nationalism was begotten in the mixture of admiration and loathing for the French Revolution. The culture-nation became an anti-French, and by extension anti-Western, rallying site.

The humiliating and destructive French occupation of German lands, not long following the flowery rhetoric of the French Revolution, solidified anti-Western elements in the incipient nation-building process.[21] Already in 1791, Wilhelm von Humboldt rejected French rational constitutionalism in favor of the "specific historicity of each people," a development in which historian Alexander Schwann sees "the first national, simultaneously somewhat anti-Western, anti-rationalistic component in German liberal thinking...."[22] Resistance against France became the call to national awakening. "A people becomes the People (Volk) through wars and through fighting them together. He who does not share in the current war [against France] can through no decree become incorporated into the German People" wrote Fichte, whose messianistic writings pitted the superiority of culture against the baseness of politics.[23] If this was the birth of the modern German nation, it was born in hate, a glorious hate which gave meaning to life. Already in 1803 one of the towering inventors of the German nation, Ernst Moritz Arndt, wrote:

> I want hate against the French, not just for this war, I want it for a long time, I want it for ever. Then will Germany's borders be safe without artificial defenses, then will the People (Volk) always have a unifying point, whenever the restless thieving neighbors want to overrun us. This hate glows as the

---

20 The notion of a "culture nation" was problematic from the beginning because the ethnic and linguistic notion of German cultural belonging overlapped the existing national boundaries. See Dann, 1994: 36-38.

21 For the influence of the Napoleonic wars on the major intellectual progenitors of the German nation see Kohn, 1949a and Kohn, 1949b.

22 Schwan, 1987: 74.

23 Johann Gottfried Fichte, quoted in Giesen, 1991: 302ff. The original reads: "Durch die Kriege und durch gemeinschaftliches Durchkämpfen derselben wird ein Volk zum Volke. Wer den gegenwärtigen Krieg nicht mitführen wird, wird durch kein Dekret dem deutschen Volke einverleibt werden können."

religion of the German people, as a holy illusion in all hearts and preserves
us always in our loyalty, honesty, and courage....[24]

Thus, unlike the familiar narrative where civic nationalism emerges from a
democratic impulse, German liberalism and nationalism encountered each
other as antagonists in an atmosphere charged with hatred toward the enlightened enemy, which was at the same time France and the Enlightenment itself.[25]

The significance of the culture-nation concept for us lies in its creation of
the nation as a sphere independent of the nature of the state.[26] Bernhard Giesen sees in this split that "the identity of the nation was next-worldly, eternal
and exalted; the statist present, however, was this-worldly, finite and contingent....The "nation" in Germany turned into a depoliticized and porous idea
which could be filled with the sundry and contradictory."[27] The looming nar-
rators of German identity—Herder, Arndt, Fichte—situate Germany's specific historicity in the embodiment of "das deutsche Wesen" (German "being"
or innate character).

The German "Wesen" represents the untapped potential of an exalted ancient people, and the creation of a German state would serve this end, and allow their potential to emerge for the betterment of humankind.[28] In this romantic view the striving for a state was merely a stage in the fulfillment of a
cultural mission, which in turn was embedded in a world historical mission
summed up most poetically (in German) in the imperial adage 'Let the German essence heal the world '—Am deutschen Wesen soll die Welt genesen.

---

24 Ernst Moritz Arndt, from his infamous 1803 book *Über den Volkshaß und über den
Gebrauch einer fremden Sprache* On People's Hatred and On the Use of a Foreign
Language, p104, quoted here in Giesen, 1993: 160-1. The German reads: "Ich will den Haß
gegen die Franzosen, nicht bloß für diesen Krieg, ich will ihn für lange Zeit, ich will ihn
für immer. Dann wird Deutschlands Grenzen auch ohne künstliche Wehren sicher sein,
denn das Volk wird immer einen Vereinigungspunkt haben, sobald die unruhigen
räuberischen Nachbarn überlaufen wollen. Dieser Haß glühe als die Religion des deutschen
Volkes, als ein heiliger Wahn in allen Herzen und erhalte uns immer in unserer Treue,
Redlichkeit und Tapferkeit..."
25 See Greenfeld, 1992.
26 Though this is not to be confused with "civil society," which accepts its existence as
dependent on, though separate from, the state.
27 Giesen, 1993: 147. The original reads: "[D]ie Identität der Nation was eine jenseitige,
unendliche und erhabene; die staatliche Gegenwart hingegen war diesseitig, endlich und
kontingent....Die "Nation" wurde so in Deutschland zu einem entpolitisierten, porösen
Begriff, der mit Vielfältigem und Widerspruchlichem gefüllt werden konnte."
28 See Giesen, 1993: 74-75. See also Hoffmann, 1994.

INTERNAL AND EXTERNAL REASONS FOR THE FAILURE TO ESTABLISH A
LIBERAL STATE

The state became viewed as a means for the nation to unfold. Yet the vehicle
for creating such a state was not readily apparent. An attempt to follow the
French and English models with the boisterous liberal revolution of 1848
failed dismally.[29] We have already seen how romantic nationalist sentiment
situated itself as anti-Enlightenment. This was certainly a main reason why
the liberals, with their ideas of human rights and popular sovereignty, faced
internal opposition from both monarchists *and* nationalists, who smelled
French perfume in the aborted constitution of the democrats. This liberal-
national debate articulated the ideological cleft between a "Western" and a
"Germanic" orientation, and led to a rejection rather than institutionalization
of liberal values, values which came to be seen as "Western" (i.e. foreign)
values in nationalist discourse.[30]

But there is an important second reason for the failure of the liberal revolution which connects the nationalist ideologies to the geopolitical trap. While
internal pressure doomed the democratic delegates, external pressures against
a German nation-state set the stage for the future Germany's *geopolitical* dilemma. The royal Concert of Europe had come to regard the weakness of the
German states as a boon for European stability. In the era which birthed the
balance of power as an analytical concept, as long as the largest German
power, Prussia, remained uncertain of her borders and wary of war on her
many and vulnerable fronts, France, Britain and Russia felt secure in the mutually beneficial order of 1815. A German nation-state, even if founded on
liberal principles, would upset the balance. "The peaceful activity of the
Frankfurt Paulskirche delegates seemed to the cabinets in London, Paris, and
Petersburg" reminds historian Hagen Schulze, "to be sheer revolt against the
holy principles of the balance of power in Europe. French envoys demanded
guarantees of the continuation of the sovereign German independent states,
British warships demonstrated in the North Sea, Russian troops marched up to
the east Prussian border, and the German Revolution of 1848...foundered not
least on the threat of a danger of intervention by the three powers."[31]

A STATE AFTER ALL, BUT WHAT KIND OF STATE?

Nature, according to axiom, abhors a vacuum, and perhaps power loves
nothing so much as a vacuum. The nineteenth century blooming of the Westphalian nation-state system created a vacuum in its geographical midst. The

---

29 On the revolutionary events of that extraordinary year in Europe see Langer, 1971.
30 See Müller, 1993.
31 Hagen Schulze, "Europe and the German Question in Historical Perspective" in
Schulze, 1987: 188-89.

German lands were not only an administrative anachronism: its industrial and intellectual elite found themselves plunged into the social churnings of modernization without the mooring of the nation-state, which was fast attaining the epistemological status of an element of nature. The process of "naturalizing" the nation is wonderfully expressed in 1815 by a certain long-named Count Schlabenrendorf an Varnhagen, exclaiming in a letter written while sojourning in Paris: "For countless years there were no nations at all! Today, as I must read, they all stand there fixed and finished."[32] The 'fixing and finishing' of these nations occurred around an amorphous center. The identity-conferring borders of France, the Netherlands, Denmark, Poland (Russia after 1795), and Switzerland all faced the three hundred German states and the barely harnessed imperial desires of the Hapsburgs and Hohenzollern.

Thus Imperial Germany arose to fill a power vacuum in the ambiguous spaces which modernity cannot tolerate (Nature may abhor a vacuum, but modernity is our medium for observing nature). This is not to be understood merely as a rational reaction to an external security threat—it was a question of faith: If, as nationalism proclaims, nation-states are the instantiation of nature—whether God's will or evolutionary design—the clumsy conglomeration of German states became, by the nineteenth century, simply unnatural. This proved untenable over time, and despite the endeavors of the European Concert for the status quo and their ruin of the liberal German revolution unification was forestalled for little more than a generation.

When the state finally came, it arrived not on wings of lofty universal principles of democracy—however fickle such principles may prove in practice—but through the meticulously organized regiments of Protestant Prussia. Unification in 1871 came as the result of war rather than democratic revolution. Appropriately, perhaps, Germany's official entry into state sovereignty rested on Prussia's humiliating defeat of France, the arch-nemesis who was also Germany's mirror. This ascendancy of Prussia was, for Schulze "a tragedy of German history"[33] wherein German sovereignty arrived not as a liberal nation-state but under the heel of Prussian authoritarianism. But keeping in mind the balance of power tactics of the Concert of Europe, he perceptively questions whether, even had the internal obstacles been overcome, the European powers would have allowed a peaceful unification.

The national character of the German state was in this way defined by the "nature" of the system that engendered that very vacuum, above all by the

---

32 Quoted in Günther, 1990: 44. The somewhat exasperated tone of the colloquial German reads: "Wie viele Jahre sind's denn, und es gab noch gar keine Nationen! Heute, wie ich lesen muß, stehen sie alle fix und fertig da."
33 Guenther, 1990: 189.

intuitive logic of the balance of power. Germany is a clear product of the Westphalian state-system. In part because he cleverly and forcefully overcame obstacles to unification, Bismarck's brilliant success in 1871 summoned the deepest fears from the Great Powers.[34] And under their suspicious eyes Germany understood itself as constrained from birth, forbidden by the fears of the rest of Europe from developing "naturally." Such a perception might lead to war (as it later did), but at first Bismarck's legendary diplomacy kept Germany out of war with its wary neighbors. But external coolness belied internal combustion. Germany was finally a nation-state, but rather than the fulfillment of the nationalist dream the territorial nation-state became the casement for more nationalist development.

Prussia had settled in 1871 for what is known as the "small German" solution, a German state without the German lands held by Austria (with the exception, of course, of Silesia, won by battle in the Austro-Prussian war). Bismarck's Realpolitik and his famous palliative that Germany was a satiated country with no territorial European claims, contrasted with the resurgence of nationalism as a mission to make the nation-state congruent with the cultural nation. For despite having achieved a modicum of "normalcy" the German nation-state was controvertible in its borders and disparate in any common understanding of the country's larger role. Was the German state now one of the Great Powers with similar if competitive interests with the other powers? Should Germany be a bulwark against the decadent West and the feudal Slavic East? Should it be a bastion of Protestantism surrounded by Catholics (although the south of Germany is Catholic, pointing to an inner-German tension which persists to this day), or should the current state be viewed merely as a stage in the search by a chosen people for the right context for full self-realization? All of these ideas circulated in Imperial Germany, and these images conjure up a reactive nation, trying to get out from under others, to blossom and bloom as its poets prescribed.[35] The only consensus, it seems, revolved around the geopolitical observation that "God," as Bismarck declared,

---

34 Schulze quotes Disraeli before the English Parliament in 1871 on German unification, which for him amounted to a "German revolution, a greater political event than the French revolution of the last century. ... There is not a diplomatic tradition which is not swept away. We have a new world, new influences at work, new and unknown powers and dangers, with which we must deal, and which, at the present, like every thing new, are still not understandable." Schulze, 1987: 189.

35 It is not hyperbole to present poets as priests, for the soul of the German nation was seen to reside in the ability of its national poetry to express the unexpressable. See Giessen, 1993, and in general about this romantic characteristic of nineteenth century Europe see chapter two of Mosse, 1988.

"placed us in a position in which we are prevented by our neighbors from slipping into dullness and inertia."[36]

THE DIALECTIC OF GERMAN IDEOLOGICAL ORIENTATION

The ideological currents of Germany's identity develop within this first incarnation of the German state. We already have the outline for the dialectic of Germany's role as a state: the simplified thesis, as it were, is Germany as a culture-nation, defined by the specific historicity of the German "being" to transcend its temporal secularness and achieve redemption through the instantiation of the eternal nation. The romantic German gaze—with awe and fear— is turned here toward France and the Enlightenment. The state is profane, the nation sublime.[37]

The simplified antithesis, as it were, is Germany as a state-nation on its way to being a Great Power, a world power (*Weltmacht*), an autonomous state bent on power maximization in a Darwinian world where "the law of the strongest exerts a similar power over the life of states as the law of gravity does in the corporal world."[38]The *Realpolitik* gaze—unsentimental and competitive— looks at Britain, ruler of the seas, trading power, and master colonizer, with green envy. The state is paramount, the nation develops to fit the state.[39]

And synthesis, sublimation, *Aufhebung*? The birth of the territorial state became the spatial locus for the search for synthesis. Within sovereign state borders both aspects coexisted, if uneasily. The increased war-fighting ability of the state institutionalized Fichte and Arndts' supplications for forging identity through facing a common enemy. In doing so, the territorial state also cemented the notions of inside and outside which have come to define the anarchic system of sovereign nation-states.[40] As Giesen writes,

> The nation-state marks...the most extreme border between inside and outside, war and peace, enemy and ally which were imaginable from the per-

---

36 In Dijkink, 1996: , 19. Dijkink is actually quoting Ratzel quoting Bismarck in his 1898 book *Deutschland. Einführung in die Heimatkunde*.

37 This corresponds to van der Pijl's concept of the "Hobbesian" state representing patterns of capitalist accumulation which tether civil society to a strong state in a corporatist structure. The Hobbesian state is rigid, and "foster[s] economic and cultural autarky in relation to liberal capitalist society, interacting with war." van der Pijl, 1994: 173.

38 L.A. Rochau, quoted in Giesen, 1993: 219. The German reads: "Das Gesetz der Stärke übte über das Staatsleben eine ähnliche Herrschaft aus wie das Gesetz der Schwere über die Körperwelt."

39 In van der Pijl's political economy this antithesis would represent the "Lockean" state, where the locus for accumulation is not state control, but civil society, protected in its contracts and property by the state. van der Pijl, 1994: 173.

40 The theoretical traits of sovereignty are dealt with in detail in Chapter Two.

spective of the autonomous unfolding of power. These borders simultaneously enabled a civilizing of relations within society. Violence and power were pulled out from internal societal relationships and pushed beyond the border into inter-state circumstances: society [became] the sphere of the regulated free self-determination of reasonable individuals, [while] the inter-state anarchy [became] the empire of pure violence and the will to power.[41]

Giesen notes that this emphasis on the natural togetherness of a people within the clear borders of a nation-state boosts the power projection capacity of that territory, so that the "primacy of foreign policy"—thusly formulated by Leopold von Ranke—becomes the logical extension of melding nation and state.[42]

The key to the first successful German nation-state, however, was projecting power without actually having to use it. Because of Bismarck's keen conception of power, and not least because of the potential array of powerful enemies, war with Germany's neighbors was strategically out of the question (until, of course, the final unraveling of Bismarck's ill-managed legacy in 1914). Significantly, this approach left the dynamic of power projection and power attainment to the realms of colonialism and imperialism. If Germany was destined to be a great power, it had best "catch up" with the existing powers whose concerns had constrained Germany autonomy. The "belated nation" (Helmuth Plessner) went in search of its infamous "place in the sun."[43] True to the function of inside/outside, colonialism was seen as filling both the need for international status and internal consolidation of a badly fragmented political landscape. "It appeared to politicians and political commentators of all sorts," writes Woodruff D. Smith, "that...colonialism could be used to appeal to many different classes and social groups simultaneously in a way that no other readily available ideological set could do."[44] Imperialism accompanied the colonial impulse and served analogous functions.[45]

The tension between the culture-nation and the nation-state came to express itself through the contesting world views of *Weltpolitik* and *Lebensraum*, the

---

41 Giesen, 1993: 224. On the theme of inside/outside see Walker, 1993. Giesen's original German reads: "Die Staatsnation markiert damit die äußerste Grenze zwischen innen und außen, Krieg und Frieden, Gegnern und Verbündeten, die unter dem Gesichtspunkt autonomer Machtentfaltung vorstellbar war. Diese Grenze ermöglicht gleichzeitig eine Zivilisierung der Verkehrsformen innerhalb der Gesellschaft. Aus den internen gesellschaftlichen Beziehungen werden Gewalttätigkeit und Macht herausgezogen und jenseits der Grenze in die zweistaatlichen Verhältnisse verschoben: die Gesellschaft als eine Sphäre der geregelten freien Selbstbestimmung vernünftiger Individuen, die zwischenstaatliche Anarchie als Reich der reinen Gewalt und des Machtwillens."
42 Giesen, 1993.
43 Pleßner, 1959.
44 Smith, 1986: 33.
45 Ibid.: 35.

two dominant ideologies of German foreign policy from the first unification to the Second World War. Given the "primacy of foreign policy" in the identity-seeking atmosphere of the new empire, it is not surprising that the policies of *Weltpolitik* and *Lebensraum* became central to defining the role—internal and external—of Imperial Germany.[46]

WELTPOLITIK

Weltpolitik, literally "world politics" or "world policy," conveys the essence of economic imperialism within the Lockean heartland.[47] As Foreign Secretary and later Chancellor Bernhard von Bülow reflected, "...I understood by *Weltpolitik* merely the support and advancement of our industry, our trade, the labor-power, activity, and intelligence of our people...We wanted only to protect the vital interests that we had acquired, *in the natural course of events*, throughout the world."[48] Or as Smith encapsulates, *Weltpolitik* for von Bülow and his compatriots at the turn of the century reflects "a foreign policy worldwide in scope, aimed at the protection and expansion of the external connections of the German industrial economy. ... *Weltpolitik* was, first and foremost, external policy in support of German commerce and the industrial sector."[49]

Wholly within the idea of the nation-state as a power-maximizing unit within a competitive system, *Weltpolitik* presaged elements of recent international relations with almost uncanny familiarity. It was an ideology of modernity and modernization, employing "the values of science, reason, and progress," to control the expansion of social and economic change, while maintaining coherence with a balance of power approach.[50] In its dealing with the non-(West) European world "the foundation of the structure was a view of the relationship between peripheral areas of the world economy and the central industrial ones in the process of economic *development*. We are, in fact, dealing with one of the direct ancestors of modern development theory."[51]

In its diplomatic guise it conjured up disingenuous platitudes reminiscent of less distant addresses. At the inauguration of the German parliament Bismarck pronounced the pure principle of sovereignty, where Germany's claim

---

46 A full discussion of the inside/outside function of foreign policy appears in Chapter Two.

47 On the "Lockean Heartland" see van der Pijl, 1994.

48 von Bülow, reflecting in his 1930 biography about his views on *Weltpolitik* during a 1900 parliamentary debate. He was Foreign Minister from 1897-1900 and Chancellor from 1900-1909. Quoted in Smith, 1986: 53. Emphasis added.

49 Smith 1986: 53.

50 Smith 1986: 55-60.

51 Smith, 1986: 66.

for its own independence (*Selbständigkeit*) relies on "willingly acknowledging the independence (*Unabhängigkeit*) of all other states and peoples, the
weak as well as the strong."[52] At this Wolfgang J. Mommsen, the eminent
historian of imperial Germany, comments:

> But this was in good part only lip service, with limited significance. The
> provisionally incurable differences with France alone hint at the direction of
> the German Reich toward a state-based power politics which focuses pri-
> marily on armed power and the weight such power brings to international
> relations. Nevertheless [the German Reich] needed a circumspect diplomacy
> which carefully weighed the interests of the other great powers in order to
> secure the independent position of the German Reich in the middle of
> Europe for a long time. In the background, however, lurked the explosive
> nationalism of the rising bourgeois stratum, whose energies were no longer
> primarily concentrated on the erection and consolidation of a constitution-
> ally governed national state, but rather on the increase of the German
> Reich's position in the world.[53]

Weltpolitik was thus in a sense ahead of its time, a strategy for imperialism
during the final century of colonialism. *Weltpolitik*'s focus was informal control of large parts of the world's economy which could be used for investment
and as markets, not the territorial administration of captive markets.[54] There is
no doubt that Britain was the model for German imperialism. Smith notes
how in Britain class and economic differences seemed subsumed by the notion of a national interest, a national mission, suffused with the sense of superiority, leading German *Weltpolitiker* to "almost universally [draw] the conclusion from the British case that one of the main solutions to fragmentation
was imperialism."[55]

---

52 Quoted in Mommsen, 1993: 15. The quote in Mommsen reads: "...[Es] hieß unter
anderem, daß Deutschland die "Achtung," die es für seine eigene Selbstständigkeit in
Anspruch nehme, "bereitwillig der Unabhängigkeit aller anderer Staaten und Völker, der
schwachen wie der starken," zolle."
53 Ibid. The original reads: "Aber dies war gutenteils nur ein Lippenbekenntnis, dessen
Bedeutung begrenzt war. Tatsächlich verweis allein schon der vorläufige unheilbare
Gegensatz zu Frankreich das Deutsche Reich auf die Bahn einer staatlichen Machtpolitik,
die in erster Linie auf die bewaffnete Macht und deren Gewicht in den internationalen
Beziehungen setzte. Gleichwohl bedurfte es einer umsichtigen, die Interessen anderen
Großmächte sorgfältig abwägenden Diplomatie, um die unabhängige Stellung des
Deutschen Reiches in der Mitte Europas auf Dauer zu sichern. Im Hintergrund aber lauerte
die Sprengkraft des Nationalismus der aufsteigenden bürgerlichten Schichten, der seine
Energien nicht länger in erster Linie auf die Errichtung und den Ausbau eines
konstitutionell regierten nationalen Staates konzentrierte, sondern auf die Steigerung der
Weltstellung des Deutschen Reiches."
54 See Smith, 1986: 66, 70-71.
55 Ibid.: 74.

While closely modeling itself after British imperialism, the claim that *Weltpolitik* anticipated the imperialism of the twentieth century (i.e. imperialism without an imperium, without an overseas empire) rests precisely on the greatest difference between Germany and Britain—the lack of a substantial and long-standing overseas empire. While Germany would try to compensate for this both through the conquering of colonies and a furious race for maritime superiority, she would never succeed in truly "catching up." This was partly because of the constraints which the above-mentioned constellation of European power imposed on the new Germany. So even while trying to 'catch up,' notes Mommsen,

> The foreign policy of the German Reich since 1871 was directed toward the principle that it was territorially 'saturated;' the strategy of diverting tensions on its periphery required that the German Reich hold back in overseas regions and not present itself as competition for the other powers.[56]

While this strategic principle did not entirely stop Germany from in fact becoming a competitor (ultimately vindicating the wisdom of the principle, since abandoning it led to the Great War), it did account for its peculiar brand of economic imperialism, including the creation of the European customs union (*Zollverein*) and detailed plans for the first European economic union.[57] Germany needed a world-wide free trade system with access to natural resources whose smooth functioning did not depend on the possession of colonies. It was also, as Dijkink describes it, "the search for self-realization through materialism," the materialist swing of an identity-seeking pendulum which swings between the rationality of economic superiority and the emotion of cultural superiority.[58] The clearest expression of the tenacity of this *Weltpolitik* world-view, formulated as we saw already in 1871, comes as an eerie echo of late twentieth century neoliberalism: World politics, remarked German Chancellor Bethmann Holweg, is in the final analysis economic politics.[59] And economic politics implies the possibility of common economic in-

---

56 Mommsen, 1993: 56. The original reads: "Die Außenpolitik des Deutschen Reiches war seit 1871 auf das Prinzip ausgerichtet, daß es territorial "saturiert" sei; die Strategie der Ableitung von Spannungen an die Peripherie setzte voraus, daß das Deutsche Reich sich in den überseeischen Regionen zurückhielt und nicht selbst als Konkurrent anderer Mächte auftrat."

57 See List's original plans for the custom's union in List, 1966. On the customs union in general see Hahn, 1984. An interesting article examines Germany's plans for *Weltmarkt und Weltmacht* world markets and world power from the 1870s through World War I, especially regarding their plans for dominating Eastern Europe. See Gutsche, 1972.

58 Dijkink, 1996: 23.

59 Reichschancellor Theobald von Bethmann Hollweg in communication with the German Ambassador in Constantinople, April 23, 1914. Cited in Mommsen, 1993: 293. The full quote in Mommsen reads: "[U]nser Nationalvermögen nähme so zu, daß wir in

terest and compromise, enabling an era when economic interests preclude territorial wars. These optimistic sentiments were voiced in April of 1914, scant four months before the anxiety-ridden continent engulfed itself in paroxysms of violence.

LEBENSRAUM

Weltpolitik embodied the Lockean nation-state ideal; its themes of balance of power, free trade, and sovereign statehood are intuitively familiar for those of us raised in Cold War realist/liberal tradition. *Weltpolitik*, however, was not just a new idea but also a reaction to the anti-modern forces of the culture-nation school, whose influence in imperial and Weimar Germany was far from negligible. Following Smith's use of the term *Lebensraum* (literally: living space) to designate this world-view, *Lebensraum* is an ideology whose overarching aim is to "protect and enhance" Germanness (*Deutschtum*). It is the cultural/intellectual antinomy of "soulless materialism" promoted by *Weltpolitik*.[60] This is to be achieved through a policy of establishing and settling colonies with the what now seems rather odd notion that true German culture could only bloom in an agricultural setting no longer attainable in rapidly industrializing Germany, and so true German culture must be recreated and preserved in the colonies. The conjunction of alienating but inevitable industrialization in the Fatherland and rejuvenating affirmation of the German *Wesen* in the colonies was the envisioned vehicle through which the German character would rise to its natural place atop the hierarchy of the world's people.[61]

Like anti-Semitism, notes Smith, where Jews become scapegoats for the problems of modernity and capitalism while leaving the inherent problems of capitalist society morally unscathed, "*Lebensraum* effected the trick of disparaging aspects of modernity without threatening modernity's beneficiaries by displacing the images of a traditional society to colonial settings."[62] Fundamentally anti-modern cultural determinists were confused and confounded by the seemingly unstoppable social changes effected by the axial shift to the capitalist mode of production.[63] An ideology of cultural displacement allowed for a narrative in which the culture-nation could fit in the state-nation without being usurped. While *Weltpolitik* revered Britain as a model to be emulated

---

zehn bis fünfzehn Jahren alle Nationen überholt hätten. Dann würden wir in der Weltpolitik, *die letzten Endes Wirtschaftspolitik wäre*, an gesicherter Stelle stehen. Unsere Aufgabe wäre es, uns ohne große Konflikt durch diese Zeit durchzuwinden." Emphasis added.

60 Dijkink, 1996: 23.
61 See Chapter Five in Smith, 1986.
62 Smith, 1986: 92.
63 See Van der Pijl, 1994.

(and eventually surpassed), advocates of *Lebensraum* could not admit a common bond of stewardship and interests conferred by great power status. The specific historicity, the world-historical potential, the messianistic mission of the German People allowed for no compromise, no cooperation, in the epochal struggle for self-realization. In the service of self-realization, Bismarck's claim that Germany was territorially "saturated" held no quarter.

Territorial acquisition was initially limited wholly to colonies. Seizing an idea first articulated by Friederich List, however, the notion of "inner migration" (as opposed to "migrationist colonialism") became increasingly popularized by the nationalist Pan-German league starting in the 1890s.[64] This idea focused on expropriating large aristocratic properties in the East to be resettled with farmers. The existing land, however, was quickly perceived as too limited, and the aristocratic class was hardly supportive. Following the logic of national superiority the notion of inner migration quickly transformed into the not-to-subtle notion of "annexation." As the name implies, annexationists sought the expansion of German lands, but only to the area directly to its East. The Eastern border is geopolitically, as Dijkink notes from Ratzel's writings, the "kind of border which is attributed to historical empires: zones of transition to the world of barbarians, a kind of atmosphere becoming thinner and thinner"[65] It is not surprising, then, that "annexationism was," writes Smith,

> ...essentially migrationist colonialism projected spatially into eastern Europe and temporally into the future. And it was clear what the precondition of that future was: a major war. Whether the war came because of Germany's need for additional farming land or for other reasons, one of the main *results* of a successful European war should be large-scale annexations in the east.[66]

If *Lebensraum* had remained merely a radical agrarian movement it would perhaps have faded into a romantic relic in the face of *Weltpolitik*'s rational scientific approach to international relations and international political economy. A perverse reverse of priorities evolved, however. If the origins of the First World War lie in *Weltpolitik*'s balance of power gone askew, those of the Second World War lie the fulfillment of annexationist appetite. The beginning of this reversal lay in the ability of *Lebensraum* advocates to convince industry that annexation held benefits for them as well. As dissatisfaction grew with the turmoil of modernity, syntheses of *Weltpolitik* and *Lebensraum* types of imperialism were advanced by the most respected of scholars, including Friederich Naumann and Max Weber, and publicists such as Paul Rohrbach and Friederich von Bernhardi. Scientific and pseudo-scientific le-

64 Smith, 1986 On the Pan-German league see also Wertheimer, 1971 and Usher, 1913.
65 Dijkink, 1996: 17.
66 Ibid.: 109.

gitimations of all aspects of *Lebensraum*, from Friederich Ratzel's detailed geopolitical theories of migration to the advent of social science as a legitimating discourse, lent it valuable support.[67]

All this notwithstanding, without the loss of the First World War *Lebensraum* would have remained unacceptable for proponents of *Weltpolitik*. *Lebensraum* triumphed in the dying days of the war, when the political leadership of Germany succumbed to what was essentially an army coup in early 1917.[68] From then until Hitler's takeover of power the two ideologies of German imperialism existed in an agitated relation with each other. While both ideologies retained their respective purists, there was a far more serious incentive for synthesis. Following his disciplinary predecessor Ratzel, the geopolitician Karl Haushofer played perhaps the key role in providing a scientific theory which integrated the previously opposing concepts: "It was possible, if Haushofer's ideas were interpreted in a certain way, for one to pursue the basic *Weltpolitik* aims of economic network building and market and investment security without rejecting the notion that agricultural living space was a long-run necessity—indeed, while playing the latter idea for all it was worth."[69]

This blend of economic and cultural imperialism created a vision of Germany-in-the-world which was not inconsequential for the approaching era of National Socialism. Following Haushofer, the ideal view was concentric, consisting of a Greater Germany (comprising its postwar losses and Austria) with a strong domestic industrial base, sitting in the dominant position in a European economic union of its own making, and control over substantial colonies. "The aim would not be" writes Smith, "in fact, absolute economic autarky, but rather a sufficient degree of centralized German control over the union and empire that economic interactions between Germany and the major industrial states would not threaten Germany's political independence and power. The system of external economic relations had to be so constructed, however, that temporary autarky in the event of major war would be possible."[70] This scenario is not the Nazi approach itself, but Hitler and the Nazi planners drew significantly from Haushofer, and the realm of geopolitics and

---

67 See Smith, 1986: 144-146. On 145 Smith writes that "The emergence in the late nineteenth century of new social sciences, largely but not entirely in an academic setting, and the simultaneous appearance of a class of academically qualified social scientists and theoreticians with a journalistic bent provided the means by which the legitimation of the imperialist ideologies could occur."
68 See Smith, 1986: 187-195.
69 Smith, 1986: 222.
70 Smith, 1986: 223.

the roots of Nationalist Socialist foreign policy are evident in the interwar advance of the *Lebensraum/Weltpolitik* mélange.[71]

YESTERDAY AND TODAY

Weltpolitik and *Lebensraum* are the traditions of German foreign policy which form the background for the identity-defining debates of the postwar era. Given *Weltpolitik's* common roots with late twentieth century political realism and its precocious articulation of neoliberal economic ideas it would seem conceivable that Weltpolitik could serve as a positive tradition. However, it is compromised not only by being linked to German aggressiveness, but also by its uneasy alliance with *Lebensraum* in years preceding Hitler.

If *Weltpolitik* and *Lebensraum* could truly be isolated from each other, then we could posit a link between the former and the new Germany of the 1990s, and a link between the latter and the years of the Nazi dictatorship. While Weltpolitik would have to be critically assessed, such a distinction would emphasize the victory of the nation-state model over the culture-nation, the acceptance of the logic of sovereignty over the logic of messianic cultural historicism, the roots of the German state in the categories of Western Enlightenment rather than in the romantic search for cultural perfection. In short, *Weltpolitik* could overcome its negative associations with German imperialism to become a positively-charged testimony to Germany's status as a great *Western* power.

Were it only so straightforward! The cohabitation of *Weltpolitik* and *Lebensraum*, however, makes such disjunction difficult. The tension here points us toward the heart of the ongoing postwar German identity crisis: what caused National Socialism to triumph in Germany? Interestingly, and importantly, the question about National Socialism's origins is simultaneously a debate about National Socialism's aftermath. What is the "normal" to which war-weary Germany sought to return? Does returning to "normal," given the discrediting of *Lebensraum*, mean returning to *Weltpolitik*? Can *Weltpolitik* thus be separated from *Lebensraum*? This line of questioning also affects views toward unification: Is a "united Germany, whole and free" a state which the divided Germany sought to return to, or a utopian state which the postwar generation sought to create? The answers turn around the divisive question of whether National Socialism signifies a break with or an extension of German history.

---

71 Smith, 1986. On Haushofer and his influence and limits see Jacobsen, 1979 and Norton, 1968.

National Socialism—Break or Continuity?

GERMANY AS WOUND

There is no debate about the terror and destruction wrought by National Socialism. It left Germany a wound which became physically manifest in the nation's division.[72] The War was always more than just the military machine. From its ideological origins to its ignominious end the War symbolized Germany's identity crisis in its every manifestation. As Stephen Brockmann writes:

> It was not only in the technical and legal sense that the Second World War did not end in 1945. It did not end morally, spiritually, and emotionally for German culture either. Much of postwar German culture became an attempt to understand and to treat the open, bleeding wounds that the war had caused. 'The war' here is not simply the military conflict that lasted from 1939 to 1945; it is the enormity of Germany's moral, spiritual, political, military, cultural, and economic catastrophe.[73]

The imagery of Germany as wound insinuated itself in German literature, from Böll to Enzensberger to Walser, who saw caring for wounds as a national mission.[74] In a land where literary and political culture are closely linked, Martin Walser's view of the postwar German national mission as caring for wounds has considerable political import—since Germany is itself a wound, its national mission involves caring for itself. As regards Germany, the word 'caring' is perhaps somewhat misleading. Caring can be understood as healing, but in this context it also assumes the double meaning of 'tending,' as one tends a fire. Tending a fire means keeping it going, and for Walser, caring for Germany's wound has the double meaning of tending it, keeping it open, keeping the consciousness of division—and therefore the desire of unification—alive.[75]

'Keeping the wound open' allowed unification to be seen as the acceptable healing, the cure for the wound. Not allowing the wound to heal is the metaphor for refusing to accept the postwar status quo, no matter how self-evident it might seem. But not allowing the wound to heal also means not allowing the past to become past. This can be interpreted positively, as in not allowing Germany's culpability in the war and the Holocaust to become a taboo for public deliberation. But it can also be interpreted negatively, in that viewing

---

72 See the treatment of wound metaphor in Brockmann, 1996.
73 Brockmann, 1996: 30.
74 Ibid.
75 Ibid.

the division of Germany as the manifestation of the wound gives unification—as utopian as that may have seemed before 1989—a disproportionate significance as the cure for the wound. Focusing on unification conflates the self-inflicted wound of Nazism and the externally-inflicted wound of division.

Consequently, the actual (if unexpected) unification of Germany would be expected to heal "the wound called Germany." More religiously-minded Germans have remarked in private that the division of the nation into enemy alliances was a form of penance for the transgressions of the German nation against humanity and against itself. If the division kept the past alive, then the past should pass with the end of the division. Finally, without the artificial truncation of the nation, the terrible past "which has in fact established itself as the present, and which hangs above the present like a sword of judgment," can return to its grave and free the nation from its allegedly unhealthy obsession with twelve distant if significant years of its rich history.[76] Yet the desire to make the Federal Republic of Germany a "normal" state arose during the revisionist debates of the preceding decade before unification even entered the realm of possibility.

THE HISTORIAN'S DISPUTE AND THE CULTURE OF GUILT

This desire to make the past past is consistent with the position taken by the historian Ernst Nolte (from whom the above quote stems) and his supporters in the infamous "Historian's Dispute" of the 1980s. Although the dispute carried great significance for interpreting national socialism's legacy, the Historian's Dispute began as a debate about National Socialism's origins, or more precisely, its uniqueness in world history. The revisionist critique had two directions: in one the Holocaust was set in the context of other historical crimes and techniques; in the other, Hitler's attack on the Soviet Union was portrayed less as unqualified aggression than as a pre-emptive strike.[77] If Hitler's crimes, horrible as they were, were not unique, then the German people must reexamine, and recognize as inappropriate, their 'culture of guilt' about the war.[78]

Against these claims rose a chorus of complaint and outrage, leading perhaps to the clearest articulation of the competing claims of civic and ethnic

---

76 Nolte, quoted in Brockmann, 1996: 32.

77 See the collection of original texts in 1987; and 1986. In English see Maier, 1988, and Jarausch, 1988. For German commentary see, among others, Kühnl, 1987.

78 See Schwarz, 1985 and Schwartz, 1990 for taking the Germans to task for their culture of guilt, and Rainer Zitelmann and his colleagues decry this perceived neurosis even more intently. See, for example, Zitelmann, 1993. For an insightful look at the approach to guilt in Germany outside of the backbiting of the German debate see Buruma, 1994.

nationalism in public discourse. For at its heart, the Historian's Debate was a debate about the nature of national identity, about whether the nation is defined by blood or by citizenship. Jürgen Habermas became the eloquent advocate of "constitutional patriotism," the identification of national identity with the values of political society rather than the metaphysics of ethnicity.[79] In doing so, he also became the bête noire of the emerging "intellectual right."[80]

It is significant that the Historian's Dispute arose prior to unification, for it sets the stage for the identity-defining debates of the 1990s, including foreign policy. Despite sharing a similar desire with keepers of the wound to make the past past, the revisionist historians are especially notable because they break with unification as the main trope for achieving this. Rather than call for unification, the revisionists shied away from a focus on division, not because it was politically incorrect but because focusing on the division highlighted Germany's "abnormal" nation-state status.[81] Given the unprecedented acceptance of the existence of two Germanys and severe public skepticism toward the possibility of unification during the 1980s, it is perhaps none too far fetched to regard the rise of revisionist historiography in the eighties as a form of giving up on unification as the healer of Germany's wound.[82] The continued institutionalization of the bipolar conflict created a situation where the search for "normalcy" became uncoupled from the dream of unification.

If at first, for the nationally-minded, keeping the wound open strengthened Germany's consciousness as one nation, as time wore on keeping the wound open seemed rather to erode Germany's consciousness as a nation. Keeping the nation alive meant keeping the bitter past alive to the point where, as Brockmann writes, "it would be no exaggeration to say that reflection on the Nazi past has become *the* primary intellectual and spiritual contribution of the Federal Republic of Germany to world culture, indeed a source of its very identity."[83] With such reflection defining identity, nationally-minded intellectuals such as Nolte and Michael Stürmer feared lasting stigmatization of Germany as a petty bourgeoisie nation mired in paralyzing guilt. Keenly aware of growing German power, Stürmer exclaimed exasperatedly in 1987:

---

79 See Habermas, 1992a.

80 See the biting criticism of Habermas' views in Schwilk and Schacht, 1994.

81 It is important to note that there was always an implicit two-level approach in West Germany's civic nationalist rhetoric, since ethnic national identity *was* maintained and officially sanctioned by the FRG's standing offer of citizenship to *all* Germans. Thanks to Katalin Fábián for raising this point. Lutz Hoffmann, 1994 also discusses this seeming paradox.

82 In, 1987 only 3% ! anticipated unification in the "foreseeable future." See Merkl, 1995: 4.

83 Brockmann, 1996: 30.

"We cannot stand up in the middle of central Europe and be the strong man in NATO—and do it on our knees."[84]

For revisionists and their supporters, to make (West) Germany "normal" meant once and for all to draw a line under the past, to make the past past, and to develop a "healthy" sense of nation, of patriotism, of national pride, one where the sentence "I am proud to be a German" (*Ich bin Stolz, Deutscher zu sein*) would no longer be the sole provenance of the radical right. The revisionist historians were at great pains to explain that this did not mean disavowing the past, but merely letting the past be past. With the wisdom of the past divorced from its burden, Germans could once again, as the legendary Bavarian politician Franz Josef Strauss was fond of saying, be "somebody again" ("We are somebody again!"—*Wir sind wieder wer!* — was one of his infamous slogans). Being someone again meant knowing how to combine power with responsibility. As the title of political scientist Hans-Peter Schwarz's 1984 book complained, the postwar era lead the Germans from obsession with power to the ignorance of power (*Von Machtbesessenheit zur Machtvergessenheit*).[85] Already in the 1980s we can see the emerging nexus of power-responsibility-normalcy.

All of the issues which came to play such a central role in German debates after unification—the nature of national identity, the lessons to be drawn from the German past for future behavior, the question of what is, and whether it is desirable to be, a "normal" nation with a "healthy" sense of patriotism and pride—had thus all emerged in the previous decade. The irony, of course, is that they emerged then precisely because unification ceased to be seen as a serious option, and intellectual energy was being directed instead toward searching for normalcy in a world defined by the status quo of bipolarity. When, against all honest expectations, unification re-emerged not merely as an option but as an almost immediate fait accompli (formal unification occurred less than a year after the Berlin wall fell) the issues raised in the Historian's Disputes of a few years before encountered a surreal resurrection.

THE NEW ZERO HOUR?

The guiding "socio-psychologically necessary historical myth" of postwar West Germany was the notion of the Zero Hour, the moment between the apogee of dictatorial destruction and the beginning of democratic renewal.[86] The concept of a Zero Hour enabled the psychological reconciliation of post-

---

84 Quoted in Brockmann, 1996: 33.
85 Schwarz, 1985.
86 von Dirke, 1996. On the issue of socially necessary historical myths see Barthes, 1986, and also, from a quite different perspective, Cassirer, 1979. The role of narratives for national identity is the focus of the next chapter.

war stability and prosperity with wartime insanity and moral poverty. The idea of a complete break with the past, a complete and utter new start on a clean slate, provided a basis for the will, the energy, and the motivation to rebuild the vanquished, vilified, occupied, and morally bankrupt country. How else could one explain the apparent success of democracy so soon after dictatorship? As Sabine von Dirke writes, "the notion of the Zero Hour became the conceptual working hypothesis for a country which found it impossible to site its cultural reconstruction in the past."[87]

Given Hitler's thanatopic urges, it seemed only fitting that a defeated Germany should be seen as a corpse, as dead. "Faced with the smoke-blackened picture of this European landscape of ruins, in which human beings wander aimlessly, cut loose from all outdated bonds, the value systems of the past turn pale and lifeless" writes Hans Werner Richter in his radical depiction of the moment of no return, quoted in Brockmann:

> Any possibility of connecting up with what went before, any attempt to begin again where the older generation left its continuous developmental path in 1933 in order to surrender to an irrational adventure, seems paradoxical in the face of this European picture....Because of the complete dislocation of life feeling, because of the violence of the experiences which have become a part of and which have shaken the younger generation, this generation believes that the only possible source for spiritual rebirth lies in an absolute and radical new beginning.[88]

This "absolute and radical new beginning" constructs a clear break with the Nazi past. A clear break, however, did not match the realities of power and politics in the early Federal Republic. Denazification had significant limits and former Nazis occupied prominent positions in government, the judiciary, and industry. By the 1960s, the Zero Hour came not only to signify the myth of rebirth, but also the silent acceptance and tabuisation of the past. For the student activists of the 68 Generation the Zero Hour came to represent a failure of coming to terms with the past (*Vergangenheitsbewältigung*). Against the radical break as posed above by Richter they saw only authoritarian wine in new bottles, mostly labeled anti-Communism.[89] For them the Zero Hour became a burdening rather than enabling myth, conflating coming to terms with the past with consigning the past to a kind of prehistory where it loomed, incomprehensible, as an atavistic anomaly.

The critical voices of the 1960s became absorbed into mainstream German culture, partially because of the moral authority ascribed to critics of fascism,

---

87 Ibid.
88 Quoted in Brockmann, 1996: 18.
89 See von Dirke, 1996: 76.

partially because of the legacy of literature, philosophy, and politics which the period bore, and partially because the identity of West Germany became inseparable from the dialectic of break and continuity. The present came to be openly defined through its perceived relation to the past. The intellectual fervor of the 1960s restored, in a way, the past to the present, instilling in the public consciousness a sense that the Nazi years cannot be overcome through rhetoric of a new beginning alone, that those years indeed cannot and should not be overcome. To deny the Nazi past is to deny self-knowledge, an integral part of the self. Günter Grass made Auschwitz the dominant metaphor for postwar German identity, stating unflinchingly that "We will not get around Auschwitz. We should not even attempt such an act of violence, no matter how much we might wish to do so, because Auschwitz belongs to us, it is a permanent scar on our history, and it has, on the positive side, made possible an insight which might run like this: now, finally, we know ourselves."[90]

As Brockmann astutely notes, the linking of postwar identity with the "permanent scar" of Auschwitz meant "that to oppose the writers and their critical consciousness meant to oppose the Federal Republic itself."[91] Thus even throughout the bitter Historian's Dispute the Federal Republic itself was never an object of criticism, only the interpretation of its role was at stake. But suddenly unification makes it possible to oppose the established critical consciousness, even if it means opposing the Federal Republic. This is one of the greatest paradoxes of unification: while underscoring the self-evident nature of Germany's Western ties, unification also provides the opportunity for questioning the legitimacy of the Bonn Republic which situated Germany in the West in the first place. Was the Bonn Republic at best an outgrown stage and at worst a deviant "special path" enforced by outside powers?

ADIEU BONN?

The displacement of the Bonn Republic as synonymous with postwar German identity is a function of the search for a new foundational myth of unified Germany. Unification brings with it a discursive disorder, where the terms left and right are torn from their traditional moorings.[92] Claudia Mayer-Iswandy observes that the "new *Unübersichtlichkeit,*" by which is meant the disarray of conventional ideological categories, benefits and is manipulated by the intellectual right, who see *1989* as a New Zero hour. The intellectual right, as noted above, are the heirs to the reactionary historians and are continuing the debate about Germany's break and continuity with the Nazi past. The new

---

90 See Grass, 1990. Quoted here in Brockmann, 1996: 31.
91 Brockmann, 1996: 34.
92 Mayer-Iswandy, 1996.

twist is that the Bonn Republic now starts to appear as the deviation from the norm.[93]

If the "68 Generation" seemed to have the upper hand in the Historian's Dispute, the so-called "German-German literary debate" brought the major subtext of the Historian's Dispute into the 1990s with considerably more success for the right. The literary debate initially concerned the legacy of Christa Wolf and other East German writers whose works, once celebrated as expressions of courageous creativity under the oppressive Communist regime, came under attack as politically-compromised "state literature" blown out of proportion by Western leftist writers more interested in a canon of political correctness than literary merit.[94] This criticism of Eastern writers quickly spread to include Western postwar writers, most importantly Günter Grass, whom the intellectual right particularly sought to topple from his pedestal of moral and literary authority. The attack, led by *Frankfurter Allgemeine Zeitung* critic Frank Schirrmacher, is part of a general conservative reaction against the literary movements of the 1960s and 70s from which sprang variations of deconstruction, postmodernism, feminist and postcolonial studies.

Seen together with the general conservative backlash against "multiculturalism" and "political correctness" and in the context of the Historian's Dispute, a larger agenda emerges from the intellectual right's fomenting of the German-German literary debate. The hidden agenda, as von Dirke points out, concerns the entire legacy of the Sixties, which itself is shorthand for the political culture of West Germany as it developed until 1989. Against the "Generation of 1968" Brigitte Seebacher-Brandt posits a "Generation of 1989," and proclaims along with Schirrmacher that 1989 signifies a new Zero Hour which can yet redeem Germany from the misplaced dogmatism of the 1960s.[95] The primary transgression of the 1960s was its location of the Nazi past squarely within the definition of German identity. Thus at heart, writes von Dirke, the conservative criticisms "circle around the issue of the Nazi past." In a sense the new Zero Hour tries to fulfill the mythic task of the failed original one: the erasure of Nazi Germany as the focal point for a new identity.

Defining 1989/90 as the true Zero Hour drains Germany of an uncomfortable cultural heritage—a literary intellectual discourse which had forced the Nazi past back onto the FRG's public agenda. The new Zero Hour rhetoric, if successful, will kill two birds with one stone: eliminating the 1960s from

---

93 See Mathiopoulos, 1995, also Habermas, 1995.
94 Heidelberger-Leonhard, 1991.
95 See Seebacher-Brandt's contribution in Schwilk and Schacht, 1994.

collective memory will also remove the Nazi past, which the generation of the Sixties had brought into seemingly permanent focus.[96]

The function of the New Zero hour is to return Germany to a position of normalcy, where normal means rediscovering the nation as a positive endower of identity. The search for normalcy is not new—it was an issue through the debates of the sixties and a key element of the Historian's Dispute. But unification has both intensified and altered the normalcy discourse. It is intensified politically because both the telos of European integration and the exigencies of the "international community" call for a Germany safely entrenched in the "normalcy" of the West, including the ability for joint military intervention. The search for new foundational narratives and a meaningful identity as "German" also intensifies the discourse. This quest for a meaningful identity results in the alteration, because the discursive disorder created by unification allows for a connection between normalism and positive national identity, where the concept "nation" becomes reinscribed with premodern values. As Mayer-Iswandy notes, the term "nation" in post-unification intellectual discourse has

fully relegated that with what the idea of the nation-state was once introduced—the protection of civil rights in the framework and afterward of the French Revolution, the *nation civique*—to the background, and is wrongly replaced (*verstellt*) with questions about "identity" and ethnicity, the homogenous nation and national pride. The discourse goes thusly back in the premodern. ... The nation éthnique celebrates its return in speeches of us and others, of foreigners and alienation. This is reminiscent of the turn from the cosmopolitanism of the Enlightenment, as Fichte undertook in his *Addresses to the German People*, and is hardly encouraging for the peaceful living together of diverse population groups in one country.[97]

The blurring of the categories of left and right, Mayer-Iswandy concludes, is a project which serves to rehabilitate right-wing values, moving a formerly marginal discourse to a position in the political center.[98] With this perhaps unforeseen effect of unification the debate about Germany's identity ratchets up to a more intense level: in the power struggle over who defines normal the legacy of the Federal Republic itself is open for redefinition. As the conservative critic Ulrich Greiner aptly points out, "he who determines what was, also determines what will be."[99]

---

96 von Dirke, 1996: 83.
97 Mayer-Iswandy, 1996: 509.
98 Ibid.: 516.
99 Quoted in Mayer-Iswandy, 1996: 512. "Wer bestimmt, was gewesen ist, der bestimmt auch, was sein wird."

The years following unification are an especially important time for determining what was and what will be. The interpretive struggle in Germany, especially the debate about how to commemorate the fiftieth anniversary of the end of World War Two, reminds Dan Diner of the battles over symbols in the third French Republic, "it was first in this debate that the commemoration of the French Revolution of 1789 was lifted into public consciousness as a part of national self-understanding. The symbolic determination currently underway in Germany is of similarly great import for the self-understanding of the country. The symbols, which are being determined today, are, so to speak, the mold for future common character."[100] This ongoing symbolic determination is the context for the following examination of national identity and foreign policy in post-unification Germany.

---

100 Diner, 1995: 547. The German reads: "[E]rst in diesem Streit ist die Errinerung an die Französische Revolution von 1789 als Teil des nationalen Selbstverständnisses ins öffentliche Bewußtsein gehoben worden. Die symbolische Festlegungen, die gegenwärtig in Deutschland erfolgen, sind für das zukunftige Selbstverständnis des Landes von ähnlich großer Bedeutung. Die Symbole, die heute festgelegt werden, sind sozusagen die Muster des künftigen Gemeinwesens."

2. Of Narratives and Nations: The Challenge of Discursive Disorder

A Brief Excursus on Narrative and Discourse

For nearly forty years American tourists clambered up on wooden platforms to gaze onto the "death strip" behind the Berlin wall. Through binoculars and cameras they sought the eyes of young border guards, who watched them back from their whitewashed watchtowers. The guards duly observed viewers of all stripes gawking on the perimeter of the "anti-fascist protective wall." Aesthetically speaking the scene was grim at best, yet the view exerted a magnetic tourist attraction. The Berlin Wall was the material instantiation of stories told by ideologies–here American tourists could see 'live' the dangers of the other side from an opulent perch. West Berlin was beloved by Americans because, among other attributes, it was a living metaphor for the bipolar world: West Berlin as the West in microcosm defiantly celebrated wealth and consumerism in the shadow of an apparently impoverished enemy. Its atmosphere of cosmopolitan normalcy was protected by a huge military that remained, for the tourists, mostly invisible (and also by Bonn subsidies that were equally invisible). The population was openly and sincerely indebted to the United States and its allies for the air lift of 1948 and the commitment to West Berlin's status. For US tourists Berlin was a kind of theme park where the good guys could literally thumb their noses at the bad guys only yards away.[1]

More than a metaphor for the division of Germany, the attraction of the Wall for US tourists is testimony to the power of narratives in structuring our understanding of the world. Both East and West Berlin told a story about who was good and bad. The story told by East Berlin was ultimately less convincing, not because it was not told well, but because it failed to resolve or displace contradictions, material and logical, which made the story untenable. Once untenable, overt coercion and cynicism replaced conviction and acceptance. In this particular historical situation the outcome was the implosion of the regime and its state.[2]

---

1 For a general overview of the bizarre and fascinating double-life of divided Berlin see Wyden, 1989.

2 On the collapse of the GDR see, among others, the treatment in Görtemaker, 1994. For a critical view see Unger and Klein, 1994.

The power of narrative lies in its ability to create and sustain social reality; it is no exaggeration to say that narrative structure is a foundation of human experience. The role of narrative in the construction of subjectivity has been dealt with at length elsewhere, especially in the writings of Paul Ricouer, but also through the work of White, Brunner, Kermode, Kerby, Carr, and many others.[3] For this work two related aspects of narrative are particularly salient: narrative as constitutive of collective identity and as constitutive of the context in which politics is played out. Borrowing loosely from Kuhn's paradigmatic distinction between normal and revolutionary science, we can state, rather banally, that some political change takes place within accepted and expected bounds, while some political change confronts and provokes novel and unfamiliar situations.[4] During the former, policy formation tends to follow social rules that, to a certain degree, are discernible and predictable.[5] In the latter instance, however, the rules that guide policy formation within a paradigm are of less use in grasping the situation. On the contrary they may blind analysts to new developments.

Both 'normal' and 'revolutionary' politics (in Kuhn's sense) consist of stories–about why the Clean Air Act is important, or why welfare should be cut, and so forth. In this significant sense, policy making is a narrative exercise. Narratives, however, serve different functions at different times and places. A simplified analytical distinction can be drawn between the 'action-coordinating' language of 'normal' policy narratives and the 'world-disclosing' language of 'revolutionary' politics.[6] While the two are never completely distinct (all language is in some sense 'world-disclosing'), one can nonetheless focus more on one form of language or the other. Interpreting

---

3 Ricouer's work is almost paradigmatic here, especially Ricoeur, 1979; Ricoeur, 1983-5. Ricouer's sense of temporality, however, is indebted to Heidegger's *Being and Time*. Definitive work extending the study of narrative from literary studies to philosophical, historical and social anlysis has also been done by Carr, 1986, Kerby, 1991, Kermode, 1967, White, 1981, Brunner, and Coste, 1989. On the role of narrative in the natural sciences see Ormiston and Sassower, 1989.

4 A decision to increase penalties for drunk driving, for example, while mustering proponents and opponents is unlikely to lead to major changes in the perception of the U.S. governmental system. Indeed, such a policy change tends to reinforce dominant strains of thought about the politics of alcohol. The decision to integrate the U.S. army, however, challenged fundamental ideas about what the US government is supposed to do. This decision was both a reaction and a challenge, and had a profound effect on race relations in the US.

5 On social rules see, among others, Onuf, 1989.

6White, 1991 makes this distinction in chapter 2. "Action-coordination" language is the domain of theorists in the "speech act" tradition of Searle, 1969 and Austin, 1975, while "world-disclosing" language corresponds to the continental phenomenological tradition of Heidegger and Derrida.

'world-disclosing' language during 'revolutionary' circumstances is particularly important, for it allows glimpses of paradigm formation (or more accurately discursive formation)–the context which makes 'normal' politics possible.

Germany during 1989/91 embodied revolutions at many different levels: the literal level of the East German internal revolution, the revolutionary developments of unification, and the revolutionary effects of the fall of communist regimes from East Berlin to Moscow on both German policy and the international system. In addition to problem solving, policy makers struggled to grasp, and control, events with overtly metahistorical significance. My exploration of German foreign policy and national identity since 1989 focuses on the narrative essence of political change. Looking at the narratives woven into and from German foreign policy discourse allows us to look behind the action-coordinating issues to larger issues of paradigmatic value, in particular what conception of the German nation-state, and its national identity, prevails and how it does so. This 'world-disclosive' focus allows us to address both meta- questions of German identity and narrower questions about why and how certain policies developed at particular times, including speculation on what this augurs for the future.

To better situate this story about Germany's discursive disorder and its effect on foreign policy, it is helpful to review the primary functions of narrative as they pertains to the construction of social reality. To this end I develop four dialectically-related functions: Ordering, the ontological function which engenders subjectivity; Delimiting, the epistemological function which creates discursive formations; Perpetuating, the hegemonic function which sustains narrative integrity; and Challenging, the counter-hegemonic function which represents the margins of discourse. This overview creates the basis for a narrative notion of nationhood and the role of foreign policy as one of its key discursive constituents. The chapter then returns to the particular paradoxes raised by the restoration of legal sovereignty in Germany after the fall of the Berlin wall.

THE FOUR FUNCTIONS OF NARRATIVE

Ordering: The ontological function

Harnessing Temporality

Should you be inclined to examine the medieval annals of Gaul from the eighth to tenth century, you would most likely be extremely frustrated with the list of events penned therein. Hayden White explains why: the events lack a sense of connection. The text, while "referential," possesses no central subject, no well-marked beginning, middle, and end, no peripeteia, and no identifiable narrative voice. ... Social events are apparently as incomprehensible as natural events. They seem to have the same order of importance or unimportance. They seem merely to have *occurred*, and their importance seems to be indistinguishable from the fact that they were recorded. In fact, it seems that their importance consists of nothing other than the fact that they were recorded.[7]

To make "sense" of the era (presumably the motivation for such arcane delving), you would have to order the events in a meaningful way, such that Duke Gottfried's death (whoever he was) followed from a hard winter, and without his leadership a battle was lost, which in turn caused.... This is an example of how narratives bind temporal events together such that meaning can be ascribed to a pattern. The organization *of* time itself endows meaning to events.

Thus narrative is, first and foremost, the human instantiation of temporality. "Time becomes human," writes Paul Ricoeur, "to the extent that it is organized after the manner of a narrative; narrative, in turn, is meaningful to the extent that it portrays the features of temporal experience."[8] Without narrative we would have little meaningful sense of time, no sense of past, present or future. This ordering function of narrative is the ontological function which creates meaning. By articulating our temporality we gain a significant element of control over our existence. This control gives us the ability to go beyond the instinctive urges of every day life (sleep, eat, sex, etc.) and give our actions context by the means of emplotment within a telos, an ending.

This sense of an ending is the key feature of temporal ordering: knowing the end (or at least the desired end) sets us searching for the best path toward that end. Frank Kermode, in *the Sense of an Ending*, writes that plot "presupposes and requires that the end will bestow upon the whole duration and meaning."[9] In other words, the end justifies the meaning. The type of telos, and the way in which the telos is arrived at, thus acquire a disproportional importance to other elements of the narrative. Understanding the projected end (which is often closely related to an illusionary origin) of a certain group, say a doomsday cult, or a society whose security is based on nuclear deterrence, becomes central to understanding their actions, be they erratic behavior or policy formation.

In the Beginning there was...Language

The ontological aspect of narrative's ordering function is most clearly visible through its reliance on language. Language is arguably the attribute which

---

7 White, 1981: 7,8.
8 Paul Ricouer, quoted in Kepnes, 1992.
9 See Frank Kermode, 1967. Quoted in Kepnes, Ibid.:88.

makes humans human, although the origins of language are far from clear.[10] We conceive of meaning through language: words form non-arbitrary linguistic structures which characterize the world for us. Our subjectivity is predicated on, indeed generated by language: "The self is essentially a meaning construct deriving from language and conversation, generally, where language must be seen as essentially "material," that is, as an extension of the sphere of activity of the human body."[11] In the Heideggarian phenomenological vocabulary, where "the world is the symbolic ordering of the disclosure of Being," language is the means of disclosure.[12] It is in this sense that we spoke earlier of language as "world-disclosive."

If language gives Being form, then it cannot be merely representational of reality, but is itself a manifestation of reality. And "reality" is a narrative experience. To the extent that humans, after birth, are cast into the world, "thrown" into the "clearing of Being," they have no *a priori* identity or direction (beyond instinct).[13] Language enables narratives, and in turn narratives–through their ability to emplot and mimic events and thereby endow them with meaning–give position, direction and identity to the condition of "Being-in-the-world" (*Dasein*).[14]

Delimiting: the epistemological function

One story or many?

The second function of narrative is an epistemological function and a logical extension of the ordering function. Although, as Kerby points out, "lived time has a quasi-narrative character, and this is why it is not amenable to just any telling," the possibility of narrative says nothing about the necessity for a *single* narrative.[15] Yet multiple alternatives make us nervous, or seem simply implausible–imagine your child is taught that both evolution *and* creationism, or both Ptolomeic *and* Copernican astronomy are true. If presented with *either/or* then most of us would have no problem–either/or promises that somehow it is possible to judge which one is, in fact, true. But say *and* and we confront the problem of incommensurability. The persistence today of creationism despite a century of scientific evidence to the contrary hints at the stakes

---

10 On the debate surrounding the origin of language see Steven Pinker's evolutionary approach in his Pinker, 1994. For a wonderful overview and also a good summary of Pinker see Trabant, 1995.

11 Kerby, 1991:112. For a detailed explanation of how subjectivity is formed by language see Kerby, chapter 3.

12 Murchadha, 1992: 126.

13 See Kepnes, 1992: 96-7.

14 Ibid.

15 Kerby, 1991:42.

involved in narratives: which theory we believe depends on which story we tell, not necessarily on objective facts. And which story we tell depends on which story tells us (i.e. our salient identity as a scientist, fundamentalist, etc).[16]

Multiple stories about the same event thus threaten the truth-claims of a given narrative and potentially undermine its function as a giver of direction and identity. At a more abstract level, the inherent elasticity of language always threatens to make meaning indeterminable.[17] The epistemological function of delimiting counters this by creating a system for intelligibility. This system can be seen as a master narrative, in which a coherent web of smaller narratives can complement, rather than contradict, each other. For Jean-François Lyotard, narratives in a respective society "define what has the right to be said and done in the culture in question, and since they are themselves a part of that culture, they are legitimated by the simple fact that they do what they do."[18] Narratives delimit the available interpretations, and in doing so they provide a coherent schema for the ordering of experience. Ordering is incomplete without delimiting–it would be like an alphabet without grammar.

Delimiting sifts the multiple possible orders so that a salient identity and direction can take root and establish a material base. Yet the monocausal tendency of delimiting struggles against the inherent ambiguity of multiple possible narratives, what Kermode refers to as the opacity of narrative.[19] Delimiting exists in constant tension with ordering. The upshot of this tension is that intelligibility is not a thing in itself. Rather it consists of a bargain, where the price of narrative coherence (and, therefore, the price of identity and direction), is the obscuring of contradictory, alternative, or unpleasant aspects inherent *in* a particular story, and the elision of alternative ways of seeing or thinking.

This "price" may be inevitable–the cost of understanding *per se*. Yet the possible universal inevitability of delimiting says nothing about its particular instantiation: in some cases the price of delimiting may be perfectly acceptable, such as narratives associated with grieving (narratives of fate, afterlife, etc.). In others, such as narratives which posit Jews or African-Americans as

---

16 Here is the connection between narrative studies and philosophy of science regarding theory building. The classic debates center around Popper, 1958, Kuhn, 1970 [1962], and Lakatos and Musgrave, 1970. For creative and provocative variations on those debates see Feyerabend, 1993; Rouse, 1987.

17 For perhaps the preeminent postmodern statement on the elasticity of language see Derrida, 1976.

18 Lyotard, 1989:23.

19 Kermode, 1967.

racially inferior to Christian Caucasians, the price of narrative coherence can be unacceptable (for most).

The way it is: discursive formations

Delimiting–the creation of narrative coherence at the (necessary) expense of other possible narratives–enables the making of truth-claims. This is its essential epistemological role: it takes the harnessing of temporality (ordering) and turns one possibility into "the way it is." This is not done arbitrarily: one cannot tell just any story and expect it to resonate. What is perceived as true must, depending on one's philosophical predilections, cohere or correspond to expected outcomes. The difference between representational and narrative theories of truth is *not* that, for the former, truth is "true" and for the latter truth is, somehow, relative. The difference lies in *where* the basis of truth resides. For representationalist approaches, social truth exists in a realm independent of linguistic representation, a realm "out there" which language helps describe. Narrative theories of social truth see truth emerging from linguistic representation, and thus locate the basis of truth at the level of discourse.

The location of truth at the discursive level is manifested in and through "discursive formations" (also referred to as discursive orders, or communities).[20] The discursive formation is the epistemological framework in which statements are possible. As Linda Martìn Alcoff writes, "The rules of discursive formation do not mandate specific truth-values for specific statements, but open up a *delimited* space in which some statements can be meaningfully expressed and understood."[21] The actions which inscribe the rules of the respective order are discursive *practices*, for example the criminalization of homosexuality in modern society, or its acceptance in ancient Greece.[22] These discursive practices form the boundaries of the imaginable.

Delimiting is the connection between the discursive and the material (the non-discursive). The difference between rich and poor is clearly material, but the creation of value–and who falls into these categories–represents a particular *relation* between material goods and discursive formation. "Dominant discourses," writes David Goldberg:

---

20 See Foucault, 1970 and Foucault, 1994.

21 Alcoff, 1996: 123. Emphasis added.

22 Alcoff uses this example to illustrate how discursive formations makes statements statable: "For example, it is likely that in the dominant discourse of Greek citizens in the fourth century B.C., a statement condemning homosexuality as a sexual malfunction would result in puzzlement rather than rejection. The concepts necessary to generate the statement, for example, "homosexuality" as a sexual identity, as well as the discursive rules necessary to determine its truth-value, did not exist in that discourse. Therefore, the statement would have been meaningless." Ibid.

–those that in the social relations of power at some moment come to assume authority and confer status–reflect the material relations that render them dominant. More significantly, they articulate these relations, conceptualize them, give them form, express their otherwise unarticulated yet inarticulate values. It is this capacity–to name the condition, to define it, to render it not merely meaningful but actually conceivable and comprehensible–that at once constitutes power over it, to determine after all what is (or is not), to define its limits. To control the conceptual scheme is thus to command one's world.[23]

In short: if the ordering function of narratives constructs social reality, the delimiting function of discourse regulates social relations.

Locating truth-claims at the level of discursive formations significantly alters social scientific analysis.[24] Rather than searching for meaning in the propositional content or subjective intentionality of statements, one looks instead at the discursive formations which legitimize propositional statements, intentions, etc.[25] "An evaluation at this level," writes Alcoff, "will involve as a central consideration the relations between statements, objects, subject positions, and strategic choices."[26] Those discursive practices which "give rise to the systems of meaning and value from which actions and policies are directed" [27] become a locus for analysis, rather than the actions and policies *per se*.

Perpetuation: the hegemonic function

Once a discourse is delimited, perpetuation or reproduction of the discourse is essential for its continued existence. A discourse seeks self-evident status *through* repeating, reinforcing and reifying. Once self-evident, a discourse draws around itself a cloak of normalcy. What is normal seems natural, and to question the normal and natural is to invite marginalization, ridicule, condemnation, or even punishment. The act of perpetuation is not pernicious in itself. It is a necessary part of delimiting. However, the very fact that a discourse has to be *imposed* in order to achieve narrative coherence necessitates an actor which is capable of imposition. Discourses do not impose themselves: a community uses social pressure, institutions create frameworks for the legitimated use of power, groups of persons can use violence or control information–the methods are manifold.

---

23 Goldberg, 1993: 9.
24 See Bach, 1994a.
25 See Alcoff, 1996.
26 Ibid.: 127.
27 Shapiro, 1989: 13.

Not all forms of imposition are similar. It is axiomatic that, for example, imposition through brute force is seldom the most effective long-term method of control. Brute force tends to lack the subtlety that lends itself to analyzing complex social relations. The workings of discursive practices are perhaps best interrogated where narrative primacy is sought by the establishment of discursive dominance: the claim of one group to legitimately, if not solely, interpret events.

The establishment of discursive dominance is similar to what Gramsci coined hegemony: order based on consent rather than coercion.[28] Consent is forged in the realm of civil society–that part of society consisting not of coercive state apparatae such as the police or the military, but of legal norms, educational systems, leisure activities, science, arts, religion, and social activities.[29] Civil society and state apparatae influence and, if hegemony is successful, reinforce each other. For example, the pre-civil rights discourse of racial superiority in the USA was entrenched in civil society: codified in law, maintained by segregation, bolstered by religious convictions, supported by (pseudo) scientific research (such as phrenology), and re-presented through some forms of art (e.g. jockey statues), literature, and myth, as well as enforced by the police and coercive groups such as the Klan.

How does the dominant discourse become dominant? The quick answer is through a combination of coherence with existing narratives and control over resources, both material and rhetorical. Regardless of the ideological spin, there is little question that dominant narrative is usually beneficial to its keepers, and involves a significant degree of self-interest. Yet were it simply a matter of self-interest, game theoretic analysis might suffice for studying social reality. Self-interest requires a high degree of transparency and, importantly, a sense of end, a telos–strategies of self-interest must presuppose an end in order to evaluate their usefulness. But strategies of hegemony are not so transparent. This is because hegemony operates at the level of metanarratives: the story is naturalized and internalized; it becomes "authentic" in the context of common sense.[30] By institutionalizing itself in common sense, the metanarrative legitimates itself both from below and from above and creates the conditions for its own perpetuation.

Let us briefly summarize the two reasons why a discourse must perpetuate itself in order to survive: First, the ordering function of narrative requires a sense of *process* for temporality to be articulated. Second and following from

---

28 Gramsci, 1985. See Adamson, 1980. See also Laclau and Mouffe, 1985 on hegemony.
29 On Civil Society see Keane, 1988.
30 See Gramsci, 1985. See also Gill, 1993.

the first, a discourse comes into being through repetition and reification, and *as such* is dynamic. Here we encounter the second major tension within narrative functions: tension between the sense of permanence required by the delimiting function and the risks which accompany the dynamics necessary for perpetuation.

Perpetuation can perhaps best be understood as the "constant attempt to arrest the infinite flow" of difference and thereby create a fixed center.[31] This refers to the conceptual vocabulary of Deleuze and Guattari, who see the modern condition defined by the contradictory global tendencies of flows (the fluid movement of people and ideas) and of territorialization (the fixing, the freezing, of flows).[32] Territorialization is a process of "coding" the incessant flows. But a 'fixed flow' is an oxymoron: hence paradoxically the center must always move to stay fixed.

As discussed, any fixing of meaning entails privileging interpretations. These interpretations are bound via discursive practices to signifiers which form points of arrestation, nodal or discursive points. In the case of states, for example, borders and citizenship/immigration laws are examples of the privileged discursive points. But what about the non-privileged interpretations? While marginalized often to the point of near-invisibility, seldom do they disappear entirely. On the contrary, they reappear in the constant tension between delimiting and perpetuation as the challenging, or counter-hegemonic, function.

Challenging: the counter-hegemonic function

"The death of a social machine," muse Deleuze and Guattari, "has never been heralded by a disharmony or a dysfunction; on the contrary, social machines make a habit of feeding on the anxieties they engender, and on the infernal operations they regenerate."[33] Contradictions in society are not failures or mistakes—quite the opposite; tensions between the dominant and the marginalized, the universal and the particular, the religious and the secular, the fantastic and the rational, are the motor which drives formations onward.

Part of the momentum comes from discursive displacement of negative aspects of the dominant discourse onto the marginalized narratives. For example, the anti-immigrant discourse in many Western countries represents immigrants (Mexicans in the US, Algerians in France, Turks in Germany) as

---

31 As Laclau and Mouffe describe it. Cited in Doty, 1993b: 19. See also Doty, 1996b.
32 Deleuze and Guattari, 1977.
33 Deleuze and Guattari: 151. The passage continues: "Capitalism has learned this, and has ceased doubting itself, while even socialists have abandoned belief in the possibility of capitalism's natural death by attrition."

both lazy (living off public welfare) and too hard-working (taking jobs away from the natives). Here we see both a displacement of problems (e.g. domestic and systemic causes of unemployment) and the perpetuation of the dominant discourse *through* the displacement–government and business deflect criticism to "outsiders" who threaten a way of life for which they claim responsibility, even if that way of life may be eroding under their stewardship). This is an example of how the perpetuation function exists in a dialectical relationship with the challenging function: the marginalized narratives form a background against which the dominant discourse can claim to resolve contradictions. The existence of marginalized narratives allows, in Lakatosian vocabulary, the dominant discourse to create auxiliary hypotheses to defend the system's hard core.[34] In less rarefied language: the dominant narrative uses marginalized narratives to justify their existence and deflect criticism.

In sum: The particular resolution of respective contradictions determines the mode of relations within a system. Political strategies of both consent and coercion are premised on the promise of contradiction resolution. The possibility of change resides in the ability of contradictions to persist and challenge strategies of consent or coercion through logic, debate, protest, or insurgency–in short by "decoding" the encoded world, by "deconstructing," the 'way things are,' and thereby articulating the possibilities that things can be different than imagined.

Thus, those discourses marginalized through the delimiting and perpetuating functions are in some sense always potential challenges to the dominant discourse. They are "minor narratives" (against the backdrop of metanarratives), existing despite (and partially because of) exclusion, sublimation, or suppression. Their persistence can suggest alternate depictions of familiar events, question accepted interpretations, and contest encoded structures of understanding.[35] Writing of the marginalized narrative of African-American experience, for example, James Baldwin holds a mirror to white myths:

> The American Negro has the great advantage of having never believed that collection of myths to which white Americans cling: that their ancestors were all freedom-loving heroes, that they were born in the greatest country the world has ever seen, or that Americans are invincible in battle and wise in peace, that Americans have always dealt honorably with the Mexicans and Indians, and all other neighbors or inferiors, that American men are the world's most direct and virile, that American women are pure...The ten-

---

34 See Lakatos, 1970.
35 Lyotard, 1989.

dency has been [for Blacks], insofar as this was possible, to dismiss white people as slightly mad victims of their own brainwashing.[36]

Because of their ability to challenge accepted ideas, minor narratives are associated with social activism: pointing in the U.S., for instance, to the historical exclusion of women's, black, Latino/a, or gay narratives from places where the metanarrative is perpetuated, e.g. television, churches, government, schools, textbooks, and the like. Yet one should be careful of privileging minor narratives, for they are not *a priori* morally superior, any more than metanarratives are *a priori* morally inferior. Neo-nazi, racist and fascist groups, for example, also form minor narratives which challenge the established norms of liberal capitalist society.[37]

THE INTERPLAY OF THE FOUR FUNCTIONS

Ordering creates an end, and in the creation of an end it also creates a beginning. From this stems, as Arthur C. Danto writes, the possibility of narrative and "all that narrative presupposes: the openness of the future, the inalterability of the past, the possibility of effective action."[38] Narratives are the linguistic architecture of existence. Despite their ultimate claim to seamlessly represent reality in all its material and metaphysical manifestations, narratives are structurally dependent on the elasticity of language. As such, as shown in the sections on delimiting and perpetuation, slippages, elisions, displaced contradictions, logical ellipses, inconsistencies and paradoxes are not by-products of imperfect narratives, but inherent structural elements. The struggle of political groups or social classes for control over power, culture, or territory can be approached by studying the discursive possibilities of such struggle's intelligibility. Two interwoven areas of analysis follow from this: the "coincidence of speech and listening"[39] which creates and highlights unity, identity, and stability and the disjuncture between speech and listening which creates and hides disorder, unease, and change.

Taken together, the four narrative functions presented above sketch the discursive nature of social systems. The ordering and delimiting functions form the fundamental basis for experienced reality: the linguistic harnessing of temporality creates the possibility for discursive formations which bind the material world to interpretive schemes. The hegemonic and counter-hegemonic functions express process and change within the system.

---

36 Baldwin, 1963.
37 See Rupert, 1997.
38 Danto, 1985:363.
39 Barthes, 1986:102.

In examining foreign policy discourse in united Germany I am primarily concerned with the functions of perpetuation and change. These categories, however, are not neatly separable. Let us briefly look at their interrelation. The ontological function (ordering) usually functions at the level of unquestioned assumptions. It is rarely the focus of analysis, save for philosophical investigations (especially phenomenology, hermeneutics, and (post)structuralism). In the nomothetic tradition, including traditional social science, little time is spent on metaphysical issues, save perhaps for certain branches of anthropology. Even for studies such as this one, the ontological conditions are essentially set–there exists a European philosophical tradition which, even if engaged critically, acts as the base of operations. Most scientific activity takes place at the epistemological level, where debates about what counts as knowledge seldom altering ontological assumptions. This is not to say that epistemology does not impact on ontology–new understandings of self, science (especially physics), and technology (i.e. high-speed communications) do reflect on our understanding of Being. However, it is primarily through the *encounter* with others (rather than through internal developments) that the ontological base can shift.[40]

The encounter with others, however, is circumscribed by the epistemological function of delimiting. To make sense of an encounter the other must (be made to) fit into the metanarrative. The discursive formation delimits the range of acceptable interpretations: the Aztecs saw a god in Cortez, Cortez saw heathen and gold–their encounter was shaped by the metanarratives of their respective systems.[41] Importantly, there is a hermeneutic at work in all encounters, but this is not the correct venue to explore this aspect further. The main point here is that delimiting is the level at which historical and social analysis is often aimed, in the sense of a search for origins. This level encompasses both traditional historical and more radical archeological approaches to the emergence of certain narratives (e.g. liberalism, Marxism, Christianity).[42]

Perpetuation and challenge are essentially subsets of delimiting–in the manner of a feedback loop they influence the epistemological framework. The levels of analysis appropriate to perpetuation and challenge are those parts of social science which seek to understand process, development, and change. The advantage to embedding analysis in a narrative framework is that it allows explanation, if you will, of events without abstracting them from their discursive context. This study of foreign policy discourses in unified Germany aims to capture the tension between perpetuation and challenge in a disordered discursive environment. At the same time this approach can ad-

---

40 See Inayatullah and Blaney, 1996.
41 See Todorov, 1987.
42 See for example the approach in Boroujerdi, 1996.

dress more empirical questions such as: how it was possible for the German parliament to reverse its position on the deployment of German troops in a short time span?

The narratives of perpetuation and challenge are relevant to policy formation. What options are available and chosen depend in part on the "discursive spaces" which create conditions of possibility.[43] As Sanjoy Banerjee notes,

> The production of narrative representations of events, situations, and histories is central to national policy formation and to transnational coalition policies. This is because narratives define the collective subjects that are the actors in the international arena. Shared narratives are essential for the maintenance of collective subjectivity for international coalitions, and even for individual states.[44]

The same can be said for policy at the national level. Accordingly, different modes of narrative production will result in different policy options. Different stories about Germany's role in the post-Cold War era create different realms of possibility, policy, and action. Foreign policy, as the following section illustrates, acts as a delimiter of national identity for the modern sovereign state, and thus as a locus for competing narratives of perpetuation and challenge.

National Identity, Sovereignty, and Foreign Policy

THE NATION-STATE AS A DISCURSIVE COMMUNITY AND FOREIGN POLICY AS ONE OF ITS CONSTITUTIVE ELEMENTS

From the prominence of the nation-state in the history of the last two centuries one could reasonably mistake "honor and obey thy nation" for a biblical commandment. Yet any closer look at the phenomenon of the nation-state quickly reveals how recent a development it really is. Nationalism solidified a new form of collective identity in the wake of decaying narratives of traditional society. The eighteenth century saw the decentering of traditional religious and monarchical orders and the rise of mobility in all sectors of life, from the mass production of the printed word to the selling of one's own labor. The sacred narratives of the church and of strictly stratified societies lost relevance and meaning in a context of mass mobilization, secularization, rationality, and the notion of individual rights.[45]

The upheaval wrought by new forms of production effectively "deterritorialized" identity. The old state formations (such as divine rule) no longer resolved contradictions in a meaningful manner. Marx famously cap-

43 See Bonham and Shapiro, 1994:9.
44 Banerjee, 1996:10.
45 See Habermas, 1989; Andersen, B., 1983.

tured modernity's dislocation of society: all that is solid melts into air. In the sociological language of Giesen and Junge, modernity "decoupled" the social codes, interpretive guidelines similar to delimited narratives, from process, the coherent perpetuation of codes. The trope of the nation rises as a superior code of inclusion amidst the disintegration of previously existing collectivities.[46]

The modern concept of "nation" amalgamated "the People (Volk)" and "the Nation," categories which were previously not considered identical. This new subject became the object of the new State, the nation-state, where the State, as "a regulating idea or principle in reflection...that organizes the parts and the flows into a whole," reflects and organizes flows newly coded by nationalism.[47] It is thus that we can speak of nationalism as a means of re-territorialization, a means of delimiting anew the order required for coherent social life. Sankaran Krishna addresses precisely these points when he writes:

> Nationalism is, ultimately, the territorialization of identity: it is the endowing of an inert first nature, a pre-lingual geography if you will, with content, sacrality, and the evocations of home. It is perhaps unsurprising that a practice oriented toward the creation and policing of boundaries, premised on the simultaneous and dialectical production of identity and difference, would find its discursive structure in the form of narrative. ... [Nationalism] unites and divides humanity alongside the conversion of the hierarchy of medieval, sacral space into a post-Galilean, horizontal, secular space of sovereign nation-states. The nation emerges to displace (and, unsuccessfully, to suppress) all the new found anxieties of the modern world.[48]

Let us focus for a moment here on the "simultaneous and dialectical production of identity and difference." This corresponds to the general delimiting and perpetuating function of narratives. A narrative of collective identity, of belonging, must reasonably identify members and non-members. In pre-modern narratives of belonging solidarity expressed itself primarily (though by no means exclusively) along religious, caste or class lines. Nationalism "made the shared cultural heritage of language, literature, and history congruent with the organizational form of the state," as Habermas notes, and this novel development caused a shift in primary associations of belonging.[49] "Citizen" became a new category of belonging, and with it arose a new category of outsider: the foreigner as member of another state and also those des-

46 Giesen and Junge, 1991: 256. See also Giesen1993 for a far more detailed explanation.

47 Deleuze and Guattari, 1983: 219.

48 Krishna n.d.: 50-51.

49 Habermas, 1989: 253.

ignated "non-citizen" within the state.[50] As identity became more closely tied to the nation, difference also became defined in relation to the nation.

The production of identity and difference is simultaneous because the one contains the possibility for the other; meaning is created through difference.[51] It is dialectical because the "outside" is also a creation of the "inside." An extreme example, noted in chapter one, is the notion that Lebensraum arose in large part in order to spatially displace domestic social problems. It did this by presenting the very existence of non-German countries as an external threat to Germany's existence, and these countries came to be perceived as "preventing" natural German expansion. This perception of internal threat had a significant bearing on Germany's foreign policy, and also domestic policy of the time, since opposition to this "normal" idea had to be marginalized. This is an example of a situation, as David Campbell neatly puts it, "in which internal threats made possible external dangers and external dangers controlled internal threats" thereby creating an "interpretive matrix" through which policy was carried out.[52] More abstractly, we see here the expression of the other in oneself, where "the definition of the internal other and the external other compound one another, and both of these seep into the definition given to the other within the interior of the self."[53]

The internal and external other of modern identity is projected onto the sovereign state. The state in its function as a "cerebral ideality...superimposed on the material evolution of societies"[54] is a material manifestation of modernity's response to the tension between universality and particularity.[55] Two powerful modern parallel conceptions–those of the autonomous individual and the sovereign state–work to re-channel the tension, and to resolve it through spatial displacement: inside the state people *qua* citizens can connect to the positive elements of humanity, while outside the state lurks difference and eternal anarchy.[56] This is a great paradox: the state is the particular instantiation of universal values, yet without the state there would be no framework for the realization of these values; hence, these values would be beyond reach–life would

---

50 The creation of "citizen" as a salient identity had profound liberating effects which I do not wish to gloss over. Feudal caste systems, women, blacks in the US, and religious groups, among others, were able to use their theoretical status as "equal citizens" to combat many of the accepted norms of previous systems. The fact that citizenship also necessitated new forms of identity premised on new enemies does not imply that the old forms were in some sense "superior."
51 See Connolly, 1991.
52 Campbell, 1992: 71.
53 Connolly, 1989: 326.
54 Deleuze and Guattari, 1983:219.
55 See Eisenstadt, 1991.
56 Walker, 1993. See also Ashley, 1989; George, 1994.

revert to the stereotyped Hobbesian nightmare of nasty, brutish, and short. Viewed in this way, Walker comments, the modern state rests its legitimacy on the claim that it alone

> is able to allow the citizens of particular states to participate in broader humanity, no matter whether this participation is understood to be a product of mere utilitarian prudence or some more elevated ethical or communitarian principle. ... [S]uch an account of universality within the particular community implies the acceptance of the necessity of violence and war between particular communities struggling to survive in a states system that is simultaneously universal and particularistic.[57]

The juxtaposition of universality and particularity in the nation-state relies on the creation of an exclusive space in which social practices can be, as John Agnew writes, rationalized, homogenized, and incorporated under state regulation.[58]

The narrative of the nation, like any narrative, seeks privileged points of arrestation where the flow of meaning can be channeled. The modern sovereign nation-state privileges those points which most effectively delineate the inside/outside barrier central to identity/difference. Creating and maintaining territoriality requires specific nodal points to clearly demarcate the nature of inside and outside. These are crucial to the ability of the nation-state to perform its contradiction-resolving task. Border control, diplomacy, travel restrictions and rules for contact with foreigners are some of the many nodal points which serve this function. These, among many others, are institutionalized in the context of policy toward the outside, or foreign policy, one of the most central locations for defining the identity of a nation-state.[59]

Foreign policy is the offspring of sovereignty. Sovereignty signifies the ability of a state to claim its legitimate place in an anarchical state system. Sovereignty is the sacred vessel of state identity, and its maintenance is the first line of defense against attempts to centralize the international system, either through enforceable international law or world government. It is the master narrative of inside/outside. Political science has tended to treat sovereignty as an unquestioned assumption, an ontological category similar, for instance, to the category of the human body as an autonomous realm. Indeed, the sovereign state is the anthropomorphism of the sovereign man; rational, autonomous, and self-reliant. As Ashley writes, "the sovereign figure of man ... supplies the constitutive principle of both (a) the modern state, as sovereign *subject* of rational collective violence, and (b) domestic society, as the *object*

---

57 Walker, 1993:151.
58 Agnew, 1994b:93.
59 See Doty, 1993a, also Ferguson, 1996.

domain subordinated to the state's sovereign gaze."[60] The state appears, as Ashley remarks about Kenneth Waltz's classic realist treatise *Man, the State, and War*, as the mediator between man and war.[61] And it is *as* mediator that contemporary political science discourse tends to treat sovereignty.

However, as Biersteker and Weber wonder, "Perhaps statecraft is not primarily about relations between different state units, but about the construction and reconstruction of the units themselves."[62] Perhaps, as Walker, Bartelson, and others point out, all the focus on sovereignty as mediator "encourages a certain amnesia about its historical and culturally specific character."[63] Rather than defining sovereignty as primarily the set of norms and laws which define a nation-state as an autonomous unit, we can agree with Walker's dense formulation that sovereignty "is the key practice through which a specifically modern reification of spatiotemporal relations affirms a specifically modern answer to all questions about who we could possibly be."[64] The sets of laws and norms–and attendant policies–stem from sovereignty's answer to the question of identity. And when identity is unsettled or challenged, sovereignty does not remain unscathed, rather its practices shift and change.

Foreign policy is the key practice through which sovereignty–and with it core assumptions of identity–is articulated. Maintaining one's own sovereignty, and the integrity of the system of sovereign nation-states, is the primary theoretical task of foreign policy. The principle of state sovereignty serves to delimit (and discipline) the realm of inside and outside, and foreign policy is the primary way in which the state expresses this delimiting function. Foreign policy exists in a dialectical relation with the concept of sovereignty: without a concept of sovereignty, foreign policy is meaningless, but since sovereignty is not an *a priori* given, the understanding of sovereignty is partially dependent on the practices of foreign policy.

---

60 Ashley, 1989: 268.

61 Ibid.

62 Biersteker and Weber, 1996: 5-6.

63 Quoted in Ibid.: 2., original quote in Walker, 1993:166. See also Bartelson, 1995 and Weber, 1995.

64 Walker, 1993: 154. On the same page Walker continues: "The principle of state sovereignty is less an abstract legal claim than an exceptionally dense political practice. As a response to the problems of proliferating autonomies in a world of dissipating hierarchies, it articulates a specifically modern account of political space, and does so through the resolution of three fundamental contradictions. It resolves, in brief, the relation between unity and diversity, between the internal and the external and between space and time. It does so by drawing on the philosophical, theological and cultural practices of an historically specific civilization driven by the need to realize yet also control those moments of autonomy that emerged in the complex transitions of early modern Europe."

Seen in light of its role as a privileged nodal point, there is more going on in foreign policy than the managing of external relations of nation-states. Campbell, in the most comprehensive treatment of foreign policy and identity to date, differentiates between 'Foreign Policy' as the conventionally defined task of representing a country's interests abroad, and 'foreign policy' as the process of determining the broader context of identity and difference which informs Foreign Policy. Understanding foreign policy in this way shifts our understanding

> *from* a concern of relations *between* states which takes place *across* ahistorical, frozen and pregiven boundaries, *to* a concern with *the establishment of boundaries* that constitute, at one and the same time, the 'state' and the 'international system.' ... Foreign policy ... is thus to be retheorized as one of the boundary-producing practices central to the production and reproduction of the identity in whose name it operates.[65]

'Lower case' foreign policy corresponds to the delimiting stage of narrative–here it constitutes identity through delimiting possible interpretations of global society, e.g. by hypostatizing the state as *a priori* and ahistoric. 'Upper case' Foreign Policy corresponds to the perpetuation stage, for it is concerned more with reproducing than with constituting the existing identity and, in the process of reproducing, containing challenges.[66] An analysis of foreign policy discourses illuminates the ways in which collective subjects–here the idea of the German nation–are delimited, perpetuated, and challenged. [67]

The crucial distinction between positivist foreign policy analysis and one informed by constructivist approaches is a shift in focus on the "object" of the inside/outside distinction: for (neo)realist and (neo)liberal approaches to foreign policy "inside/outside" refers to "anarchy/order" in the world system. The ensuing research questions swirl around this dualistic tension, and identity/difference is external to identity: it comes down to "us and them." For discursive approaches, inside/outside reflects the tension of identity/difference *within* the subject of research: us and them inside us.

---

65 Campbell, 1992: 69,75.
66 Ibid.: 76,78.
67 As Doty notes, foreign policy-makers act according to "social scripts." Because of the scripted nature of social action, she writes, "they are involved in a ritual production or repudiation of [their] social order. Foreign policy thus becomes a practice that produces a social order as well as one through which individual and collective subjects themselves are produced and reproduced." Doty, 1993:301.

THE SOVEREIGN PARADOXES OF GERMAN UNIFICATION

Sovereignty Redux?

German unification forced a rethinking not only of Foreign Policy but also of foreign policy, especially the meaning of Germany's status as a suddenly "fully" sovereign state. The ratification of the 2+4 Treaties on the External Aspects of German Unification officially lifted the constraints on German sovereignty imposed by the allies after World War Two. This event is described primarily in terms of 'reacquisition,' or 'restoring,' or 'regaining' sovereignty.[68] Yet the concept of sovereignty was, if anything, far less clear in 1990 than in 1945. European integration and the attendant theories of neo-liberalism promoted the dissolution of some areas of state sovereignty into supranational institutions.[69] The willingness of other European states to "give up" some sovereignty to the European Community made West Germany's postwar economic and political recovery a resounding success, and West Germany had a long tradition of sharing sovereignty in the areas of economics and social issues within the framework of the European Community.[70] German Chancellor Helmut Kohl's boilerplate adage that German unity can only happen in the context of European integration directly supported the integrationist teleology of limited sovereignty.

The tension between celebrating "regaining" sovereignty and general support for "relinquishing" sovereignty to the European Community (soon to be the European Union) gave rise to a quizzical sentiment, pithily posed by Timothy Garten Ash: having relinquished sovereignty in order to regain it, had Germany now regained sovereignty only to give it away?[71]

With this paradox Germany entered its second unification in an international context which offered no clear prescription for sovereignty or national identity. Concomitant with the struggles over the nature of national continuity discussed in chapter one, foreign policy initially offered more questions than answers about the nature of the new Germany. As a delimiter of national identity foreign policy was looked to as a source for direction and assurance. Different interpretations of foreign policy and national understanding emerged and competed to perpetuate a coherent basis for identity and policy formation.

---

68 See, among others, Szabo, 1992; Hacke, 1993; Hacker, 1995.

69 The classic neo-liberal text remains Keohane and Nye, 1977, but see also Gilpin, 1987. On the changing state of postwar sovereignty see Hinsley, 1986.

70 See, among others, Wurm, 1995 and Bulmer and Patterson, 1996.

71 Ash, 1993.

The next two chapters look at the emergence of two competing narratives of German foreign policy in light of the tension between classical and pragmatic sovereignty. The first narrative sees Germany becoming a "normal" country in the guise of a great power, and shares common assumptions with the first part of Ash's sentence: those who feel that Germany has relinquished sovereignty in order to regain it, and, accordingly, are troubled by the specter of "losing" it again to integration. The second narrative, which sees Germany's role as a motor for global governance, comes directly from the pragmatic view contained in the sentiment that sovereignty, once regained, remains to be relinquished. Common to both is an endeavor to delimit a post-unification foundational narrative as a basis for identity and a platform for policy.

3. The Narrative of Normalcy: Germany as a Great Power

In a recent speech to the German Society for Foreign Policy, German President Roman Herzog inquired after the "intellectual qualifications" (*geistiges Rüstzeug*) and "mental posture" (*mentalen Haltung*) necessary to forge a coherent approach to foreign policy.[1] His emphasis on the psychological element of the process hints at the centrality of discourses in delimiting ranges of options and action for foreign policy. This chapter explores the first of two candidates for master narratives of German foreign policy that have emerged since 1989. They are candidates, because neither narrative exerts exclusive dominance even in the high-level policy-making circles. Nonetheless, they are both hegemony-seeking and, as such, lay claim to the interpretive economy through which policies and identities are formed and formulated.

The narrative presented here relates a tale of a tragically divided organic nation-state restored through unification to its natural position as a Great Power. The criteria for being a Great Power are culled mostly from the repertoire of 'objective' facts such as geography and demography, although the nation-state requires the breath of life from its people to validate its power position. To re-attain Great Power status thus requires a process of normalization; hence the designation of the "normalization" narrative. The normalization narrative is not, in and of itself, nationalistic, although its vocabulary of sovereign states in a version of qualified international anarchy tend to privilege many characteristic nationalist understandings, such as the homogeneous state and *a priori* national interests.

The normalization narrative is given life through the writings of academics and policy-experts who influence policy based on their reputation, affiliation with think tanks, positions, and status as opinion-makers and official interpreters of history.[2] Unencumbered by the politicians' prerogative of diplomatic language, the clearest portrayal of the normalization narrative is often to be found in the texts of the foreign policy academicians and experts. I will focus in this chapter on the "mainstream" and center-right texts of the German foreign policy community authored by prominent academics such as Hacke, Schöllgen, Schwarz, Fest, and Stürmer, exploring the general contours of the narrative and its ideological heritage.

---

1 Herzog, 1995:1.
2 See Giesen, 1993.

Classical Realism Revisited

The basic narrative of the "Normalisierungsnationalisten" begins with a view of foreign policy rooted firmly in the classical realist tradition. Joachim Fest, publisher of the largest and most influential German daily newspaper, the *Frankfurter Allgemeine Zeitung*, captures this when he contends that "the fluctuating history of Europe has taught us since the Middle Ages, that every European rapprochement was only ever the manifestation of an instinct for survival. ... Of course there were other motivating forces at work, but these were always second thoughts."[3] From this perspective, a divided Germany along with the bipolar world and its highly structured security construction were aberrations which diverted attention from the basic tectonic workings of international relations. These tectonic movements remain the rudiments of classical political realism for Fest and the group I am identifying as normalists.

Classical realism proposes a worldview conforming to the positivist notion of an unbridgeable gulf between fact and values. Thus it is possible to construct two opposing worlds, the world of the *desirable* versus the world of the *possible*, and argue that politics must concern itself with the possible to avoid the utopian and dangerous paths of the desirable.[4] "A dramatic loss of touch with reality has been visible for years" complains Christian Hacke, a high-profile historian at the Leadership Academy of the Federal Army, "Increasingly fewer political scientists are capable of recognizing *what is*, because they are almost exclusively concentrated on the question of what *should be*."[5] For Hacke and fellow realists, the world of the desirable amounts to dangerous pipe dreams of peace and harmony, while the world of the possible consists of the discovery of objective facts about human nature based on the (bastardized) version of Hobbes which constructs human nature as unremittingly self-interested, and therefore driven toward a search for power which transcends space and time:

> [I]t is difficult for people to recognize the principal differences between foreign and domestic policy. Unlike domestic policy, foreign policy has no legislation or rule of law (*Gesetzgebung oder Rechtssicherheit*). Beyond state's borders there is also no common morality. Mistrust, not only trust, is a necessary currency for one's own interests. Only very few states trust each

---

3 Fest, 1994: 52.
4 Carr, 1964/1939; Morgenthau, 1954.
5 Hacke, 1993.

other and enter into coalitions or alliances to protect themselves from others.[6]

This passage contains most of the elements of classical political realism in unadulterated form. Domestic policy has legislation and rule of law; it is the ordered world of inside, a spatially and temporally secure world. Foreign policy lacks these generally-valid rules, thus it is anarchic, uncertain, and most of all has "no common morality": it is amoral. Mistrust follows naturally as a principle of interest definition, since the anarchic and amoral international environment allows for no assumptions of security, only insofar as other states join together "to protect themselves from others." This is the bottom line, even if states sometimes undergo variations from the norm, as with European integration under conditions of bipolarity. Germany benefits considerably from the European Union (see below), yet in the normalist view a revitalized reliance on power politics changes the theoretical premises of European integration, making it possible to regard European integration as an instrumental necessity of the cold war.[7]

Political union in particular is increasingly perceived as a chimera since nation-states remain the conditions for civilization and the arbiters of order. As Fest explains, "In the economic field union is really only a question of procedure," while "Common market and separate statehood are basically the norm."[8] This reinforces another key realist opposition between economics ("procedure") and politics.[9] The dynamics of this dichotomy make European political union as envisioned in the Maastricht treaty all but theoretically impossible. Nearly all of the academic normalists commit what still amounts to diplomatic heresy by claiming that the limits of political integration have been reached. Fest, from his powerful public-opinion-shaping pulpit, articulates this most provocatively: "Convinced Europeans consoled themselves over and over again with the idea that economic integration would sooner or later be followed by political union. But that was and is a simplistic Marxist illusion."[10] Of course, if the political teleology of European integration is merely a simplistic Marxist illusion, then leading Christian Democrats have either been duped or are harboring secret agendas, the very charge which German politicians take great pains to refute. Fest may be exaggerating to make his point,

---

6 Hacke, 1993: 411-12. He also writes on 553: "Schmidt [who Hacke idolizes] stands in a tradition of foreign policy realism which can be followed back from Henry Kissinger, to Hans Morgenthau, George Kennan, Otto von Bismarck, Lord Salisbury, Carl von Clausewitz, Niccolo Machiavelli and Marc Aurel to Cicero and Thucydides."
7 Fest, 1994.
8 Fest, 1994: 54, 62.
9 See Spero, 1977.
10 Fest, 1994: 54.

but his claim that political integration is an unlikely reality is increasingly shared.

Significantly, normalist skepticism of European integration is not a plea for an unraveling of existing integration in the sense that conservative U.S. Republicans in the United States Congress wish explicitly to dismantle the structure of the welfare state. Rather, it is a call to make the most out of existing integration, which is correctly perceived as largely favoring Germany, by channeling political energy into realizing Germany as a Great Power in a far more traditional sense. As the most powerful country in the EU, Germany could exceed historic levels of influence. Strengthening the European Parliament and direct elections of EU officials would play to Germany's advantage in population size, and the entry of Austria and most of Scandinavia into the EU creates the specter of a German-led bloc, which would only be enhanced by any future admission of Poland, the Czech or Slovak Republics, or Hungary, all of whom would owe Germany a considerable debt for acting as their advocate for EU membership.

A heightened interdependent context, therefore, is not presented as an obstacle *per se* to greater national power. It is when integration would seem to dissolve the very foundations of that power that integration must be halted and portrayed as utopian rather than pragmatic. "[W]hile the integration of the Federal Republic into Europe is, *for the moment*, an important common interest," writes Gregor Schöllgen, "it should not take a form which will in the long term inhibit the development of Germany and with it, the development of the continent. ... To the extent that Europe distances itself from political union, the Federal Republic must also 'become a normal European nation-state.' ... [H]owever, the Germans are not prepared for this."[11] Here Schöllgen captures the essence of the normalist approach in a nutshell: political union must not be allowed to blind the public and policy-makers alike from their task of restoring Germany to its role as an autonomous Great Power, whether within or without a system of political integration.

Being a Great Power, as everyone but the extreme right is careful to point out, does not mean being threatening or uncooperative. It means becoming comfortable in a world where 'national interest' is not a dirty word, but as natural a concept as it seems to be for US or French policy-makers. Being a Great Power does not necessarily contradict the idea of some form of further European integration, such as the "core Europe" concept or the inclusion of Scandinavia and Eastern Europe. What being a Great Power in an expanded EU does mean, representatively articulated by Hans-Peter Schwarz, is that "Germany will have to *stop imagining that its interests can be 'European'*; it

---

11 Schöllgen, 1994. Emphasis added.

will have no choice but to recognize that it has international interests and to define them as such."[12] "Realism," explains Schöllgen, "means understanding how removed from reality (*weltfremd*) the illusion of the Germans is, that power politics, at least for them, is a thing of the past."[13]

CLASSIC REALISM UPDATED: "REALIST VALUES" OR POWER BEGETS RESPONSIBILITY

Sophisticated, modern-day realists are concerned with not seeming nostalgic for a return to the multipolar uncertainty of the sort which heralded World War One. Assumptions of amorality and mistrust in international affairs, however, leave little hope for any idealistic way out of the security dilemma through, for example, collective security measures or a dissolution of the nation-state. But any realist solution is also trapped by the amoral status of its own foundations embodied in balance of power arguments to address "power vacuums" and other threats. German realists, or any other, would deny that amoral is equivalent to immoral, yet here is precisely the source of a real realist problem. Few realists would argue today that military or military-backed strength is the source of cooperation in the world, for that would expose most democratic rhetoric as hollow. So a problem for modern realists, and especially for Germans grappling with the legacy of two world wars, is how to reconcile the ethical elements of a liberal world order with the foundational amorality of a realist ontology. One solution for modern realists is to seek recourse in the putatively non-moral realm of the rational actor: to act rationally is to act realistically, and the one encourages the other. It is at this locus where German realists, attempting to resolve the tension between their pessimistic prophecies of eternal atavism and their commitment to creating a peaceful world, smuggle morality into a purportedly amoral world-view.[14] The values of the "Atlantic" or "Western" Civilization (self-reliance, patriotism, piety, among others) are the values which allow the security dilemma to be mitigated while being retained as the theoretical centerpiece. In post-wall Germany these 'realist values' result in a vocabulary shift from the amoral term 'power' to the moral term 'responsibility' through the following narrative:

The risks of a realist world are to be navigated and controlled through the active projection of values because these values allow for the recognition of an enlightened self-interest which can mitigate the security dilemma. The more power a country has, the greater its ability to assuage the negative but natural effects of realism. While policy makers cannot deny our base instincts,

---

12 Schwarz, 1994: 86. Emphasis added.
13 Schöllgen, 1993: 15.
14 Thanks to Naeem Inayatullah for the metaphor of "smuggling."

they can adopt utilitarian principles to move toward a realm of enlightened self-interest instead of the expression of self-interest through naked power. This implies an "evolution" from a war of all against all to an awareness of our plight as self-interested persons, where the awareness of our common self-interest enables us to control, though not fundamentally change, our own worst attributes. This control leads us away from the proverbial state of nature to a plane where it is rational to be moral. Conversely, and importantly, it is also moral to be rational. Thus, it is moral and rational for a state to strive to create the best possible environment where its own self-preservation is secure. The process of control of naked power through the recognition of transcendent values can be extended beyond the apocryphal state of nature to the workings of the international realm. Thus, the projection of values allows actors to move beyond the simplistic and traditional concept of balance of power premised in an amoral universe to an imperative. This imperative is a *responsibility* for mitigating anarchy, not for reasons of good will, but out of self-preservation. The move from power to responsibility is cast as analogous to the move from short-term self-interest to long-term self-interest in the state of nature, whereby the basic ontology need not be questioned, only the strategies dealing with its consequences.

Gregor Schöllgen articulates perhaps best the realist view of responsibility:

> [O]vernight the Federal Republic has once again been catapulted into the role of a continental great power with global significance. This situation requires the Germans to cope with their new power, and thus *calls for a special responsibility*. The prerequisite is a *realistic, sober*, and above all, fully aware recognition that German foreign, security and economic policy, even its policy on asylum-seekers, *is power policy (Machtpolitk)*.[15]

"New power" calls for "special responsibility." One could indeed claim on ethical grounds that responsibility is central to the exercise of power, in that power consists *inter alia* of the ability to influence other's lives, but this leads away from a view of power as amoral and constrains it within a moral framework. Schöllgen, however, claims that the prerequisite for responsibility, rather than a moral grounding, is power policy (*Machtpolitik*).[16] The dictionary definition of being responsible offers both "having a capacity for moral decisions and [being] therefore accountable" and "being capable of rational thought or action."[17] Responsibility is thus a concept which straddles the ethics of moral obligation and the amoral elements of rationality. For the normalists, conflating power and responsibility enables power politics to apply

---

15 Schöllgen, 1994: 40.
16 See Lukes, 1986.
17 Random House Dictionary, 1987.

ethics as a form of procedural rationality. This is a version of having one's cake and eating it too: foreign policy and the workings of the international environment continue to be seen as ultimately amoral, yet power politics can express morality (and thereby gain democratic legitimacy) if one understands power as begetting responsibility. 'Power' has negative connotations, 'responsibility' has positive ones. Thus, Hacke can write that

> Germany strives with his greater economic, geopolitical, demographic and total political weight *not for more power, but for more responsibility.* Germany wants to contribute to Europe's being able to rightly assume his responsibility for the creation of a new world order.[18]

Here note how power (as a product of "greater economic weight" etc.) does not beget "more power" but, rather, power begets "responsibility." However, Hacke proceeds to equate the two terms by openly chiding Genscher for once presenting responsibility as the *rejection* of power politics: "Postulating 'power' and 'responsibility' as opposites is a fatal misunderstanding of German history."[19] Genscher might, Hacke admits, be "morally unassailable" by making such statements, but Genscher is mixing morality with foreign policy, and thereby confusing the issue. Eventually Hacke synthesizes his two understandings into the term "responsible power politics," clearly denoting the power element of responsibility.[20]

This is a way of rehabilitating the concept of power from its associations with brutality and repression. Realist theory assumes power as the primordial human element and presents it as empty of moral content in axiomatic formulations such as "power is a factor in the lives of humans, peoples and states."[21]Power here is a morally neutral concept waiting to be filled. Thus, writes Schöllgen, power contains within itself both the "danger of its misuse and the chance for its use (Einsatz) for life-saving, peace-maintaining, civilizational purposes."[22] "Responsible power politics" (Hacke) can clearly only work with the latter. Indeed, the argument starts to turn itself around – "life-saving," "peace-maintaining" and indeed civilization (both its spread and its continuation) depend on the proper, that is responsible, use of power. To be good world citizens in this context necessitates rejecting "fear of power" in favor of "responsible power politics." The recent currency of responsibility serves to rehabilitate the burdened term of *Machtpolitik* (power politics).

---

18 Hacke, 1993: 467.
19 Ibid.: 472.
20 Ibid.: 585.
21 Schöllgen, 1993: 154.
22 Ibid.

REVISITING THE 'SPECIAL PATH'

The rehabilitation of *Machtpolitik* has a potentially profound effect on dominant interpretations of German history. The concept of the German *Sonderweg* (special path), throughout most of the Cold War a stable trope in West Germany for the perditious excesses of power politics, has entered a period of contestation barely ponderable five years earlier.[23] Until the 1980s the Federal Republic was regarded not only as an opportunity for a new beginning after the Third Reich, but also as the correct, normal, and desirable incarnation of the German nation. "The successful history of the Federal Republic as a constitutional state, civil society and political economy," explains Manfred Henningen, "represents the answer to the historic pathology of Germany."[24]

National Socialism added cultural ignominy to a prostrate German nation, since widespread popular support for Nazism and unsuccessful resistance to Hitler eroded the semantic distinction between "Nazi" and "German" for most outsiders. A new democratic national identity was required for the new state to break with its past, and this identity was carefully and successfully cultivated. *Westbindung*, ties to the West, became the catchphrase for commitment to Western democratic values, free-market economics and the parliamentary political system. Championed by Adenauer and the Christian Democrats *Westbindung* became the dominant middle, tarnishing critics on the left and the right as anti-democratic idealists. By the mid-1950s, especially after the historic Social Democratic Party Congress in Bad Godesberg in 1959 when the SPD accepted West Germany's integration into NATO, social-democratic opposition to *Westbindung* faded and being tied to the West became a stable part of West German identity.[25] Syllogistically, to doubt a full commitment to the moral, economic, and political systems of the West was to cast the legitimacy of the West German state into heterodox doubt.

The surreal months of occupation and extrication from rubble following unconditional capitulation in May 1945 became the *"Zero Hour"* (*Stunde Null*), the mythic origin for the phoenix-like resurgence and rehabilitation of the Federal Republic. If two abortive attempts at military domination separated by one misshapen democratic experiment showed the wrong paths the nation had taken, the Federal Republic was now sticking to the straight and narrow path, summarized succinctly in Adenauer's campaign slogan: No Experiments!

The inglorious Weimar Republic bequeathed the Federal Republic no proud democratic tradition to fall back upon, causing National Socialism to be

---

23 See Niethammer, 1997.
24 Henningsen, 1995: 589.
25 See Hess, 1986; also for a sociological approach see Schweigler, 1973.

viewed less as an episode of anopsia than a culmination of historical tragedy. The contention that the Third Reich was less an anomaly and more the result of structural flaws in the concept of the German nation-state was supported by the controversy surrounding the historian Fritz Fischer in the 1960s, whose works and students highlighted the continuities between Wilhelmine Germany's imperialist foreign policy and the goals of national socialism.[26] The more Imperial and Weimar Germany became tainted as steps toward National Socialism (for fundamentally different reasons), the more the Federal Republic became constructed by its founders as a fundamentally new entity, with "its unique (*eigenen*), stable, and civil self-consciousness which did not deny the past but understood the Federal Republic as a new beginning."[27]

West Germany became the "real" Germany, morally whole though territorially truncated. This is clearly expressed in the attitude of the Federal Republic to the GDR. The automatic extension of West German citizenship to East Germans, the Hallstein Doctrine, and, last but not least, the very act of incorporation of the GDR as "five new *Länder*" into the existing and unchanged structures of the Federal Republic all testify to the view that the "real" Germany was West Germany, while the GDR remained a variation of the "Soviet Occupation Zone" (*SBZ*, or often simply, "the zone"). *Westbindung* was synonymous with the Federal Republic, and the Federal Republic was Germany.

What began to change in the mid-1980s, especially among young conservatives, was the fundamental acceptance of *Westbindung* as synonymous with the identity of the Federal Republic.[28] The goal of West German policy, domestic and foreign, had been to promote the Western orientation of the Federal Republic in administrative, judicial, security, and economic areas, making *Westbindung* the counterweight to fear of a German 'special path.' To this end, the Federal Republic was constructed precisely *not* as a provisional state. But it is as precisely that which a spectrum from the "intellectual right" to prominent mainstream academics and media are increasingly interpreting the old Federal Republic. Hermann Rudolf writes in the *Süddeutsche Zeitung* of the "special path existence of the Federal Republic;" Christian Hacke talks of "The German 'special path' until 1989."[29] The restoration of full sovereignty is seen as restoring continuity with the Germany of Bismarck: the situation in which Germany finds itself today is "not so different from the situation facing Germany between 1871 and 1945" writes Arnulf Baring – "Germany is like before, or newly again, Bismarck's empire, although in the form given to it by

---

26 On the Fischer controversy see Moses, 1975 and the protagonist's controversial work itself: Fischer, 1986.
27 Naumann, 1994: 437.
28 See Zitelmann et al., 1993.
29 Rudolf quoted in Naumann, 1994: 441, Hacke in 1993: 545.

the Adenauer Republic."[30] "Seen in power-political terms," concurs foreign-policy expert Jochen Thies, "the Federal Republic finds itself since the summer of 1992 again in the same concealed, half-hegemonic position as she did in the Bismarckian empire after 1871 and the Weimar Republic after 1922 with the conclusion of the Rapallo Treaty."[31]

There is a fine line between recognizing the novelty of European politics after the Cold War and proclaiming the Federal Republic of 1949-1990 as a "special path." Jürgen Habermas, a strong critic of this form of "normalization," is afraid historians will come to reduce forty years of the Bonn Republic to, as Habermas puts it, a "not entirely serious Rhein-based federated entity in the shadow of world history. (*Eine nicht ganz ernst zu nehmende Rheinbundexistenz im Schatten der Weltgeschichte*)."[32] Hacke lends credence to Habermas' fears when he writes that a "political birth defect (*Erbfehler*)" of the old Federal Republic was that

> She could not develop her own national identity, *little more than the GDR could*. The Federal Republic and the GDR were "rationale states," they were founded (*Teilgründungen*) by the victorious powers with the goal of preventing a German nation-state from easily rising again.[33]

This passage contains two important elements of normalist thought. First, it equates West and East German identity, giving the impression that both states were equally provisional constructs between 1945 and Germany's "return" in 1990 ("Germany is back" as Gregor Schöllgen phrases it[34]). Secondly, it unsettles the dominant interpretation of the Federal Republic as the "real" Germany by emphasizing its provisional nature and even equating it with the GDR. It is surprising that a prominent historian such as Hacke would present the division of Germany primarily as an explicit attempt to prevent the recreation of a German nation-state, especially since the division resulted precisely not from allied consensus but rather from disagreements about the nature of a unified Germany.[35] But more important than the historical details is the way in which elements of a relatively firm identity are being thrown open.

---

30 First part of the quote in Baring, 1994: 1; second half of the quote in Naumann, 1994: 442.

31 In Zitelmann et. al, Westbindung, quoted in Glotz, 1994. p.69. The original quote reads: "Machtpolitisch gesehen, befindet sich die Bundesrepublik Deutschland seit dem Sommer, 1992 wieder in jener verdeckten, halb-hegemonialen Stellung, wie sie das Bismarck-Reich nach 1871 und die Weimarer Republik, 1922 mit Abschluß des Rapallo-Vertrags besaßen."

32 Habermas, 1995: 172.

33 Hacke, 1993: 537.

34 See Schöllgen, 1994.

35 See Klessmann, 1986.

The historian and publicist Karlheinz Weissmann in his recent book *"Rückruf in die Geschichte. Die deutsche Herausforderung"* includes parliamentary democracy in a list of many stages which Germany has experienced, including modern variations of traditional monarchy and right- and leftwing dictatorships, leading Jörg Lau to comment that "One should let the way in which parliamentary democracy is treated here as a mere transitory phase dissolve slowly on one's tongue; merely a phase of the German soul on the way to itself, like Wilhelmism, National Socialism, and real existing socialism."[36]Weissmann's allusions are a powerful echo of revisionist historians such as Ernst Nolte, who claim that "at some point the famous-notorious final line *(Schlußstrich)* must be drawn ... the National Socialist past should become primarily the property of science and reflection and not become an object of continual polemic and eternal accusation."[37]

Although *sotto voce*, claims like Hacke's and Weissmann's open the space for the implication, if not directly imply, that the Federal Republic's democratic system was a form of government forced on a defeated Germany, similar to the Soviet imposition of socialism in the East. The German people, then, contrary to popular belief, have not been able to freely determine the shape of their nation-state.[38] These claims add to the sense of rapidly breaking taboos in a culture steeped in protocol and proscriptions. Indeed, "new beginnings without taboos" is how Brigitte Seebacher-Brandt welcomes the emergence of an intellectual right.[39] Attempts to view the West German experience as a 'special path' complicates the negative connotations which heretofore have been associated with the term, since both Hitler's suicidal psychosis and Adenauer's painstaking democratic groundwork can both be subsumed under the concept. Removing taboos on the past, the historian Klaus Naumann fears, will come at the cost of imposing taboos on the old Federal Republic.[40]

---

36 Lau, 1994: 913.

37 Ernst Nolte in *Der Spiegel*, October 3, 1994, cited in Henningsen, 1995: 389.

38 While Hacke does not take this to its extreme, Naumann points out that Rainer Zitellmann et. al. do by claiming that the 'Western community of values' is a totalitarian utopia because it claims to ideologically influence the entire population by presenting them with a teleology rather than allowing for, as Brigitte Seebacher-Brandt calls it, "new beginnings without taboos." In Naumann, 1994: 435-36.

39 Quoted in Naumann, 1994. See also Zitelmann and al., 1993, Zitelmann, 1994, and Schwilk and Schacht, 1994. Glotz speaks of the de-tabooization of war in Die falsche Normalisierung, 1994: 47.

40 Naumann, 1994: 446. Naumann writes: "Die Entwertung von 40 Jahren bundesdeutscher Geschichte verbindet sich mit eimen Verbindlichkeitsschwund aller jener Negativerfahrungen, die bislang unter dem Signalwort 'deutscher Sonderweg' oder 'Sonderbewußtsein' Gültigkeit gehabt hatten; eine Annullierung, die über die NS-Zeit hinaus auf macht- und realpolitische Traditionen zurückgreift. ... Die 'Entabuisierung' der Vergan-

If the old Federal Republic has no more claim to the German nation-state than the GDR, then how can the new Germany reject the Bonn Republic yet expect to be accepted as a non-threatening, democratic great power? The answer to this conundrum lies in the normalist school's appropriation of political realist theory as the universal and amoral basis which defines responsibility and normalcy. This is combined with a view of internal cold-war era psychological constraints as responsible for a surfeit of "pacifist-moralistic internationalism" now endangering the nation's progress toward normalcy.[41] If German special paths are at an end, the end is a condition of normalcy. But what is 'normal'?

Defining the Normal State

The word 'normal' has, outside of the natural sciences, two basic meanings: 'not deviating from an established norm' and 'naturally occurring.'[42]While these definitions are not mutually exclusive (something naturally occurring could still be perceived as deviating from an established norm), the inner logic of discursive formations connects the two. The requirements of social cohesion often dictate that what is naturally occurring be considered coeval with non-deviation from norms, especially since those norms form the basis for what persons consider reality. The normalist's 'normal' state expresses the desire to be part of an established international norm for naturally occurring reasons.

The established international norm to which German normalists aspire is perhaps best summarized by Winston Churchill, who proclaimed: "The governments of the world must be entrusted to satisfied nations, who wishing nothing more for themselves than what they had. If the world-government were in the hands of hungry nations, there would always be danger.... Our power placed us above the rest. We were like rich men dwelling at peace within their habitations."[43] Churchill wrote this in the aftermath of World War II, when Germany, in both the sense of the expansionist ideology of its recent Nazi leaders and the "hunger winter" endured among the rubble of its cities, was one of the "hungry nations." Fifty years later one of Germany's leading foreign policy politicians proudly explained to me that Germany today was "a

---

genheit, die damit bewirkt wird, hat die Tabuisierung bundesdeutscher Zeitgeschichte zur Voraussetzung."
41 Hacke, 1993: 541.
42 Websters, 1941 edition: 677.
43 Quoted in Wolin, 1995: 419.

saturated (*saturiertes*) country," adapting Bismarck's well-known term from
era of *Weltpolitik*.[44]

The naturally occurring reasons for Germany's satisfied (or saturated) normalcy are, as Michael Stürmer alliteratively alludes, the four "G's:" "Gewicht
und Größe, Geschichte und Geographie," or Weight and Size, History and
Geography.[45] Under "normal" conditions, that is, a hierarchy of states whose
positions are defined by geographic, economic and military indicators, Germany is by its nature (territory, economic strength, population, etc.) a Great
Power. Germany is thus both *becoming* normal and *returning* to normalcy:
becoming normal because, as a sovereign nation it is following the rules
which insure acceptance in the international community, and returning to
normalcy because, as Schöllgen tells us, the German nation-state "always was
a Great Power, until its dissolution terminated this status. ...[Now] a half-
century after the Second World War Germany was again united, again a nation-state, and *through this* (*und damit*) also again on the way to a European
Great Power."[46]

The question arises how the old Federal Republic, once considered the very
model of the modern nation-state and the most normal of the German Nation's turbulent and cataclysmic incarnations, is being reassessed by the normalist camp as an abnormal special path. The most obvious ways in which the
old FRG was not normal are because: 1. external foreign powers imposed
limitations on German sovereignty; 2. the existence of two German states created an anomaly for the identity and representation of the German nation-
state; and 3. the Cold War created an exceptional security situation which
maintained a permanent, frozen front line. The full reversal of these situations
leaves Germany, in the most basic sense of international law, more normal
than it had been under the conditions of the Cold War. But 'being normal'
does not rest on the mere removal of these 'obstacles.' This fairly self-evident
point enjoys wide agreement; the point of contention surrounds what it takes
to complete the transition from a recently divided country to varying conceptions of the modern German nation-state.

For the normalists, Germany is now free to regain its rightful role as a Great
Power, becoming 'normal' in the same sense that France, Great Britain, or the
United States are "normal" powers who do not balk at talking candidly about

---

44 Personal communication with Karsten Voigt, Winter, 1995.
45 Stürmer quoted in Schöllgen, 1993:140.
46 Schöllgen, 1993: 27, 24. Emphasis added. The original reads "...der [the German na-
tion-state] eben immer auch Großmacht war, bis seine Auflösung zugliech diesen Status
beendete." ... "Ein halbes Jahrhundert nach dem Zweiten Weltkrieg war Deutschland wieder vereinigt, wieder ein Nationalstaat und damit wieder auf dem Weg zu einer europäischen Großmacht."

national interests. Günther Gillessen provides a characteristic overview of the normalist position on "normalcy" and interests:

> Germans feel tempted to negate their nationhood in a vain attempt to flee from the shame which Hitler and his followers brought upon their country. But those who want to forget in fact feel ashamed and do remember in a round-about way. And those who try and run away from their nationality into a 'European' identity remember too, in a different manner. *No attempt at flight will help. Germany will have to become a 'normal' nation among other nations. ... A bad collective conscience will not serve as a guide. ... Identifiable national interests are the basis of continuity, credibility and trust. ...* For the guilt-ridden collective national conscience, the term 'national interests' is banned from the domestic debate and widely regarded as 'politically incorrect' language. *Yet a nation which is not able to talk about its national interests openly and clearly will appear to pursue a hidden, and perhaps suspect, agenda. ...* A country which cannot define its interests properly and set its policies accordingly will be regarded by others as unpredictable and if, in addition, that country is powerful, as dangerous.[47]

So a normal German nation, in order to form national interests, must neither reject the past nor feel guilty about it? Is the hallmark of a normal nation not feeling guilty about terrible deeds committed in that country's name? Such rhetoric seems guaranteed to alarm Germany's neighbors, yet the normalists argue that, quite to the contrary, such an approach is the only way to affirm a non-threatening future. A normal Germany will be non-threatening because of the transparency of its interests, and most importantly because the post-Cold War geopolitical situation is now seen as allowing for the compatibility of German power and European security interests. Schöllgen writes that Germany's security interests were historically incompatible with Europe's security interests *because* "the logic of Germany's political, economic, military, and even geographical position meant that a German nation-state would *always* be a great power and even a possible world power."[48] But this fundamental incompatibility supposedly no longer holds true given European economic integration, security cooperation, and common Western values. Germany can therefore be a 'normal' Great Power without being a threat to Europe. More to the point, it is *only as* a 'normal' power that Germany can fulfill her responsibility to the "European responsibility for peace."[49] Only by becoming more self-interested can Germany become 'normal,' and only by becoming 'normal' can Germany prevent itself from going on a 'special

---

47 Gillessen, 1994: 30-31.
48 Schöllgen, 1994: 37. Emphasis added.
49 Hacke, 1993: 466.

path.' In the interest of European peace, then, this all leads to "one quite simple conclusion" according to Schwarz:

> In the future, Germany will find itself compelled on *objective grounds* to make its foreign policy, and also its European policy, more self-centered, more tightly budgeted and less flexible than it has been, all in the service of a rather narrowly defined national interest. ... [T]his will not occur because Germans have lapsed into old nationalistic habits....[50]

It is not nationalism, because a narrow definition of national interest is interpreted as a natural part of being normal. Furthermore, nationalism implies irrationality, whereas defining national interests conjures up images of rationality. The path toward normalcy is to be sober and realistic. It is Schwarz again who best represents the binary opposition of rational/emotional which typifies this type of realist thought:

> National interest, which always implies the existence of other nations, starts out as *a thoroughly rational concept*: the analysis of one's own interests and the probable reactions of one's partners *demands dispassionate and level-headed* thinking. Interests are a utilitarian category, and the more utilitarian the approach governments take toward achieving them the better. Yet it is also true that *emotional components* such as pride, *group identity*, ... enter into citizens' perceptions of themselves as a nation. Sometimes antipathies and hatred of other nations, and occasionally, self-hatred, play a role. *Wherever disturbances in the emotional dimension exist, rational analyses of self-interest will be more difficult.*[51]

This is a significant insight into how this brand of realist thinking can present itself as non-nationalistic because of the syllogism that emotions have no place in politics, nationalism is emotional, realism is not emotional, therefore realism cannot be nationalistic. As the historian Christian Meier maintains it is only "the continued immaturity of the Germans, that is, their incapacity to deal with a great power, [that brings one] to the conclusion that a German national state is damaging."[52] The normal state here is a state which accepts its natural role in the great distribution of capabilities dutifully and rationally. The central part of this natural role is defining national interest which, despite certain general overlaps, is by definition unique to a nation's history, context, and character. Yet precisely these ingredients for national interest are far from dispassionate, rational occurrences, and therein lies a conundrum even for those who believe emotion is antithetical to ideal politics: how can one disentangle history, rife with consequential emotions and passions, from those

---

50 Schwarz, in Baring, 1994: 117.
51 Ibid.: 129.
52 Quoted in Ely, 1995: 91.

contemporary configurations of a given nation-state (borders, modern language, relations with neighbors) which form the basis for definitions of national interest?

IDENTITY ANALOGIES

We have seen how the normalizing discourse presents Germany as a great power in a context where power begets responsibility. We have also seen how the "objective" facts of Germany's strength entitle it to a power status equal to those countries which make up the power center of the international community as presently organized. How does the normalist approach view Germany in relation to other Great Powers? Germany comes across at least as powerful as France or Britain, far more stable than Russia, though lacking Russia's brute force, and is most similar to the United States, which is widely perceived as entering a state of decline, or at least reduced international activity.

This view of a normal Germany leads to what at first may seem an odd comparison: unified Germany as analogous to the United States in eras when isolationism seriously challenged US foreign policy. "Germany," for Hacke, "potentially a great power with world-wide responsibility, parallels, in the mid-1990s, the USA during the interwar years of 1919-1939."[53] Schwarz picks a different era, that of Republican opposition to NATO and the Marshall Plan: "In some respects one could compare the position of re-unified Germany to that of the United States after WWII."[54] Three elements are at work in these comparisons. First is a quiet equation of US and German potential for power and responsibility which ties into the view of German civilization as paradigmatic. Second is an implicit statement of German interests. Third is a criticism of domestic forces which are being set up to parallel the isolationists of the interwar and immediate postwar United States.

The equation of German and US potential for power and responsibility is not meant to suggest that the capabilities of each nation are in any direct sense identical, but it does suggest that for a variety of reasons Germany is better poised to assume the role of the United States in world affairs should the US, for reasons of decline or isolationism, relinquish its responsibilities. This assumption rests on a vision of Germany as the most economically and culturally powerful country in Europe, such that whether at the head of a unified Europe or even a loosely associated one, Germany would still be the leader of one of the world's most populous and powerful regions.[55] Germany's exces-

---

53 Hacke, 1993: 517.
54 Schwarz in Baring: 127.
55 See Agnew and Corbridge, 1995: 151-155.

sive dependence on exports, which account for a third of the German economy, gives it excellent reasons to be concerned, in the fashion of the United
States, about insuring global free trade. The normalists also take very seriously former President George Bush's offer of "partnership in leadership,"
and feel that this underscores their political right to be the special partner, if
not the heir apparent, to United States leadership, power, and responsibility.

Schwarz sees Germany's "true national interests" as lying in the stabilization of its surroundings, much in the way, he writes, that the United States
saw creating stability in Western Europe as a priority despite the lack of a direct threat to the US mainland.[56] In order to be a stabilizing power Germany,
together with other European countries or even alone, must become a benign
hegemonic power (which is generally how normalists perceive and often ad-
mire the United States), an approach whose basis lies in theories of
hegemonic stability.[57] Repeatedly, normalist literature makes clear that all the
ingredients for an assertive, enlightened, and active Germany fulfilling its
destiny as a European Great Power, eventually as *primus inter pares*, are at
hand.

So how does the normalist discourse, more than five years after unification,
explain that this vision seems far from reality? Why does Germany not seem
poised to lead Europe to stability? If all the "objective" factors are in place for
Germany's new position of power and responsibility, and if all the external
constraints have been removed in the 2+4 Treaty, then what is preventing this
realist vision from being realized? What, from the normalist perspective, is
missing?

NORMALCY WITHIN: THE OTHER OTHER

In a brief sentence Schöllgen identifies the problem: "The Germans have unlearned (*verlernt*), indeed had to unlearn (*verlernen müssen*), how to think in
categories of power." That Germans "had to unlearn" is a particularly noteworthy point, because it helps identify a pattern visible across most all of the
normalist literature. We can see this pattern with Schöllgen's portrayal of
sovereignty as the most important characteristic (Eigenschaft) which will allow Germany to deal "appropriately" with its new power position. The most
salient element of this most important characteristic, however, is not the external recognition of German sovereignty under international law: "Sovereignty is especially also a question of the inner bearing (*Haltung*) of the
population, which expresses itself in quiet composure (*ruhiger Gelassen-*

---

56 Presumably he means, for Germany today, Russia and Eastern Europe.
57 On the concept of hegemonic stability see Gill and Law, 1988.

heit)."[58] The problem is that this "quiet composure" was never available during the division of the nation. During this time the Allies seem to have succeeded in preventing the German people from having the posture or will to achieve world leadership as part of a (at least originally) calculated plan to prevent Germany from regaining power. The German people, in the title of Schwarz's famous 1985 book, have trodden the path from obsession with power to ignorance of power (from *Machtbessesenheit* to *Machtvergessenheit*).[59] The geopolitics and historical necessity of Germany's role, however, pushes Germany into world leadership even against the disposition of its people, who "have fled only too willingly into the moral impulse, into the emotional reflex 'no war.'"[60] Germany can thus only become a normal Great Power if the will of its people to this task is recreated.

To do this, normalism turns inward, creating classes of persons whose thinking is dangerous and counterproductive to the German return to normalcy. "In Germany today, powerful isolationist forces exist which argue against involvement and intervention on historical, moral, constitutional and budgetary grounds," writes Schwarz, clearly condemning the "isolationist forces" and warning against "German self-isolation based on legalistic and *crypto-pacifist* attitudes." For a 'normal' Germany, a passive or pacifist approach to the use of power leads to a *sonderweg* of isolationism: "In the middle term, the threat of self-isolation comes not from neo-Wilhelminian arrogance but from *pacifist weakness.*"[61]

Here the nationalist-normalist school is most clearly fulfilling the function of a hegemony-seeking discourse which tends to make its own perspective invisible while highlighting a group which becomes the 'Other.' In attempting to universalize the dominant discourse as the norm it disables other interpretations of German politics and history by relegating them to positions of "abnormality," with the corollary implications of immaturity, foolishness, and even danger. The real problems are shown to lie *within* German society. National consciousness has been spoiled by decades of neglect leading to the dangerous illusion that a unified Germany could or should exist as anything less than a major power with global responsibilities. The SPD and the '68 Generation are particularly singled out for creating this undesirable situation, though even conservative politicians are not entirely spared.[62] A pacifistic approach for most normalists is pegged as a psychological holdover from the

---

58 Schöllgen, 1993: 34.
59 Schwarz, 1985.
60 Major General Johann Adolf Graf von Kielmansegg in *Truppenpraxis*, Nr.3, 1991, quoted in Wette, 1994: 199.
61 Schwarz, in Baring, 1994: 122.
62 See Hacke, 1993.

traumatization of Hitler's excesses. While no normalist would deny Hitler's crimes, they consider staying the course of the old Federal Republic tantamount to basing the foreign policy of a great power on a legacy of collective guilt which in effect consigns Germany to an eternal 'special path.'

This trend towards a disavowal of military action, generally ascribed by normalists to a combination of wartime guilt, the peculiar security concerns of the Cold War, and the overzealous anti-nationalism of the left, began to be perceived as "crypto-pacifistic" and attacked in the mid-80s by Schwarz and others. In a unified, sovereign Germany such "crypto-pacifistic" attitudes have become perceived as more than counter-productive, they become obstacles to progress. They undermine and enervate the will to be a world power. Hacke crystallizes this argument:

> The foreign policy failures in the Yugoslavian crisis and in the Gulf War and elsewhere have their origin in the inability of German politicians to adequately grasp the international aspects of their own German identity since 1990. While France pursues Great Power politics without possessing the necessary means, while the USA often militarily pursues world-power politics without possessing the corresponding financial means, Germany possesses the requirements to act as a great power and disposes over the economic means to practice world-power politics, *but* it possesses no corresponding *will* for international responsibility.[63]

If only Germany had the will, Hacke seems say, it could take its rightful place not only next to, but above France and the United States. The difference between these countries is thus not only capabilities, but *will*. Paradoxically, this lack of will leads Hacke to reassess his original title for his most famous work, *World Power Against its Will*: "Can one, against this background of foreign policy mistakes, missed opportunities and dramatically changed domestic situation even talk at all about Germany as a 'world power against its will'?"[64] Yet would not his title, if anything, apply better now than when the book was first published in 1989? After all, the "objective" factors of sovereignty, territory, and population have only worked in Germany's favor. How can Hacke then claim that without the will to being a world power Germany is no longer a world power against its will? This sounds hopelessly tautological, unless, before 1989 the wanting will for being a world power was a function of external constraints, whereas now the lack of will is an internal matter which allows no excuses.

Hacke's normalist discourse does its best to berate the "pacifist-moralistic internationalism" of the SPD and other misguided Germans whose "neglec-

---

63 Hacke, 1993: 521.
64 Ibid.: 522.

tion of the national question," among other transgressions, set the ground work for the current dearth of will: "Before 1989 the old FRG was *weakened from within*, without powerful political leadership, without vision and courage for sacrifice or even the readiness to take risks. *The foreign policy of the FRG until 1989 missed the connection between power politics (Machtpolitik) and responsibility.*"[65]After 1989 this internal weakness has caused "Germany's standing in the world [to be at] a low point. ... [Germany is] cowardly, indecisive, unsympathetic and self-pitying," not to mention "impotent."[66] It is hard to imagine how the newly united Germany, widely praised and feared for its economic and political strength, can be viewed as at a low point, considering competing historic analogies for this designation. But Hacke and other normalists are working within a normalist logic which intimates, in the final analysis, that the defining characteristic of a world power rests not on 'real' capabilities but on the metaphysical concept of 'will.'

As the above quotes indicate, the normalist discourse attributes the lack of "will" in German society to a crisis of identity. The basis of normalism in political realism does not allow for ambiguity at the ontological level, because a strict fact/value distinction tolerates a blurring of its own borders at the cost of questioning its legitimacy. Thus one hallmark of 'normalcy' is a firm national identity which is not "plagued by crises of self-doubt" or been "damaged" by overexposure to "pacifist-moralistic internationalism:"[67] "He who, as a German, says that it is all the same to him whether he is German, suffers from a loss of identity or an identity disturbance. *On this basis the country is unpredictable in foreign policy and cannot develop an adequate national interest.*"[68] Worse, as the maverick Alfred Mechtersheimer succinctly puts it, "People without national identity are not pioneers of a new world order, but victims of foreign interests."[69]

While the form of identity (self-assured, proud, sober, firm) is resolutely reiterated throughout the normalist discourse, the content of the desired identity is far more obscure. Although Hacke speaks of the centrality to the Constitution of the concept of "being German" he would hardly consider Habermas' "constitutional patriotism" an adequate sense of national identity. "Being German" is a tremendous territory which must, if it is large enough to allow commendation, allow condemnation as well. Self-criticism, however, is viewed as a weakness if its conclusions do not mesh with realist interpretation. Ironically, the normalist fear of self-criticism undermining national

---

65 Ibid.: 424. Emphasis added.
66 Ibid.: 520-521, 533.
67 Ibid., 1993: 503, 538, 541.
68 Ibid., 1993: 556. Emphasis added.
69 In Dijkink, 1996: 34.

identity is itself an indication of insecurity, for what identity is more secure than one which can weather critical reflection?

A key to why the particular normalist construction of identity is averse to any self-criticism lies in their ultimate reliance of interests on identity. The definition of interests belongs to the realm of rationality and sobriety. Interests, as both the classic realist authors and the modern German realist-normalists point out, are based on 'objective' factors.[70] Yet a firm national identity is necessary for the definition of national interests. Working backwards, if national interests are based on 'objective' factors, then national identity must also be an 'objective' factor, that is, a given which must be recognized, rather than a construction which is always in process. National identity thus becomes the static first principle of the realist nation-state. Yet while a national identity can serve as a requirement for the existence of a nation, this requirement alone says nothing about what constitutes a nation and about the relations of the people (das Volk) to the state. Rather, it begs the question. This is where political realism remains uncomfortably unclear. Perhaps the best way to ascertain the identity content of the normalist approach is to examine the dichotomies of self and other which they set up.

Dichotomies of self and other are one of the basic ways in which meaning is created through difference.   From within the normalist school Schöllgen writes that "Every [European] country needed an adversary, with the border and the rival just beyond; *it was only these conflicts that made each people refine its own identity*."[71] One indication of the 'adversaries which make people refine their identity' are the fears expressed about what will happen to one's own society if dogmatic tenets are not upheld. The normalist literature prognosticates dire consequences for European society if the primacy of the nation-state is ignored. This normalist theme is most clearly visible in Hacke's handwringing about the impending collapse of Western civilization.

DEFENDING WESTERN CIVILIZATION FROM ITSELF

In Western Europe since the 1950s, complains Hacke, there has been an increasing unwillingness to use military power for reasons other than self-defense. Germany is the most egregious case of such reticence in two senses: first because these sentiments are most pronounced in Germany, and second because Germany's leadership potential is seen in normalist discourse as a historical advantage coextensive with the soul of the nation.[72] Reticence about using military power "has historically *always* led to the decline of great civili-

---

70 See Morgenthau, 1954, and Stürmer, 1992, on this point.
71 Schöllgen, 1994: 64. Emphasis added.
72 See the work on German attitudes toward foreign policy in Asmus, 1992.

zations," claims Hacke, an axiom which leads him to conclude that "Germany and Europe are obviously in a phase of civilization decline."[73]

Central to civilization is the use of military power in pursuit of national interests. Failure to acknowledge this endangers not only 'national interests' but especially national identity, since the former is premised on the latter. The 'inside' of domestic order requires acceptance of the 'correct' interpretation of the 'outside,' the external (dis)order. Thus, the most pernicious threat to a society becomes primarily not *external* threats, which can be dealt with matter-of-factly (e.g. by recalling ambassadors, sending troops, terminating aid), but internal threats which might prevent the 'correct' way of interpreting the outside world. Our worst enemy is ourselves:

> Obviously the Atlantic civilization after the breakdown of communism is falling victim to its own weaknesses and powerlessness. Will the West go the way of the Roman Republic, after it successfully overcame Carthage and Hannibal at the end of the second Punic War? Are we letting today, like then, our guard down after decades-long strenuous effort? Is the will to self-preservation bending to the tendency for egoism and diversions (*Zerstreuung?*)[74]

It is particularly interesting how criticism of German "unlearning" of power politics extends to a critique of Western civilization. Normalist discourse accepts the integrationist axiom that democracies do not wage war against each other, making war between members of the European Union unlikely, if not impossible. Furthermore, the identities of European nation-states are considered to be fully formed (even if currently lost or damaged in Germany); note how Schöllgen phrases his earlier description of the role of conflict in refining identity in the past tense. Since European nation-states possess stable identities, and since the only wars they might encounter involve non-(Western)European countries, threats to the identity of a particular European country are also a threat to Europe as a whole. All European countries, however, are not equal: Germany's role in the new world order is to lead Europe, so German abdication of power politics is even more deleterious to European civilization than, say, Danish.

This argument allows criticism of what might otherwise at worst be seen as innocuous idealist ideas of pacifism and disarmament; dangerous ideas which threaten, in the long run, all the achievements of Western Civilization. We have become too comfortable, too concerned about our own wealth and peace, to realize that without proper vigilance "Global problems can reach a level which will endanger the survival of *our* civilization into the next mil-

---

73 Hacke, 1993: 502, 566. Emphasis added.
74 Hacke, 1993: 589.

lenium"(emphasis in the original).[75] The Atlantic or Western (these terms are used quite interchangeably) civilization is hence threatened at two levels, by internal criticism and external threats. As with national identity, this approach begs the question of what constitutes an Atlantic or Western Civilization. This, however, is somewhat easier to answer because the nature of the threats set up fairly clear binary oppositions. Atlantic civilization is democratic, wealthy, tolerant, orderly, rational, non-belligerent, and future-oriented. Its weakness stems from indulgences of its own strengths: decadence. Here we hear echoes of the historic legacy of Germany as a bulwark against Western decadence, but this time with a twist–not to oppose the West but to save it from itself.[76]

Strains of Carl Schmitt

One curious intellectual source of the normalist discourse resides in the writings of the philosopher Carl Schmitt. Schmitt, a controversial political and legal theorist born in 1885 and who died in 1986, was an active theoretician for the National Socialist regime and admirer of Ernst Jünger, a conservative author of similar notoriety and longevity. Recently Schmitt has experienced a revival not just among right-radical organizations, but also in the conservative circles out of which normalist thought emanates.[77] "Insofar as one can identify a renaissance of national conservatism in Germany today," writes John Ely, "Schmitt's influence is a signature feature."[78] Ely charts a

'Schmittian' constellation extending from the FAZ [*Frankfurter Allgemeine Zeitung*] and conservative politicians like Edmund Stoiber, Peter Gauweiler, Wolfgang Schäuble, Alfred Dregger, Michael Glos, Rupert Scholz, Manfred Kanther, and Heinrich Lummer on the one hand to the *Junge Freiheit* and Franz Schönhuber's 'Republican' ideology on the other. Characteristic features include the following: emphasis on the strong state as the solution to political problems and laissez-faire economic policy; a presidial or Bonapartist view of 'decision making'; a Hobbesian view of sovereignty; a strong emphasis on the state as a *homogeneous* entity congealed by its 'national identity'; the development of a nationalist sphere of influence in the East; the 'reform' of state policies on asylum; and the situation of foreigners in the country.[79]

---

75 Hacke, 1993: 591. Emphasis in the original.
76 See, for instance, the examples of anti-Western German thought in Hobsbawm, 1962, and also Müller, 1993.
77 See Lilla, 1997. See also Neocleous, 1996.
78 Ely, 1995: 83.
79 Ibid.

This Schmittian national conservatism is what Hans-Martin Lohmann calls "extremism from the middle."[80] What makes Schmitt central to normalist discourse is not merely, or even consciously Schmitt's penchance for an ordered, authoritarian state, but his attempt to construct a political ontology which can deal with the failures of democracy. In Schmitt's time it was the frantic shenanigans of the Weimar Republic that seemed to point to the failures of democracy. For the normalist discourse today it is the lack of will among the electorate to embrace the responsibility concomitant with the historical necessity of a Great Power. Schmitt's writings contain an insightful critique of the major structural incompatibility of mass democracy and advanced capitalism: the privileged position of interest groups promoting private interests at the expense of an ever-increasing hypocritical myth of parliamentary debate anchored in rationality.[81] There is no democratic resolution to this problem: "Democracy seems fated to destroy itself in the problems of the formation of a will."[82] Schmitt's critique of democracy shares significant elements with the normalists critique of the legacy of the old Federal Republic. Both lack the will to make political decisions, and both engage in "avoiding the need to face up to danger."[83]The will to make political decisions is the decisive characteristic of the truly political state, according to Schmitt. The political for him is a relationship based on friend-enemy relations rather than an arena in which certain kinds of activity take place. Gowan explains:

> [T]he friend-enemy relationship does not denote mere conflict between groups over policy or over material interests or resources. For Schmitt, all such conflict is sub-political, it is mere competition. The political involves a qualitative breakthrough to a total antagonism between groups. Furthermore, the friend-enemy relation between groups does not necessarily involve any physical conflict between them at any moment. It simply entails an awareness on the part of one group of the identity of the other as alien and hostile, as "the other," and thus as potentially involved in total conflict. Schmitt proceeds to apply this new concept of the political to the state. Not every state is genuinely political: to become so it must possess the capacity to practically distinguish friends from enemies, in other words the capacity for political decision. A state which has lost this capacity in relation to its internal affairs is threatened with disintegration. One that has lost it in external affairs has lost its political character in international relations.[84]

As Gowan points out, in this way Schmitt connects the internal transformation of the state to the state's external purposes. Schmitt's legacy combines a

80 Lohmann, 1994.
81 See Gowan, 1994: 104.
82 Originally in Schmitt's *The Concept of the Political*, quoted in Ibid.: 100.
83 Ibid.
84 Ibid.

conservative national program with direct foreign policy applications, one reason why Schmitt's work lends itself as an intellectual foundation for normalist discourse. Interestingly, while many normalists such as Hacke and Schöllgen also consider themselves classic realists, Schmitt's appropriation of Hobbes is somewhat different than the dominant, if misleading, view that the state of nature within specific spaces is to be overcome by political organization into nation-states. For Schmitt, politics is not the escape from the state of nature, rather it is *of* the state of nature: "the political is not the alternative to Hobbes' state of nature, it is the actuality of the war of all against all."[85] The state of nature is only overcome to the extent that friend-enemy relations are transferred from an individual level to a communal level. Politics is the constant refining of the psychological and physical borders of friend-enemy. This refining necessitates a strong state, and a democratic state is not strong enough because of its tendency to fall victim to private interests which are at odd with state interests. To quote Gowan again, for Schmitt

> the state is not the expression of society or of the people's will: it is the precondition for a unified community and is the creator of any popular will. With this new conception of the political, we can see that *the state's role in creating a community consists precisely in distinguishing those that can be incorporated into the friend-community from those who are alien, other – enemies.*[86]

This is perhaps an extreme and rather simplistic version of the role of the state, and not one promoted as such by individual normalists. Yet it is not difficult to hear strains of this role of the state in the vocabulary of the normalist discourse: firm and sober national identities trying to surface against inner enemies of the nation who through their moralizing and emotion are eroding the foundations of no less than Western Civilization, while beyond the core of democratic industrialized countries new threats of migration and terrorism are already battering at the door.

The revival of Schmittian thinking is significantly related to the challenges facing democratic societies after the end of the Cold War. Among the reasons why Schmitt is being revived today, writes Mark Lilla, is that "his political preoccupations–sovereignty, national unity, the dangers of ignoring enmity between nations, constitutional stability, war–have once again become the central themes of European politics."[87] Although analogies of united Germany to the Weimar Republic are found sorely wanting, there is a more general parallel between the two eras in the broader sense of a crisis and reorganiza-

---

85 Ibid.: 111.
86 Ibid., 110. Emphasis added.
87 Lilla, 1997: 40.

tion of authority in the democratic-capitalist world. Paul Kennedy describes how political authority, no longer nestled in the capitals of nation-states, is being allocated upwards toward supranational organizations and downward toward regional economic groupings.[88] The cohesion of national identities are particularly challenged by this reallocation of authority, as national identities were challenged by the principles of the failed social-democratic ideals of the 1920s. Then, as now, center-right opposition to social democracy focuses on the allegedly deleterious effects of the welfare state on the moral integrity of its citizens. But in the process of improving moral fiber the center-right tends to support a version of economic libertarianism with serious consequences: "the destruction of social-liberalism then as now entailed a freeing of the capitalist state from all obligations to society and enabled it to more effectively dominate its society in capitalist interests."[89]

Romantics in Disguise?

Like the center-right critiques of Carl Schmitt in the 1930s, the normalist discourse is thus also a reaction to the challenges with which the international political economy confronts the nation-state. In its most sophisticated form, for example Fest and Stürmer, the normalist discourse incorporates the language of integration and globalization, but remains suspicious of any hint of idealism, separating and subordinating political integration to economic integration. The unambiguous (though occasionally contradictory) anger of normalist theorists such as Hacke and Schöllgen highlight a fear present in the discourse which takes it beyond a mere recapitulation of classical realist tenets and differentiates normalism from realism. To be sure, the normalist discourse is built upon a firm foundation of political realism, but its preoccupation with the inadequacies of a nation which has "unlearned" power and sacrifice and consequentially threatens the survival of Western civilization revives romantic nationalist themes quite at variance with the discourse's privileging of sobriety and rationality. I do not mean to suggest here that the normalist discourse falls short of achieving its desired level of rationality. The problem, rather, is with the idea that rationality is a tool for recognizing truth, a method that will lead policy-makers and the public to recognize Germany's proper role as a 'normal' nation-state. To support their particular view of the nation-state becomes rational while alternative approaches become emotional and dangerous. The derivation of the normalist view of the nation-state stands out as contradictory. Odd as it may sound at first, there are distinct Romantic themes which underlie the normalist world-view:

---

88 Kennedy, 1993.
89 Gowan, 1994: 127.

In their claims to be anti-rational, the Romantics counterpoised rationality and naturalness, asserting it was not natural to be rational, if being rational meant smothering emotion. Yet following emotions was not 'irrational,' it was 'anti-rational.' Rationality, for the Romanticists, was often a synonym for modernity, for science, for those developments which harbinge the de-mythologizing of the world. But the Romantics held to a hierarchy of val-ues, defining and ranking emotions. Patriotism, as Josep R. Llobera reminds us, was foremost in this hierarchy: "love of country was natural, nearly in-stinctive, except that cosmopolitanism had killed those feelings and had to be reinstated so that the natural course of things would follow. For this a certain amount of voluntarism was needed."[90]

Compare Llobera's reminder of the high Romantic value of patriotism to Hacke's writings on Germany's wanting will to being a world power. Pre-cisely voluntarism, in the form of will, is lacking. It is sorely needed to restore the love of country, once instinctive until the modern form of cosmopolitan-ism (in the form of "pacifist-moralist internationalism") killed those feelings. And the anti-national effects of cosmopolitanism threaten the unfolding of the natural course of things. If rationality can be defined as the exercise of good sense and reason, then it certainly is rational to be patriotic, if patriotism is a requirement for the proper unfolding of the natural order of things.

Llobera sets out three additional themes from the last quarter of the Eight-eenth Century which later formed the core of Romantic thought: pluralism, nostalgia for the past, and organicism. All of these themes resonate resoundly with the normalist discourse. Pluralism is perhaps the most interesting, be-cause the Romantic conception of pluralism differs from Anglo-American democratic discourse. Following Isaiah Berlin, Romantic pluralism refers to "the incommensurability of the values of different cultures and societies." This is pluralism in the Herderian sense. Although Herder took pains to deny any moral hierarchy among the different nations of the world which he helped categorize, the insistence on each nation's uniqueness tempts comparison with other nations. Combined with later bastardizations of the Hegelian no-tion of the world spirit (*Weltgeist*) being realized historically through the na-tional spirit (*Volksgeist*), pluralism as incommensurability serves as an excel-lent basis for ethnic nationalism.

In the normalist discourse, pluralism as incommensurability becomes the excuse for adopting a form of "difference politics." John Ely, writing about national conservatism in the *Frankfurter Allgemeine Zeitung (FAZ)*, the pri-mary media location for normalist discourse, notes that

---

90 Llobera, 1994: 174.

> The *FAZ* provides an example ... of the new phenomenon of a politics of 'difference' as 'differential racism,' which French writers such as Pierre-André Taguieff and Etienne Balibar have observed in the French Right. With a rhetorical focus on difference per se rather than some essential causes, this form of the politics of difference divides the world into a geography of ethnic communities founded on a core/periphery model. In the *FAZ*'s version, the Schmittian or even Prussian focus on land and territoriality rather than sea serves to make this ethnic quality more evident. The *FAZ* imagines Germany as the center of a new geopolitical balance of power, a layered gradient of declining, increasingly distant national and ethnic groups.[91]

The distinctiveness of (the German) people becomes a way of understanding the extremely contentious issues of migration and asylum as threats not only to jobs but to identity. Normalist opposition to further European political integration also stems from the fear of losing the distinctiveness of nationality. In a direct attempt to confront this fear, German Government information designed to boost enthusiasm and create support for European integration often focuses on how the cultural distinctiveness of different German groups (e.g. Bavarians, Swabians, Lower Germans) have been preserved through Germany's federal structure.

The second theme Llobera identifies, nostalgia for the past, is also abundantly present in normalist discourse. History becomes a representation of the past which is also the path to the future. Llobera quotes Friederich Schlegel: "A historian is a prophet facing backwards."[92] There are two elements to romanticist historiography, both relevant to normalism: 1. uncovering a forgotten country and 2. "celebrating the past of a powerful nation."[93] In the first instance the normalist discourse creates the divided Germany as the era in which "Germany" was lost, both territorially and psychologically. The first has been restored, the second remains lacking. In the second instance, the consistent normalist analogies of Germany in the 1990s to the Germany of Bismarck raises "the past of a powerful nation" as a point of comparison. The third theme, organicism refers to a holistic concept of the nation, a concept implicitly shared by a realist reliance on nation-states as the international unit of comparison, the conveyer of identity.

The recurrence of these themes – a pluralism which stresses difference and national uniqueness, a heroic representation of the past combined with admonitions of deficient national pride, and an organic conception of the nation – suggests that the normalist narrative's filiation is more with Romantic themes

---

91 Ely, 1995: 87.
92 Llobera,1994: 172.
93 Ibid.: 173.

than the classic realism of Morgenthau. That normalists could be romanticist sounds contradictory, since they explicitly reject the notion of romanticism, using the term to pejoratively evoke images of idealist, utopian thinking in contrast to real(ist) understanding. Yet Romanticism is not synonymous with political idealism. Rather, it is in part a reactionary response to economic, technological, and political forces which anticipate shifts in identities. The logic of the world economic system in the first half of the Twentieth Century culminated in crises which produced responses as varied as Keynsianism, Corporatism, Communism and National Socialism. The logic of the globalization of the world economy in the last quarter of the Twentieth Century, with the concomitant reallocation of authority and blurring of borders and allegiances, is in the process of producing its own responses. The normalist discourse is one of these responses, and it is particularly powerful, combining the seemingly faultless rationality of realism with the identity-affirming allure of romanticism.

4. The Liberal Narrative

The normalist discourse of the last chapter expresses its uniqueness through opposition to those whom, as they see it, deny the primacy of national identity. The normalization function of the narrative requires the acceptance of their categories as self-evident truths. The construction of arguments through exclusive truth claims is a key characteristic of hegemony-seeking discourses --this is why the normalist narrative can conceive of denials of the desirability or primacy of national identity, as Hacke put it, as "distortions of identity."[1] The major competing narrative also maintains the claim to exclusivity yet it reverses the terms: here, to think primarily in national terms is to fail to accept the supranational teleology of the postwar West. Both the normalist and its opposing discourse, which I will call the 'liberal discourse,' are particular German reactions and expressions that are embedded in, and embodied through, larger Western metanarratives. This is not to diminish their uniqueness: no other history could have produced the particular reactions and resistances of the German narratives described herein. Yet their uniqueness lies precisely in their reaction and resistance to the metanarratives of nationalism and liberalism which constitute the environment which engenders those ideas.

I present the counter-discourse to "normalism" as liberal rather than as a narrative of exceptionalism or historical responsibility *per se* because the main glue of the counternarrative is that of a universalist secular teleology. The German "liberal" discourse incorporates a wide swath of ideas, all of which, however, rest on the assumptions of civic nationalism as traditionally defined: the nation is not an end in itself, but a necessary phase in the progress toward a global order based on democracy, the rule of law and individual human rights. Like the normalist discourse, the liberal discourse also employs an operative vocabulary of "normalcy" and "responsibility" but with a different set of assumptions and expectations. "Normal" is future-oriented (normalcy as adaptation to conditions of globalization) rather than past-oriented (normalcy as a return or recovery of great power status); "responsibility" is framed in terms of responsibility *to* the past, which can be positively engaged, rather than responsibility *for* the past, which connotes collective guilt.

The liberal discourse is represented by two primary groups, the centrist mainstream of the Bonn Republic's liberal consensus (prominently repre-

---

1 See Hacke, 1993: 556. He also speaks of "damaged" national identity on: 538.

sented by leading members of all major political parties), and the center-left party wings, research institutes, and academicians. As with the normalist discourse, the foundations of the liberal discourse are articulated by intellectuals who, either through direct participation or intellectual authority, influence the environment in which policy-decisions are made. In this analysis of the discourse I will focus on examples of the discourse from the works of authors such as Ernst Otto Czempiel, Dieter Senghaas and Dieter S. Lutz. As individuals these authors differ considerably, however I wish to draw out common elements which link them to overall assumptions behind the liberal foreign policy narrative.

The general outline of the liberal narrative, in severely abbreviated form, is as follows: the positive roots of the German nation lie in the failed liberal ideals of 1848, when nationalism was presented as a force to move the country toward democracy. The perversions of the idea of a German empire, especially the Third Reich, saddled Germany with a dangerous legacy which necessitates the prominent privileging of democratic values. While West Germany had 'learned its lesson' during the prosperous years of the Bonn Republic, the unified Germany retains a responsibility to itself, to its history, and to the international community, to use its *de facto* power as a force for peace and democracy in Europe and beyond. Peace and prosperity cannot be achieved through traditional power politics, but through recognition of new opportunities presented by collective action in an era of globalization. German foreign policy, accordingly, must avoid succumbing to the traditional tools of power politics, above all the military, and emphasize economics, politics, culture, and collective action. These approaches must be used to strengthen integration and cooperation in Europe and to spread the ensuing democratic values to non-Western parts of the world to reduce conflict, increase trade, and promote democracy. This will encourage a more peaceful world based on liberal democratic values and commonality of universal interests.

Foundations of the Liberal Narrative

CIVIC NATIONALISM

In an article on citizenship and national identity, Jürgen Habermas exhorts that "The nation of citizens does not derive its identity from some common ethnic and cultural properties, but rather from the *praxis* of citizens who actively exercise their rights."[2] This sentiment stems from his notion of "con-

---

2 Habermas, 1992b: 2.

stitutional patriotism," or the fealty of a nation's citizens to its democratic constitution rather than loyalty to essentialized national characteristics. It is more, however, than a concept of loyalty--Habermas is claiming that the identity of a nation (of citizens) arises from their constant reaffirmation of normative principles. This is akin to Renan's famous portrayal of the nation as "a plebiscite of everyday" and his notion of the nation as a "great solidarity."[3] Habermas' concept of constitutional patriotism is one of the clearest expressions we find of the notion of civic nationalism.

Civic nationalism is the privileged term in a binary opposition with its 'evil twin,' organic nationalism.[4] Organic nationalism is based historically on ineliminable notions of blood and language. The superiority of civic nationalism over organic nationalism resides in its claim to realize the ideals of the Enlightenment, to valorize reason and purge myth, and allow for the development of a nation based not on organic criteria but on the calculable will of the individual. Renan once again captures this disposition: "We have driven the metaphysical and theological abstractions from politics. What remains? Man remains, his desires and his wants."[5]

The power of civic nationalism lies in its claim to explain and tame the excesses of organic nationalism while retaining the logic of the nation-state. This notion was particularly attractive to postwar West German intellectuals and politicians in their search for instruments of social cohesion in the aftermath of national socialism. Socialism in the GDR was also attractive to an extent because of its claim to reject, explain, and overcome the legacies of German organic nationalism. The anti-national stance of socialism initially elevated its acceptability in Germany as a whole. The attraction of socialist internationalism in the West, however, was severely tempered by totalitarian Soviet leadership and the Western Allies' anti-Communist orientation, both aggravated by the division of Germany and, in 1961, the building of the Berlin Wall.

LIBERAL FOREIGN POLICY

Socialist internationalism, under the tutelage of the Soviet Union, solidified itself in the GDR, and the GDR's foreign policy became embedded in Soviet anti-imperialism, despite occasional serious differences between the GDR and the Soviet Union, especially during Gorbachev's rule in the USSR. In West Germany, the civic nationalism of the United States became the model, both in opposition to the GDR and in conjunction with the values of the Western

---

3 See Renan's famous essay "What is a Nation?", reprinted in Kohn, 1965: 139.
4 On the Janus face of nationalism see Nairn, 1975.
5 Renan in Kohn, 1965. For a broad discussion of these themes see Smith, 1983.

occupying powers. Federal German foreign policy was accordingly influenced by developments in US foreign policy. In the perennial debates between realist and liberal foreign policy approaches in the United States, the liberal aspects held a special attraction for German foreign policy analysts of the mainstream and center-left, because it 1. held out the hope of resolving the division of Germany through peaceful means and 2. envisioned a state system based on norms rather than nations.

Liberal foreign policy derives directly from civic nationalist ideas. Consider Woodrow Wilson's linkage of US war aims and liberal ideals: "We are glad now that we see the facts with no veil of false pretense about them, to fight thus...for the rights of nations great and small and the privilege of men everywhere to choose their way of life and of obedience." Why? Because "A steadfast concert for peace can never be maintained except by a partnership of democratic nations."[6] True, the idea of democratic peace can be attributed to Kant, but Wilson was the first policy-maker to introduce these ideas as justification for national interests. It is also true that Wilson's rhetorical attraction diminished precipitously twenty years later, after his vision of democratic peace dissolved into cataclysmic war. Yet the idea of predicating peace on "a partnership of democratic nations" is perhaps even more popular at the end of the Twentieth Century than at the beginning.[7]

COMMON SECURITY

Divided Germany's precarious security situation created a natural incentive for favoring liberal ideas over classic and structural realist foreign policy approaches. The latter at worst viewed war as a natural evil in world politics, and at best envisioned a secure but lasting bipolar stalemate--in other words a perpetuation of the division. Realism could be attractive when invoking balance of power arguments against European force imbalances. Yet the specter of the two Germanies as ground zero in even a limited nuclear war between NATO and the Warsaw Pact tapered political enthusiasm for the cold war status quo. Hence the particular, and persistent, German emphasis on détente, *Ostpolitik*, and common security. *Ostpolitik*, with its leitmotif of "change through *rapprochement*" (Egon Bahr) became the mainstay of Federal German policy toward the GDR and, by extension, other members of the Warsaw Pact.[8] The notion of common security, however, was not adopted by Chancellors Schmidt and Kohl, and became instead a *cause celebre* of the Social Democratic left and the nascent Green Party. The architect of *Ostpolitik*, Egon

---

6 Wilson, 1918.

7 See, among others, Doyle, 1983; Benoit, 1996; Chan, 1997; and Clifton, 1993.

8 For a basic overview of *Ostpolitik* see Griffith, 1978. For a more recent and contextual evaluation see Ash, 1993.

Bahr, was also the initial visionary of common security through the mechanism of a "security partnership," which "starts with the insight that war can no longer be won and that destruction cannot be restricted to one side....The consequence of this insight is that there is no reliable security *against* an opponent, but only *with* an opponent. There is only common security, because everybody is partner in it, not despite potential enmity, but *because* of it."[9]

EUROPEAN INTEGRATION AND THE CONCEPT OF "EUROPE"

All three of these foundations of current liberal discourse--civic nationalism, liberal foreign policy, and common security, are premised on the assumption of continued European integration. More than just providing a psychological and economic boost to postwar German development, European integration constructs "Europe" as a conceptual category which fulfills at least three important identity-related functions.

First, it allows a troubled national identity to be subsumed (and at times, perhaps, evaded). By offering "being European" as an acceptable, and accepted, category next to "being German," official designations of identity are able to transcend the limits of national identity and provide a psychological comfort zone for expressions of belonging. "Europe" is a somewhat vague yet positively coded category, implying cultural achievement, common heritage and enormous political and economic potential. Feelings of loyalty toward Germany were unseemly -- "I'm proud to be a German" was a statement attributed to right-wing supporters, whereas "I'm proud to be a European" was a non-controversial remark.[10] "Europe" moved from phylum to phenotype, from a descriptive term to a salient identity characteristic. Importantly, the extension of "Europe" as an identity is nearly exclusive to Western Europe. Just as West Germany represented the "real" Germany vis a vis the GDR, Western Europe represented "Europe" which the countries of the East, in the language of the transition from authoritarian rule, could "join." This creation of a "Europe" which countries territorially and historically within Europe need to join is a prime example of the construction of the concept of "Europe" as a normative community.[11]

Second, "Europe" fills the function of a new historical goal in which Germans can partake in. The normative imperatives of "Europe" require viewing it as a teleology--the value community of Western Europe can only pretend to the title of "Europe" as long as the potential exists for extending its operative concepts to the rest of territorial Europe. Building "Europe" takes the place of

---

9 Egon Bahr, quoted in Risse-Kappen, 1995: 197.
10 See the survey data in Merkl, 1992.
11 See Nelson, Roberts, and Veit, 1992 especially chapters 2, 5 and 6.

nineteenth-century nation-building as the historical task confronting current generations. Rebuilding the German nation-state can thus be conceptualized as a subset of building Europe. In this way, German patriotism becomes a subset of European patriotism. Pre-unification mainstream public sentiment in Germany identified strongly with the European teleology: 73 percent of the population in a 1989 poll from the conservative Konrad Adenauer Foundation envisioned a confederation or a federation as the future of Europe, and only 22 percent anticipated a future consisting of nation-states.[12]

Third, not only can Germany take part in realizing the European teleology, but it can play a leading role. Here "Europe" becomes the legitimate context for German leadership. Again this is important for a double reason: it contests damaging historical images (where previous German attempts at European leadership have been set in terms of conquest and racial superiority) while offering an outlet for expressing *de facto* German power.

Thus the three main identity functions of European integration for postwar West Germany have been to subsume burdened national identity in a supranational identity, present its fulfillment as a historic telos, and provide Germany with a leading role in a historically legitimized project. The liberal discourse in post-unification German foreign policy is a compendium of these forces. The leading idea of the discourse--common security systems with the goal of global democratic peace--is the progeny of the Kantian-Wilsonian emphasis on democratic peace and the civic nationalist sentiment of European integration against the backdrop of German organic nationalism.

COLD WAR INFLUENCES AND REGIME THEORY

The security position of divided Germany suggests good reasons for a general German predisposition for liberal explanations of international relations. With hundreds of nuclear weapons and hundreds of thousands of troops stationed on German soil, making Germany the world's ultimate powder keg, it is not surprising that peace and conflict studies, criticisms of nuclear deterrence, and arms control should find a particularly large echo among the scholarly and policy community. In addition, the sentiment that war should never again emanate from German lands ("nie wieder Krieg!") added a profound moral and historical perspective to criticisms of the normalized absurdity of the Cold War.[13]

---

12 Poll conducted on "German Attitudes Toward Europe's Future" in May, 1989 by the Konrad Adenauer Foundation, cited in Asmus, 1994: 45. The breakdown was 55 percent for confederation, 18 percent for federation, 22 percent for nation-states, and 5 percent "don't know."

13 See Cooper, 1996.

In the 1980s "regime theory" became increasingly popular in the German foreign policy community.[14] Regime theory in Germany differed from its counterparts in the United States, where the theory first gained currency, through its usefulness as a way out of the escalation dynamics of the cold war. Whereas in the US trade and alliance relations predominated, for Germany the issue was security. "In an American perspective," writes Volker Rittberger,

> the world may have appeared to be already one of international regimes, particularly when focusing on the relations among developed western countries (or the western world including the western-oriented developing countries). However, in Europe, directly confronted with the often troublesome relations between capitalist and socialist countries, the lack of international regimes for the management of conflicts stood out in the perception of international political life.[15]

The general goal was to extend to East-West relations "a layer of institutionalized co-operation for conflict management comparable to the one extending across West-West issue areas."[16] Of course, extending similar trade regimes across the ideological gulf of the COMECON and Western states as between the (then) EC and the US was not a serious possibility (save for quiet adherents of convergence theories). Conflict management, arms control, and human rights issues, and not primarily trade, became the main areas for the building of East-West regimes. The most novel aspect of regime theory was its repudiation of classic realist assumptions about anarchy and cooperation through the introduction of norms as adequate for regulating behavior. Regime theory saw itself as an alternative to both anarchic models of state interaction (realism) and the elusive notion of a world-state (naive idealism). Regime theory saw itself as part of a growing process of "international self-regulation," which stressed voluntary action in pursuit of common interests, i.e. long-term self-interest:[17]

> Regime theory is to explain the possibility, conditions, and consequences of international governance beyond anarchy and short of supranational government.... In the case of governance without government obligations do not emanate from a hierarchical norm- and rule-setting process (government)

---

14 See Hartwich, 1989; Kohler-Koch, 1989; and Zürn, 1987.
15 Rittberger, 1993.
16 Ibid.
17 Mayer et. al. define international collective self-regulation as "the voluntary participation by states and other international actors in collective action to achieve joint gains or to avoid joint losses in conflictual or problematic social situation." Mayer, 1993.

but from voluntary agreements to play by a set of rules which are binding in the sense that they create convergent expectations and govern behavior."[18]

The notion of a voluntary system of norms as the glue behind conflict management is of key importance for the post-cold war German foreign policy liberal discourse. Countering confrontation with appeals to universal rights provided a rallying point for overcoming the East-West divide and remains the dominant liberal strategy for dealing with the problems of the post-Cold War era. This is perhaps most evident in the way the CSCE, now OSCE, is retained as the most promising example of a norm-based international regime. During the Cold War the principles agreed to by all CSCE participants provided dissident groups in Eastern Europe with the tools of human rights agreements which they would later use against the communist governments (even while confirming existing borders and thereby extending a certain legitimacy to Soviet hegemony). After the Cold War, the value community suggested by the OSCE forms the baseline for common security arrangements as an alternative to NATO.[19]

The current liberal discourse uses the assumptions formed during the last two decades of the Cold War to deal with the threat of military confrontation in Europe: Common security was to overcome nuclear deterrence, to make it unnecessary, just as the creation of "non-offensive defense" was supposed to make war structurally impossible, leaving non-military tools as the primary forms of dispute resolution. Eastern and Western Europe lived under the same nuclear sword of Damocles, and the shared risk intensified solidarity among concerned citizens of both systems. Ecological concerns also rose to unprecedented levels of public awareness, especially after the apocalyptic Chernobyl disaster in 1986. Human rights, partially as a result of the 1975 Helsinki CSCE conference, became a way for the Federal Republic to fashion a foreign policy which de-emphasized constraints on West German foreign policy. The emphasis on human rights gave a certain moral legitimacy (and the important impression of outside support) to dissident groups, and the Federal Republic proceeded to make human rights a frontispiece of their foreign policy.[20]

Regime theory, with its concern for environmental, security, human rights, and trade, became notable because it seems the logical progression of a German foreign policy predicated on the ideals of civic nationalism, common security, and European integration. Regime theory, as Mayer, Rittberger, and others maintain, forms the basis for a new thinking in an era when neither po-

---

18 Ibid.: 393-4.
19 See Rittberger, 1990.
20 The definition of human rights at issue here are as described in point seven of the Helsinki Final Act.

litical realism nor idealism remain tenable. In a dialectical sense, regimes "bring the state back in" while simultaneously redefining the state's role in international affairs. This fits Germany very well. Consider Michael Zürn's findings on domestic sources of regime formation (in a chapter entitled "Bringing the Second Image [Back] In"):

> First, a state actor's foreign policy will result in regime formation when the state tries to correct dissatisfying outcomes in an issue area by utilizing economic and informational resources, and when it displays an orientation to reciprocity accompanied by the readiness to make one-sided concessions. Second, such a regime-conducive foreign policy is most likely to emerge in states with a corporatist domestic structure. Third, this is most likely to happen in such states after a change in domestic power constellation has taken place, and when the degree of routinization of the pre-established policy is not very high.[21]

These elements of "regime-conducive foreign policy types" point significantly at Germany: a country which relies on economic and informational resources rather than the military, which accepts reciprocity as part of the process of European integration, is arguably a corporatist state, and has just experienced a change in domestic power through unification, if not through a change in party leadership.[22] In a new world order of regimes Germany plays a central role. The firm neoliberal foundation for regime theory creates a "scientific" starting point for the development of two further dominant liberal tropes --"societalized foreign policy" and world domestic policy -- which make up the core of the liberal discourse in opposition to the normalist approach outlined in the preceding chapter.

Beyond Foreign Policy: Societal World and World Domestic Policy

THE SOCIETAL WORLD

The concept of the societal world professes to capture a new paradigm in world history, an era when the possibility of a Kantian eternal peace is no longer impossible, no longer relegated to the realm of "idealistic" and "naive" against the steely confidence of "realist" politics. The inability of political realism to predict the collapse of the Soviet Union has severely compromised realism's claims to be a superior explanatory theory of international affairs.[23] The paradigmatic claims of the societal world and world domestic policy po-

---

21 Zürn, 1993: 283. See also Table 12.4 on: 310.
22 On Germany as corporate state see Conradt, 1993.
23 On these challenges to neorealism see Lebow, 1994, also Sørensen, 1992.

sition themselves as empirically superior explanations in the nomological-deductive realm of theory choice.

Ernst-Otto Czempiel, a prominent international relations theorist of the societal world, revives sociologist Niklas Luhmann's 1960s futuristic hope for a world society brought together through communication and trade.[24] Luhmann's ideals, holds Czempiel, were on target, if premature: at the end of the Twentieth Century we *have* a world society, but only in one part of the world. In other words, the model for the future world society already exists in one region, and is in the painful process of fulfilling its telos, a truly interconnected global society.

The regional location of the societal world comes as no surprise: it is the "OECD-world," what others would call simply "the West." The societal world is to be found only in the OECD-states and their close surroundings ("näheren Umwelt"). Why only in the OECD world? Primarily because the combination of highly developed industry and liberal government (itself the result of the "dual revolution" of the industrial and the social revolutions of the nineteenth century) created the conditions for a double emancipation of society from the tyranny of politics. The first emancipation is that of social actors from the total control of a given political system; in other words, the ability of companies or individuals to act independently of government control. The second emancipation is the rise of a common consciousness brought about by interactions of individuals who are not subordinate to the government; interactions of an "autonomous" nature, such as free trade, communications, and tourism. Following Karl Deutsch's concept of "socialization," "such interactions create a sense of continuity which is constitutive of society."[25]

This emancipation is nothing short of revolutionary, for it propels the OECD region toward its telos, a societal world based on democratic government, the free market, and respect for universal human and civil rights. "Among the OECD states, the characteristic of the societal world are clearly developed."[26] Most significantly, in its trajectory toward the societal world, the OECD world leaves the nation-state behind like a snake shedding its skin: "The societal world has left the *raison d'état* of the nation-states behind them and is on the way to develop her own maxims for behavior in the international surroundings."[27] If the nation-state is overcome in the OECD world, then how

---

24 See Luhmann, 1993.
25 Czempiel, 1996a. See also Czempiel, 1993 and Czempiel, 1987.
26 Czempiel, 1996a: 43.
27 Czempiel, 1994a: 3.

to explain its persistence elsewhere, or even the fragmentation of nation-states into what the US foreign policy literature refers to as 'failed states?'[28]

> Beyond the OECD area we find two older conditions. The so-called threshold countries [NIC's in English terminology] live in the condition of the state-world, and are characterized by a high level of societal maturity, though the societies have not yet broken the foreign policy monopoly of their political systems. The stagnating countries of the (formerly called) Third World linger as before in a pre-nation-state condition, in the condition of the tribal world.[29] ... [The tribal world are] those countries which are identified with a subsistence economy and feudalism and thus *are not yet ordered as states.*[30]

Czempiel's teleology is clear here: tribal conditions constitute a form of anarchy out of which nation-states arise, both to provide territorial security and a socialization at the more abstract level of the nation. Nation-states are useful stages of development, but rather than overcoming the anarchy and chaos of the tribal world they merely contain it in a different form, displacing the war of all against all to war between nation-states. Nation-states are the middle term in a dialectic between parochial and global consciousness: the nation-state experience is socially and technologically necessary in order to create the conditions which will transform it. This progression bears obvious similarities to Marxian analyses of the national question, though it differs fundamentally in its prediction that the success of the free-market, rather than its collapse, will presage an era of a global society characterized by a common consciousness. Why certain regions of the world move more quickly through what Czempiel calls "phases of social time" than others, who "linger in a pre-nation-state condition" is not an object of explanation in this discourse: "I leave open whether these different phases should be measured according to modernity and then identified by prefixes such as 'post' and 'pre.'"[31] The decisive issue for foreign policy discourse is the 'empirical validity' of the characterizations, at best supported by comparison charts and statistics, rather than their epistemological validity. This deeply problematic omission will be the focus of later discussion.

---

28 On failed states see Helman and Ratner, 1992.
29 Czempiel, 1994a: 3. The German reads: "Außerhalb des OECD-Bereichs sind zwei ältere Zustände anzutreffen. Die sogenannten Schwellenländer leben im Zustand der Staatenwelt, sind gekennzeichnet durch einen hohen Reifegrad der Gesellschaften, die aber das Außenpolitik-Monopol der politischen Systeme noch nicht durchbrochen haben. Die stagnierenden Länder der ehemals so genannten Dritten Welt verweilen nach wie vor im vor-nationalstaatlichen Zustand, im Zustand der Sippenwelt."
30 Czempiel, 1996a: 44. Emphasis added.
31 Czempiel, 1996a: 44. Though elsewhere he opts for using the term postmodern.

Dieter Senghaas, well-known professor of peace, conflict, and development research, echoes Czempiel's view of progress. Dividing the world into "the OECD, the rest of the world, and the whole world" Senghaas also evokes a dialectical image, one where the OECD's influence on the rest of the world will transform the "whole world," now divisively divided, into a societal world. The OECD world is "incomparably homogenous and constitutes a 'societal world' and an 'economic world' which transcends the individual societies. ... [T]he so-called 'OECD peace' [has] primarily contributed to the establishment of permanent peace (defined as dependable absence of war *and* enduring coordination of politics) between the leading industrial societies of the world."[32] While not categorizing the "rest of the world" into a state world and tribal world, as Czempiel does, Senghaas nonetheless presents an image where the OECD world works while the rest of the world does not:

> In those regions [the 'rest of the world'] we *cannot* observe configurations of economic and political forces comparable with the OECD area: All experiments on 'collective self-reliance' which have been discussed since the 1960s and especially since the mid-1970s have failed. ... [M]ost countries in the developing regions of the world are characterized by weak control mechanisms and, moreover, by stagnation, regression, or even a process of mounting chaos.[33]

Within a Czempiel-like division of the world (societal--state--tribal), the globalization of the economy, communications and weapons systems necessitates expanding the first to encompass the other two. If the societal world can successfully reconcile peace with economic prosperity, then any periphery area still dwelling in a world of senseless war and economic misery will pose a threat to the societal world. This threat includes terrorism, refugees, environmental destruction, military interventions, leading to instability within the societal world itself. Enough instability could undermine the neophyte efforts of the societal world in the OECD. Wolfgang Vogt captures this fear:

> In most Western countries a crisis of purpose, identity, and progress has broken out. There is broadening doubt about the modern Euro-American process of civilization. The security and stability of the West is no longer primarily threatened through "external," military threats, rather far more through "internal," non-military risks. Long-lasting economic crises, mass unemployment and shrinking social programs, societal disintegration processes and social discrimination, rising organized crime and drug use, political apathy, loss of identity and fear of the future, xenophobia, racism and right-wing extremism create a crisis potential which can only be disarmed (*entschärft*) and overcome through structural reform and the epochal transi-

---

32 Senghaas, 1994: 108. See also Senghaas, 1990 and Senghaas, 1992.
33 Senghaas, 1994: 109, 110-111. Emphasis added.

tion into a new environmentally and future-friendly (*umwelt- und zu-kunftsverträgliches*) societal system.[34]

An OECD country, therefore, cannot pride itself on its achievements and snicker at the poor bastards elsewhere, for its ultimate well-being is connected to the expansion of the societal world. Failure of the societal relations in the OECD would mean a return to the state-world phase, a "re-nationalization," resulting from a backlash against the uncertainties of the new era or from the unchecked self-interest of business and state actors. If the primacy of the nation-state is upheld over the primacy of the societal world, "the material interdependence would recede, the institutional cohesion would be weakened and the coordination necessary for the civilizing of politics would more or less subside."[35] The state-world would return, and with it the concomitant problems of war and misplaced military solutions to economic and environmental challenges.

Thus, the societal world is necessary for three reasons: 1. The societal world expresses the highest known stage of the natural development of civilization; 2. A societal world secures the OECD states against external threats through institutionalizing peace; 3. A societal world guards against internal instabilities by creating prosperity and peace. Also of central importance is the moral imperative of the societal world: the OECD world has a responsibility to help the "rest of the world" achieve a mutually beneficial interdependency rather than a self-interest driven asymmetrical dependency. The societal world is more than a deterministic phase of world existence, it is the best and most moral answer to the problems, internal and external, which the post-cold war world faces at the twilight of the twentieth century.

The task for policy-makers and scholars is accordingly the realization of the societal world on a global level. Authors such as Czempiel and Senghaas present the world as tantalizingly within our reach, yet laden with obstacles mocking our good intentions. Czempiel wishes to emphasize that, while the global societal world transcends the notion of the ethnic nation-state, at this stage "[w]e are dealing with a process internal to states which does not question the basic division of the world into states. Even the societal world continues to be organized into states."[36] This makes a coordinated effort to spread the societal world difficult. What both authors agree on, despite minor semantic differences, is a form of world domestic policy as the antipode to traditional foreign policy.

---

34 Vogt, 1994: 27.
35 Senghaas, 1994: 106-7.
36 Czempiel, 1996a: 44.

WORLD DOMESTIC POLICY (*WELTINNENPOLITIK*)

The theoretical basis of world domestic policy is concisely summarized by Vogt:

> The traditional foreign policy of nation-states, which primarily served to further their power and interests, no longer does justice to the transformed conditions and challenges of world politics. Nation-states, which are still the main actors in the so-called 'international relations system,' constitute agents who are too small and too egotistical to overcome alone the cross-border problems and existential crises of the world risk society. The problem-laden and crisis-shaken world society requires a 'world domestic policy' that must be more than the sum of the foreign policy activities of nation-states. The point is to replace the previous foreign policy of the nation-states with a global political paradigm, to supersede it with a new, supranational level of agency. This means establishing a world domestic policy which will be made responsible for the production (*Inszenierung*) of world policy and the handling of the world's problems.[37]

Thus World Domestic Policy differs from traditional foreign policy, as Erwin Müller conceives of it, in the following way:

> World domestic politics should see to it that at least the most urgent of the world's problems be solved, if possible, not by confrontation or disparate solo forays, but through cooperative and common efforts and true to the classical game rules of domestic politics--i.e. in *civil* and *non-violent* ways in so far as the use of violence ensues from well-defined consensual legal norms. It is a question of the peaceful overcoming (*Bewältigung*) of global problems in the framework of global cooperation according to globally recognized normative guidelines. This should occur on the one hand through

---

37 Vogt, 1994: 29. The original reads: "Die herkömmliche Außenpolitik der Nationalstaaten, die vorrangig deren Macht- und Interessendurchsetzung bezwekt, wird den gewandelten weltpolitische Bedingungen und Herausforderungen nicht mehr gerecht. Die Nationalstaaten, die noch immer die Hauptakteure im sog. 'System internationaler Beziehunen' sind, stellen zu kleine und zu egoistische Handlungseinheiten dar, um die grenzüberschreitenden Probleme und die existenzbedrohenden Krisen in der Welt-Risiko-Gesellschaft aus eigener Kraft bewältigen zu können. ...Die problembelandene und krisengeschüttelte Weltgesellschaft bedarf einer "Weltinnenpolitik," die mehr sein muss als die Sume der aussenpolitischen Aktivitäten der Nationalstaaten. Es geht darum, ein globales Politikparadigma an die Stelle der bisherigen Aussenpolitik der Nationalstaaten zu setzen bzw. diese durch eine neue, übernationale Handlungsebene zu überwölben, d.h. eine Weltinnenpolitik zu etablieren, die für die Inszenierung der Weltpolitik und die Bearbeitung der Weltprobleme zuständig gemacht wird."

the containment of war and violence, and on the other hand through the elimination (*Beseitigung*), so far as possible, of their social *causes*.[38]

An extension of domestic politics to the entire world entails the universalization of the social contract. The "prevention of violence through the elimination of its social causes" requires not only understanding what these causes are, but understanding them better than the actors who themselves are enmeshed in violence. As such, world domestic policy requires a subject who can both understand and have the power to ('benignly') impose "civilized" norms on non-OECD regions. World domestic policy, in other words, is required to maintain the teleological dynamic of the societal world. It is a policy choice whose goal is the universal advent of the societal world.

The societal world is both the justification and the goal for world domestic policy. As justification it offers its subjects old Hegelian-type narratives about the unfolding of history and modernist narratives about progress. The policymakers of the OECD world are thus confronted with an enormous potential which is simultaneously a terrible burden: the world is theirs to save, but also theirs to lose. Advocates in the narrative of world domestic policy can cast themselves in the role of the avant garde, struggling against the odds to realize a world without war. Policies which serve this noble goal of world peace through the logic of world domestic policy are given priority. In this way, world domestic policy can offer pragmatic answers to perceived threats to the OECD way of life.

These threats include the common litany of mass migration, environmental disaster, nuclear proliferation, abuse of human rights, hostile anti-democratic forces, civil wars, genocide, and terrorism. Most threatening, and most important, to the future societal world is the disintegration of nation-states into civil or other forms of war. Former Yugoslavia, Rwanda, Somalia, the Chechen Republic in Russia and Georgia are portrayed as the most dangerous threats to a future societal world, for the disintegration of the nation-state into ethnic factions undermines the possibility of democratization.[39] Without de-

---

38 Müller, 1995: 2. Emphasis in the original. The original reads: "Weltinnenpolitik soll dafür Sorge tragen, dass zumindest die dringlichsten Weltprobleme nicht auf konfratativem Wege oder in disparaten Einzelgängen, sondern kooperativ und gemeinschaftlich bearbeitet und nach Möglichkeit gelöst werden können, und das getreu den klassischen Spielregeln von Innenpolitik in *zivilen*, d.h. *insofern gewaltfreien* Bahnen, als Gewaltanwendung ausschliesslich nach wohldefinierten konsensualen Rechtsnormen erfolgen darf. ... Es geht um die friedliche Bewältigung globaler Probleme im Rahmen globaler Zusammenarbeit gemäß global anerkannter normativer Richtlinien, und zwar einerseits durch die Eindämmung von Krieg und Gewalt, anderseits durch die präventive Verhinderung von Gewalt über die Beseitigung ihrer sozialen *Ursachen*, soweit dies eben machbar scheint."

39 See, for example, the depiction of threats in Stürmer, 1994.

mocratization, the societal world cannot succeed: it is premised on a shared awareness of human rights and citizen participation in politics through elections. These are necessary to achieve the "emancipation" of the particular society vis-à-vis their political system and the ensuing global "socialization" which will anchor common norms in all the world's states.

This focus on states is crucial to world domestic policy, for it makes democratization the prime policy imperative, even more than institution-building. As Müller points out, world domestic policy lends itself to three contending instantiations of the societal world: a federal world-state (*Bundesstaat*) (along the lines of world government), an advanced state-world where policy is made by international organizations, and a confederal world state (*Staatenbund*). The idea of a federal world-state is singularly unpopular, due not least to its unwieldy character. A world dependent on international organizations is seen by Müller as insufficient, since international organizations by themselves are too loosely conceived to move decisively toward a societal world. The "only remaining alternative model" to the state-world of today is the confederal world model.[40]

The confederal model has three advantages: 1. A confederation loosens, yet retains state sovereignty; 2. A confederation can be seen either as a substitute for the utopian federal world-state, or as a step towards its creation; 3. A confederation allows for the coordination of world domestic policy through the creation of a global system of collective security.[41] By retaining the state, the confederal societal world remains a product of international anarchy. International anarchy is an assumption which all of the authors discussed in this chapter subscribe to; the societal world is the 'true' method to contain anarchy. The assumption of anarchy is evident in the workings of world domestic policy in its role as enforcer of international peace. In a confederal societal world, a system of collective security has the goal "*to bring wrongdoers to reason* by violent means (*gewaltsamen Exekution*) if efforts at arbitration remain without success or are not paid attention to."[42] The task of "bringing wrongdoers to reason," more commonly referred to as (humanitarian) intervention, forms the practical centerpiece of world domestic policy.

---

40 Müller, 1995.
41 Ibid.: 10-13.
42 Müller, 1995: 10. Emphasis added in the English. The German reads "[dass ein System Kollektiver Sicherheit] Rechstbrecher auf dem Wege der gewaltsamen *Exekution* zur Räson bringt, wenn etwa seine *schiedsgerichtlichen* Bemühungen erfoglos bleiben oder nicht in Anspruch genommen werden." Emphasis in the original.

INTERVENTION

The legitimization of interference in other countries' "internal" affairs is the focal point of world domestic policy. World domestic policy is the active method for expanding the societal world from the OECD-states to the "rest of the world." The acceptance of a world divided into globalization (represented by regime building and integration), and fragmentation (represented by civil war and poverty), requires a two-pronged approach: strengthen regimes, and strengthen dispute settlement. Czempiel points out how dispute settlement is linked dialectically to the strengthening of regimes: "Cooperation within an international organization provides the only strategy possible to counter the security dilemma which presents the most important causal mechanism of violence within the international system."[43] Senghaas reminds us why this is so important: "...the settlement of disputes," states Senghaas, "is a field of action in world domestic policy that must be regarded as vital *if we are to prevent the world from sinking into militancy and chaos.*"[44]

While dispute resolution is perhaps the most common form of organized intervention, Czempiel maintains that *any interaction* between societies counts as intervention if "it influences the behavior of actors toward their political system or toward their societal world."[45] This definition is broad enough to allow for good and bad intervention. 'Bad' intervention reinforces the status quo or causes instability. 'Good' intervention works toward the emancipation of society through democratization and respect for human rights. 'Good' intervention includes creating and bolstering democratic free-market societies through development projects, humanitarian aid, and if necessary the use of political or economic sanctions or, as a last resort, military intervention to prevent human rights violations.[46] I will refer to this definition of intervention as 'liberal intervention' to mark it as a discursive trope.

Liberal intervention is required for two main reasons: 1. from a self-interested perspective it helps create a more secure world which fosters peace and prosperity; and 2. from a moral perspective it furthers the global awareness of human, civic, and political rights, and thereby helps realize the societal world.

On the first point, the liberal discourse reinterprets the concept of security as democratization strategies "whose goal is the reliable absence of all military threats in a regional or global system" rather than a purely military con-

---

43 Czempiel, 1996a: 62.
44 Senghaas, 1994: 116. Emphasis added.
45 Czempiel, 1996a: 49.
46 See Senghaas: 121-124.

cept.[47] The liberal discourse accepts the syllogism that democracies are inherently peaceful, that peace is the basis for prosperity, and therefore democratic peace is the most desirable goal for all emancipated societies. On this basis Czempiel presents as axiomatic the notion that within existing societal systems "...political systems are *obliged* to enhance the development and consolidation of democratic regimes. ... Security interests *demand* an orientation of all interaction on democratization of political systems ... [A] security policy *demands* the construction of democracies and market economies *in all states of every region*."[48] Bluntly put, "That society which is interested in its security *must* contribute to the democratic-liberal organization of all governments in her international surroundings."[49]

Since one's own security is predicated on the stability of others, the second reason for intervention is inextricable from the first: "To develop democracy in one's own country and to further it in others--this is the common ground for a modern 'international policy.'"[50] More to the point, the OECD world can and must intervene in those parts of the "rest of the world" that, for whatever reason, do not abide by the OECD world's 'universal' norms:

> On a global level, the build-up of the societal world has obviously proceeded so far that a shared consciousness has developed regarding a certain value: human rights. Certainly, this value is not equally shared, and it also meets resistance within some ethnic-cultural traditions and some religions, such as radical Islam. Political resistance, on the other hand, is of a different kind. The political systems in Asia and Africa deny the binding nature of universal human rights.[51]

These political systems, then, must change in order to secure the norms of the societal world. What is so novel about liberal intervention, according to the discourse, is that the broad conception of intervention as interaction makes changing those political systems which "deny the binding nature of universal human rights" acceptable and even *de rigueur*: "[T]he taboo of the state-world *is overcome* as a consequence of the increased interactions of the societal world."[52]

This taboo is the principle of non-interference in a sovereign state's internal affairs. Czempiel attacks this principle on two accounts: 1. Sovereignty is reconceived to reside in the people of a given state, not the political system.

---

47 Czempiel, 1994a: 6.
48 Czempiel, 1996a: 50, 54-55. Emphasis added.
49 Czempiel, 1994a: 4. Emphasis added.
50 Czempiel, 1996a: 55.
51 Czempiel, 1996a: 47. Czempiel cites Skriver and Östreich for his claims about Asia and Africa, respectively.
52 Czempiel, 1994a: 3. Emphasis added.

Since the people of a given state are also part of a societal environment, the societal environment becomes "the true agent of sovereignty."[53] Thus, if intervention is in the interests of the societal environment, the claims of a particular political system to "sovereignty" are no longer recognized as legitimate. 2. With intervention defined as interaction, the OECD-world can be viewed as *always* intervening in the internal affairs of other countries, whether the actors in the OECD world are blind to the fact or are intervening negatively. For security and moral reasons, the OECD world cannot afford to let interventions/interactions occur in an unorganized and potentially counterproductive manner. Thus, the OECD must recognize its 'leadership' role in the world and assume responsibility for its interactions. "[The OECD world] is also co-responsible; this gives rise not only to the requirement (*Verpflichtung*), but also the right (*Anspruch*) to participate in the ordering of [other countries'] internal affairs ... The ban on intervention is based on a systemic context which no longer applies in the OECD world."[54]

The OECD world is obligated to recognize its influence and use it to further the societal world. For Czempiel and Senghaas, this amounts to an intervention imperative: "[W]e can view intervention as being established (a) as a *fact* [i.e. interaction = intervention], (b) as a *responsibility* (*duty*) based on democratic legitimacy, and finally (c) as a *right* based on security claims of one's own society." The language of facts, duties, and rights constructs intervention as an inevitable, noble, and desirable element of the modern world. Even more, intervention is the purview of the OECD world in particular, for it is they who are able to positively influence the "rest of the world" through democratization and marketization, while the "rest of the world" is reduced in the discourse to offering in return primarily negative interventions such as migration, environmental disaster and war. The portrayal of intervention as a moral imperative is central to the construction of a political culture for legitimate intervention. Intervention as democratization is *a priori* legitimate:

> A modern concept of the threat to peace is based on mankind's fourfold need for protection...: protection of freedom, protection against violence, protection against deprivation [poverty], and protection against chauvinism. Therefore, a policy which prevents serious offenses against the human need for protection *is legitimate from the outset and as a matter of principle* if it credibly aims at restoring such protection.[55]

Democratization becomes the *sine qua non*, the litmus test, of an intervention's status. "Foreign policy" *becomes* democratization:

---

53 Czempiel, 1996a: 42.
54 Czempiel, 1994a: 3.
55 Senghaas, 1994: 124. Emphasis added.

[T]he foreign policy behavior of actors in the societal world must depart decisively from those aims which Clausewitz formulated for the state world.
With the advent of the societal world Clausewitzian aims and strategies
have become extinct, at least within the OECD-world. Political non-
interference and fully-deployed military capabilities for defense are replaced
by the duty of political intervention aimed at strengthening democracy and
market economy in the international environment. All actions and all interactions which are induced through the international environment by the actors of either a political system or the societal environment ought to correspond with this aim. In the societal world all foreign policy behavior must
be checked against the norm that each action and interaction has to further
democracy and its economic correlation, market economy. Other aims, for
example the preservation of the natural environment, are not excluded at all
-- as long as they do not collide with this requirement.[56] ... Foreign policy in
the societal world must be primarily and above all, if not exclusively, democratization policy.[57]

Without much embellishment, the liberal discourse could be construed as
calling for a (peaceful) crusade for democratization. The emphasis of the crusade is clearly on non-violent means, with the use of military force reserved
for the most obstinate and egregious violators of human rights.[58] Yet theories
of colonialism and imperialism have taken great pains to show the workings
of non-military forms of coercion--a colonized country is not merely con-
quered, it is coopted, constrained, conscripted and compelled by a network of
economic, social, political, and, not least, military pressures to conform to the
wishes of a 'superior' power.[59] Cognizant of this legacy of the West, and cau-
tious of appearing too zealous despite the strident tones of their texts,
Senghaas and Czempiel both try to allay any fears that the push toward a societal world will harbor such hazards.

Senghaas reassures that "'Humanitarian interventions' as a form of imperialist politics, which were a matter of course 100 years ago, will be, if at all, a
marginal phenomenon in international politics." This is because "international

---

56 Czempiel, 1996a: 55.

57 Czempiel, 1994a: 6.

58 Czempiel writes on this point: "Natürlich lassen sich daraus keine 'Kreuzzüge für die
Freiheit' rechtfertigen, wie sie einst der Präsidentschaftskandidat Eisenhower empfohlen
hatte. Es geht auch nicht um einen imperialistischen Demokratieexport, wie er von der
Administration Reagan in dem berühmten 'project democracy' versucht worden ist. In
Frage kommen überhaupt nur gewaltfreie Strategien, die sich in den Vorgängen der
Interaktion selbst darbieten." Merkur: 4. Certainly Czempiel advocates "violence-free
strategies," though elsewhere he is far less categorical about them. In 1996a on page 56 he
writes that the "elementary needs of a society supersede all demands for sovereignty of the
political system and that these needs may on occasion be enforced by violence."

59 See Nandy, 1983, also Doty, 1996a.

public opinion is getting increasingly sensitive to improper behavior worthy of condemnation."[60] These statements imply that imperialism, or in Senghaas' more telling term, "political abuse" of intervention, results from deviation from a democratic norm, from what the liberal discourse calls 'civilized norms.' Implicit in all the texts analyzed here is a firm belief that true democracy, freed from fear of war and hence the selfish manipulations of anti-democratic fearmongers, creates a space for the natural (I use that word advisedly) unfolding of humanity's virtues. Just as for Senghaas a policy which promotes the "human need for protection" is *a priori* legitimate, so for Czempiel are democratic actors, if truly democratic, all but structurally incapable of being imperialist:

> The distinguishing feature of the societal world are multiple interactions between the societal actors. These are the main representatives of non-immediate strategies which are decisive in helping create a democratic and market-oriented environment. *These actors cannot be accused of political-expansionist interests.* Furthermore, *assuming democracy*, the political system *cannot impose conditions* so societal actors *can act freely* with their counterparts in the international environment.[61]

Freedom here is constructed in the negative sense, as an absence of conditions imposed by the political system.[62] Politics is conceived in a classic liberal sense as a necessary evil to constrain humanity's base impulses. The societal world is a continuation of the telos grounded in the myth of the Hobbesian Leviathan, whose strict control allowed human's natural morality to flourish in an environment no longer plagued by anarchy. The liberal discourse accepts the logic of nation-states as localized attempts to escape the war of all against all. Nation-states can institute physical security for its citizens, but according to the liberal tradition, only democratic states contain the correct mix of security and freedom to allow the unfettered unfolding of natural morality. Thus, nation-states are but a stage on the way to democratic nation-states, which themselves are a stage on the way to an environment where morality can exist without the need for a Leviathan, governance without government: the societal world. Without fear of life and limb, without manipulation by unscrupulous political systems playing on the fear of war, with democratic procedures and the (naturally-occurring) free-market economy, national citizens will become global citizens united in their differences by acknowledgment of basic universal human, political, and civil rights. For the liberal discourse, progress toward this point is the criterion for civilization, and world domestic policy is a civilizing tool:

---

60 Senghaas, 1994: 124-125.
61 Czempiel, 1996a: 64. Emphasis added.
62 See Isaiah Berlin, 1958, on the differences between positive and negative freedom.

[The concept of world domestic policy] ultimately provokes the question of whether or not international politics will be civilized. If the civilizing of international politics could be advanced via references to a world domestic policy perspective, then the reasons for and the extent of legitimate interference in the internal affairs of countries would gradually become a marginal phenomenon, comparable with appropriate efforts undertaken within states to tackle deviating behavior. ... A great deal will depend on whether or not an adequate common understanding for the requirements of civilized politics will be achieved in the wake of the concrete implementation of [world domestic policy]....[63]

This passage from Senghaas elucidates the element of convergence implicit in the discourse. Note the key sentence "If the civilizing of international politics could be advanced ..., then *the reasons for* and *the extent of* legitimate interference in the internal affairs of countries would gradually become a marginal phenomenon, *comparable with appropriate efforts undertaken within states to tackle deviating behavior* (emphasis added)." Civilized states adhere to universal norms, hence the need for intervention would diminish relative to the degree of civilization achieved. Despite cultural differences, which the liberal discourse allows, all countries would be similar enough in democratic political and economic structure to enable any serious dissension to be regarded as "deviating behavior" and be dealt with by the "appropriate efforts" which democratic states now use. Agreement across cultures on what is appropriate and what is deviant would be close to complete. For Czempiel this is expressed through the axiom that "the legitimacy of the societal world is constituted through *the identical nature of sovereign interests*, in that the good to be protected is no longer the freedom of monarchs in respect to their internal affairs, but the freedom of society in respect to their right to democratic rule."[64]

Will truly sovereign people have identical interests? This is only conceivable in a system where sovereignty means recognizing and accepting extant truths which have been hidden because of deceit, fear, or poverty. So self-evident for the liberal discourse is the postulate that democracy and the free market create the conditions for civilization, that there is no perceived need to discuss interpretations of deviating behavior. Coming from the left of the political spectrum, it is difficult at first to understand how an author like Senghaas can have such faith in a given democratic state's use of "appropriate efforts" to check "deviant behavior." The history of the democratic governments of all the major Western powers' actions against internal dissent in the

---

63 Senghaas, 1994: 125.
64 Czempiel, 1996a: 65. Emphasis added.

1960s (and the 1950s in the U.S.) stand out as a shrill reminder of the problem of identifying deviancy and defining appropriate efforts.

Statements such as Senghaas' become easier to understand, however, when they are placed against the background of 'true' democracy versus 'incomplete' (or perhaps 'not fully civilized') democracy. Incomplete democracy exists as long as the international environment is dominated by foreign policy behavior based on Clausewitzian "aims and strategies." Even though the OECD world has moved beyond this in principle, in fact it still remains harnessed to these state-world ideas because the global nature of the world economy necessitates dealing with the "rest of the world." Until the "rest of the world" enters the societal world or, conceivably, becomes irrelevant to it, the OECD world's political system will continue to exert an undue influence on the societal actors. This then can explain why democratically elected governments can still treat their citizens in ways incompatible with the principles of the societal world: the societal actors cannot be truly emancipated until all other societies are also emancipated. This gives further power to the dynamic of civilization and concretizes the adage that 'no-one is free while others are oppressed.'

SPECIAL GERMAN RESPONSIBILITY

The arguments for world domestic policy are not only strikingly similar in form to calls in the United States for 'global governance,' but are largely inspired by the healing rhetoric of liberal brotherhood which characterizes (and caricaturizes) some trends in U.S. foreign policy.[65] As in the normalist discourse, there is a *sub rosa* propensity among the mainstream German foreign policy community to cast themselves in a leadership role analogous to the idealized picture of the United States as the leader of the free world. This analogy by no means prevents their often sharp criticism of the US, or even ire at the hypocrisy and unfulfilled promises of the 'land of unlimited possibilities,' in the German formulation of the 'land of opportunity' stereotype. On the contrary, Germany can be interpreted now as being able to adopt, and fulfill, the role of 'leader of the free world' at a time when 'civilizing' conflicts has replaced 'containing' the Soviet Union as the *sine qua non* of foreign policy -- or more precisely, when foreign policy is to be replaced by world domestic policy.

Why Germany? Dieter S. Lutz, director of the Hamburg Institute for Peace Research and Security Policy, explains in an essay entitled "End Time: Nightmare or Reality? A Plea for a German Domestic World Policy":

---

65 See the analysis of the Clinton Administration's foreign policy in Bach, 1995.

Are there not peoples (*Völker*) and/or states who have by now learned the lessons to such an extent that they are sensitive to existential dangers in a special way and feel themselves morally co-responsible for their aversion or prevention? This question is especially directed at Germany, who alone in the 20th Century plunged the peoples of the earth twice into world war.... The will of the German people for peace should be elevated to the unalterable central idea and essential character of the Basic Law in renunciation of a system which was undeterrable even in the face of offensive wars, mass murder and slavery. The German people should in the future – as already in the preamble of the Basic Law – 'serve the peace of the world' (*dem Frieden der Welt dienen*).[66]

Lutz stresses that Germany "twice alone in the twentieth century" plunged the world into war. By implicitly exculpating the Chamberlains and Molotovs this rhetoric simplifies the past in order to simplify the present in two ways: First, in answer to the concerns from abroad that Germany is attempting to put its past behind it, claiming sole responsibility becomes a public expression of guilt that silences further discussion. Guilt is admitted, let us concentrate on redemption. Second, it becomes possible for peoples to be "solely" responsible for something, be it war or peace. If the Germans in the first half of the Twentieth Century were responsible for war, now they can be responsible for peace.

Germany can and must be responsible for peace, for when responsibility becomes an imperative it becomes a duty. This becomes clearer when we look at the different way "responsibility" is constructed in normalist and liberal discourses. For the normalists, as we saw in the last chapter, German responsibility corresponds to that which any 'normal' power of Germany's stature exhibits in accordance with the constraints of the international system. In the liberal discourse, responsibility for peace is not a 'return' to Great Power normalcy, it is a necessary element of redemption; it is redemption in action. Working for peace is the proof that the Germans have "learned their lesson."

Furthermore, there is a widely shared sentiment that Germany has reaped the benefits of the end of the East-West conflict more than any other coun-

---

66 Lutz, 1993: 9. The original reads: "Gibt es nicht Völker und/oder Staaten, die ihre Lehre aus der Geschichte bereits dergestalt gezogen haben, daß sie schon heute in besonderer Weise sinsibel für existientielle Gefahren sind und sich als moralisch mitverantwortlich für deren Abwendung oder Verhütung fühlen? Diese Frage richtet sich auch und gerade an Deutschland, das die Völker der Erde allein im 20. Jahrhundert zweimal in einen Weltkrieg gestürzt hat.... Der Friedenswille des deutschen Volkes sollte in Abkehr von einem System, das selbst vor Angriffkriegen und Massenmorden und Versklavung nicht zurückgeschreckt war, zum unabänderlichen Leitgedanken und Wesensmerkmal des Grundgesetzes erhoben werden. Das deutsche Volk sollte künftig--so bereits die Präambel des Grundgesetzes–'dem Frieden der Welt dienen'."

try.[67] This forms a further ground for Germany's special debt to the principles of the West which, in the popular view, enabled German unification. Thus three elements come together to privilege Germany as the *Vorreiter* (forerunner) of world domestic policy:

- First is the epistemic deference which Germany can claim because Germans belong to those peoples who, because of their transgressions, are "sensitive to existential dangers in a special way." The more heinous the misdeeds, this epistemic privilege seems to imply, the greater the sensitivity.

- Following from the epistemic claim is a normative claim: uniquely criminal in war, the Germans must be specially devoted to peace. The replacement of the call for unification in the preamble to the German Basic Law hints at this claim--the German people, as Lutz quoted above, are called upon to serve world peace. Certainly this does not mean that only Germans can serve world peace, but Germany is the only state which has singled itself out (with the best of intentions) by adding this phrase to its constitution.[68]

- Thirdly, the perception that Germany profited the most from the end of the East-West conflict provides a double incentive for the primacy of the liberal discourse: indebtedness to and vindication of liberal principles. The failure of political realism to predict the fall of communism and the "third wave" of democratization (Huntington) creates a pseudo-scientific basis for a realist-to-liberal paradigm shift.[69]

Lutz interprets the Basic Law's call to serve world peace as a call for action: "It requires much more the engagement of singular initiative from the 'German people' in the sense of a continuous (*stetigen*) and lasting (*nachhaltigen*) policy of peace, with the goal of a permanent abolition of war as an institution and the dynamic construction of violence-free international structures."[70] This is reminiscent of Czempiel's imperative to work for democracy: "Wherever

---

67 As Lutz reflects, "Germany, like hardly any other state, has profited from the end of the East-West conflict." Ibid.: 10.

68 Perhaps all states would benefit from adding such a phrase. The point about Germany being the only one is not meant to denigrate the phrase itself, but to highlight that Germany felt it necessary and appropriate to single itself out among states as the one which raises the call to serve world peace.

69 See the discussion in Bach, 1995.

70 Lutz, 1993: 10.

actors from German society or its political system are involved in interactions, they must further democracy."[71]

Czempiel and Lutz are both aware, however, that Germany is not yet primarily a force for peace. Lutz notes that doubt is more than appropriate if we ask the question whether Germans have learned their lesson: "a leadership role (*Vorreiterrolle*) for Germany is not yet recognizable." While on one hand an understandable admission of frustration, the discursive context of this frustration signals a marking of internal friends and foes. Earlier in his essay, Lutz had painted in stark terms impending global catastrophes of various sorts. He sees no way to prevent global catastrophe, assessing "muddling through" as the seemingly inevitable and insufficient response of unprepared policy-makers. The "last hope" beyond mere muddling through is, essentially, Germany's recognition of its *Vorreiterrolle,* with the subsequent transformation of the international environment toward an approximation of a societal world.

---

71 Czempiel, 1996a: 65. He goes on to say that "Of course one cannot do so blindfolded. A 'societal foreign policy' should not help the emerging Mafia in the East, nor should drug trafficking or terrorism be encouraged."

5. The Out-of-Area Debate: Discourses in Action

The normalist and liberal discourses described in detail in the last two chapters delineate two dominant approaches in the post-wall construction of identity through foreign policy. The previous analysis focused primarily on the intellectual and academic roots of these discourses. The recognition that ideas play a central role in the creation of foreign policy has recently become more accepted, yet the notion of foreign policy as an essentially reactive exercise premised on exogenous constraints remains dominant. While foreign policy-makers obviously react to events, the approach here emphasizes both how such reactions are contingent on their broader discourse communities and how particular constructions of national identity are privileged, inscribed and reinscribed in the process.

We have seen how the nexus between German foreign policy and German national identity hinges on the perennial historical debate about the German "special path." Since unification, the debate about whether or not the German military can or should take part in missions other than territorial self-defense for Germany or its NATO partners has become the site for competing conceptions of "Germany." The appellation "out-of-area" technically refers to the use of German troops outside of the territory of the NATO allies. The "out-of-area" debate, however, subsumes many different debates under its broad heading:

- Most prominent has been the legal debate about whether the German Constitution (the Basic Law) prohibits the use of the federal armed forces for reasons other than territorial self-defense, and whether the Constitution need be amended to allow the use of German troops in United Nations peacekeeping missions. A decision by the Federal Constitutional Court on June 12, 1994 effectively settled this issue by ruling that the Basic Law can be interpreted as it stands to allow German participation in multilateral peace-keeping operations, and that no amendment is therefore necessary. Also addressed in the ruling was a debate about where competency resides in governmental organs to decide such matters (the parliament has the power to decide).

- At the level of historiography, the question of Germany drawing the correct lessons from the past is brought to the fore: should the historical crimes of the German military impose constraints on the use of German military in the future? What is the nature of responsibility to the past? Are there different, potentially incompatible, responsibilities to the victims of Nazi German aggression and West Germany's Cold War allies?

• The historiographical questions are of course inextricable from moral issues: is "Germany" morally committed to peace, or is it a matter for individual conscience? Are military operations–even in the name of peace– unacceptable on moral grounds? To what extent should policy-makers' individual consciences be reconciled with the demands of their respective political parties?

• Politically, the debate is of defining importance for party platforms: which party can claim to identify German interests better than the others? What party is the most realistic, the most pragmatic, the most moral, the most sensitive, the most authentic? This kind of rhetorical competition is, understandably, par for the course with political parties. The out-of-area debate highlights those foreign policy issues fundamental to national identity: which party most convincingly interprets the meaning of "normalcy," "special path," "responsibility" and "credibility."

The significance of the out-of-area debate thus extends far beyond technical questions of allowing German troops to participate in UN peace-keeping missions. This debate is well-situated to explore how normalist and liberal discourses manifest themselves in political action. A brief overview of the history of the debate will set the context, before turning to terms, images, and dynamics used in the articulation of the issues. I will look at attempts to classify the different political reactions through examining political parties and their key political leaders, keeping in mind the contours of the discourses described in the last two chapters. This will be followed in the next chapter by a close analysis of the parliamentary debates surrounding the sending of German troops to participate in the UN mission in Bosnia in implementation of the Dayton Peace Accord.

The Out-of-area Debate in Context

THE MILITARY IN WEST GERMANY

The very existence of an army in a country living under the dark shadow of their its militaristic excesses is a delicate issue. The Bundeswehr was conceived in the years of the Korean War, during the first multilateral military action under the auspices of the United Nations. Its implementation was planned by the fledgling NATO in an atmosphere of fear and uncertainty, when public sentiment in the US, fanned by red-baiting invective and the war in Korea, supported drastic measures to "contain" communism. Eliciting British and French acceptance of rearmament barely eight years after Germany's defeat was a task which the United States government accomplished through a variety of measures, including the clear subordination of German troops within the NATO command structure. With great effort, the Bundeswehr achieved a considerable degree of acceptability within Germany. Its soldiers were "citizens in uniform," with the status of front line soldiers along with their allies against the Soviet Union and their former countrymen in East Germany.

The rehabilitation of the military in Germany played a significant role in restoring a sense of "normalcy" to the Federal Republic as a signifier of sovereignty and (Prussian) tradition. NATO membership reduced the image of an occupied country and bolstered the idea of West Germany as a partner rather than a subject of the military alliance. For all of NATO's obvious advantages, there remained a certain veracity to Lord Ismay's oft-quoted quip that NATO's primary purpose was to keep the Soviets out, the Americans in, and the Germans down. Rather than isolation, keeping the Germans "down" included much cooperation between German and other NATO troops in addition to the limitations on structure and types of weapons imposed on the military by international law and the West German constitution.

Seeking through the military a "return" to "normalcy" while carefully organizing and representing the German military as qualitatively different in style and purpose than the "imperial" militaries of their former-colonial allies created a contradiction which ties into the broader dialectics of German identity between a "special path" and "normalcy." One manifestation of this contradiction is the desire to engage in international multilateral missions, while avoiding the negative image (both at home and abroad) of German troops in combat.

THE END OF CONSENSUS

In the late 1980s the question of whether German troops should be able to participate in UN peacekeeping missions began to be taken seriously. Ironically it was the "First Gulf War," as the Iran-Iraq War of the 1980s is known in Germany, which prominently raised the issue of German troops abroad. The United States and other West European countries had sent mine sweepers to the Persian Gulf to insure the safe passage of ships. The German federal government rejected a call to participate directly in the monitoring of the Gulf, claiming insufficient justification in the Basic Law for out-of-area actions. In order to save face, however, in October of 1987 five German navy vessels were ordered to the Mediterranean to replace U.S. Navy ships on duty in the Gulf.

Overshadowed politically by the continuing debate on the stationing of medium-range nuclear missiles on German territory, this first major out-of-area debate did not attract tremendous public attention. Yet even within the context of a still-divided Germany the question of Germany's "international responsibility" was becoming an increasingly salient issue, spurred by President Bush's May 1989 invocation of (then-West) Germany's future as a "partner in leadership." Three months after Bush's speech, and without great fanfare, the Federal Government agreed to support a United Nations peacekeeping mission by sending 50 officials of the Federal Border Patrol (*Bundesgrenzschutz*) to Namibia for non-combat related duty.

THE DEBATE MOVES CENTER STAGE

Almost one year after the decision to participate in Namibia, Iraq's invasion of Kuwait on August 2nd, 1990 catapulted the out-of-area debate to the main stage of German politics. This came at a time when in inner-German politics the unimaginable had become real, and the German Democratic Republic was living out its last chimerical minutes awaiting official absorption into the Federal Republic on October 3. These weeks before the unity were rife with bewilderment at the historical possibilities of a united Germany. Accordingly, the question of what a "partner in leadership" meant assumed a new gravitas. Before unification the out-of-area issue was primarily cast in terms of burden sharing within the Atlantic alliance. With unification the issue grew to include the world-historic role of the new Germany. The key words of normalcy and responsibility received new currency, as the previous two chapters have discussed.

At first, the (second) Gulf War seemed to impact Germany similarly to the crisis in 1987. The initial response of the Federal Government to the request to send German ships to help enforce the embargo against Iraq seemed identical to three years earlier: the Bundeswehr is constitutionally prohibited from military activities outside of NATO countries. Notably different, however, was the presentation of the constitutional limitation as an obstacle to be overcome rather than a fundamental constraint to be dealt with on its own terms. Defense Minister Stoltenberg in particular emphasized the desire of the Federal Government to change the constitution. From this point at the end of August 1990 till the German Supreme Court decision on July 12 1994, the out-of-area debate became inextricable from the search for a judicial solution.

A NEW "TWO-TRACK" APPROACH

In the absence of constitutional clarity until 1994, the government adopted two paths which shaped the nature of the debate. On the policy-front, the government made unilateral decisions to engage the Bundeswehr on, and arguably beyond, the margins of constitutional limitations. These "salami tactics," as opponents termed them, occurred simultaneously with continuing efforts for a constitutional amendment. This two-pronged approach was effective, for while the constitutional amendment rhetoric provided a public guide for policy through prominent speeches by Chancellor Kohl and Foreign Ministers Genscher and Kinkel, the actions of the government provoked the SPD and even the Conservative's coalition-partner the FDP to bring suit in the highest court against the federal government, thereby forcing the issue. It should be noted that the CDU/CSU, together with the many legal experts, held that the constitution was not in need of amendment in order to allow out-of-area missions, a position with which the High Court eventually agreed. In the absence of partisan consensus, however, and in the face of substantial textual ambiguity, the CDU/CSU wholeheartedly supported their coalition partner's clarion call for a constitutional amendment to clarify the issue.

The government's presentation of the out-of-area issue was generally compatible with a traditional normalist approach. Accordingly, the operative discourse of the debate tended to be skewed toward viewing the constitutional limitation as an obstacle to "normalcy." The emphasis on the search for a judicial solution created the impression that the problem was less political than legalistic, by implication the arcane provenance of legal experts rather than a concern for all in a democracy. The historical, moral, and political controversy of the debate was thereby downplayed. This was also the case in most of the major policy speeches given by Kohl and Kinkel (though Kinkel, as we will see, is somewhat inconsistent). Here morality and history appear solely in support of allowing German troops to participate in peacekeeping missions.

In addition, viewing the issue primarily as a constitutional problem highlights different questions. Rather than directly debating the form which the new Germany could take, including varying understandings of Germany's "interests," these issues became secondary to a debate about what Germany is or is not *allowed* to do.[1] There was doubtless a certain comfort for all parties in the abdication of difficult decision-making to the courts. If the court rules that the Bundeswehr can participate in out-of-area peacekeeping missions, they are thereby vindicating the government's position. This vindication can be all too easily misinterpreted as support, and juridical sanctification makes German participation in out-of-area missions appear more "normal."

Ironically, the government's proposed solution of a constitutional amendment would have forced politicians to have taken greater direct responsibility for sending German troops into combat situations. Kohl himself bluntly stressed the political rather than the juridical nature of the debate by ex-

---

1 Siedschlag, 1995: 206.

claiming at a press conference in 1991 that "I want the constitutional amendment, whereby I do not investigate at all whether it is [legally] necessary or not: it is politically necessary."[2] That the courts settled the problem instead of the politicians is due in part to the inability of procedural consensus in parliament, as well as differences within the government. But above all it was the government's increasing use of the German military for peacekeeping missions despite the lack of constitutional guidance that brought the issue to the courts.

The Path to Constitutional Resolution: A Narrative Chronology

During the Gulf War the German government was caught in a rat's nest of conflicting issues, which made decisive action a political nightmare aside from declarations of solidarity with the allies and financial/logistical aid. In addition to the unresolved constitutional issue, the final ratification of the 2+4 treaty on the external aspects of German unification by the then-Soviet Union did not take place until March 15, 1991, after the fighting in Iraq had ended. Demonstrating the use of the German military before the 2+4 treaty was even fully ratified seemed inopportune at best, and counterproductive at worst, if it meant that the Soviet Union would delay, or even refuse, ratification. Added to the delicate situation was wide public condemnation of German arms exports to Iraq, especially the illegal transfer of chemical weapons technology with which Iraq was threatening Israel. This macabre constellation found German technology used in producing in poison gas directed at Jews in Israel by Iraq. Public disgust extended not only to the arms export issues, but to the manner in which the war was planned and waged as a whole.

All these difficulties notwithstanding, the Kohl government was able to begin to push the boundaries on out-of-area operations by sending German military to Turkey. At the end of December 1990 Turkey requested a strengthening of the allied mobile forces in their Southeastern region. NATO responded positively on January 2, 1991. This gave Germany an unusually good opportunity to involve its military without challenging the constitution outright, since Turkey was clearly within NATO territory, yet also bordered Iraq. Four days later 18 German Air Force Alphajets with 212 soldiers were sent to Erhac in Turkey, to be followed at the end of the month by approximately 500 troops from missile defense units, who were also sent to Erhac and to Diyarbakir. While officially deployed for Turkey's defense, if needed, the NATO force in Turkey was seen by critics as potentially provoking an Iraqi attack, which would induce the first German military involvement in combat since the Second World War. This scenario never materialized, but

---

2 Quoted in Ibid.: 38.

the Bundeswehr had made its first contribution of combat troops to a potentially dangerous conflict area, even if officially within NATO territory.

As was perhaps inevitable, these actions satisfied no one. Those in favor of a greater show of solidarity through military participation in Desert Storm saw the deployment to Turkey as hesitant and insufficient, a perpetuation of Germany's isolation and "*Machtvergessenheit.*" Critics of the war and of out-of-area operations for the Bundeswehr saw the government unilaterally deciding an issue of historical importance for the whole country. The surprisingly quick cessation of the ground war in Iraq in February 1991 made the debate moot, and the out-of-area question lost immediacy as the impending disintegration of Yugoslavia and the Soviet Union gained in drama.

Between the end of the Gulf War and the next deployment of German troops in support of a UN mission a little more than a year passed, during which the out-of-area debate broke down more clearly along party lines. The CDU/CSU reaffirmed its call for supporting UN missions, while the FDP was more circumspect, declaring its readiness to accept all the duties of a United Nations member-state, noting that it would nonetheless be undesirable to send German troops worldwide as a primary duty. The SPD, on the other hand, declared a system of common security as its goal for Europe.[3] While the parties were staking out ground, an "Independent Commission on the Future Duties of the Bundeswehr" delivered a non-binding report in September of 1991 that would bear similarities to the later court decision. The commission found that no constitutional amendment was necessary to justify Bundeswehr missions out-of-area; the report emphasized political rather than legal consensus.

It was in this atmosphere of uncertainty that the first German "blue helmet" operation took place, with the sending of a medical unit to Cambodia in May of 1992. This rather delicate foray into peacekeeping missions was an important public relations test for the government. In many senses Cambodia was the perfect precedent-setting peacekeeping mission for Germany. The conflict was far enough removed from public attention that, unlike the Gulf War or Yugoslavia, it did not ignite fiery public sentiments. The image of medics reinforced the idea that German soldiers were there to help, not to fight. They were called the "angels of Phnom Pen." Perversely, Cambodia also produced the perfect first casualty, an inevitable event which politicians feared would galvanize public opposition and cause negative domestic fallout. The death of a young medic, Alexander Arndt, however, caused no such backlash. The calm dignity with which the government was able to treat his death was due in part to its non-combat nature–he was killed off duty, possibly by accident.

---

3 See Ibid., appendix.

But if Cambodia seemed to proceed smoothly, foreign policy problems seemed to mount almost immediately after its commencement. Foreign Minister Genscher, a living political legend, resigned on May 18, after eighteen defining years in that position. The out-of-area problem fell heavily on his successor, Free Democrat Klaus Kinkel, an advocate of supporting out-of-area military actions in the framework of the United Nations (though his rhetoric was not always consistent). Kinkel, admittedly following an impossibly difficult act, lacked Genscher's clout and international standing. The outgoing Genscher had presided over the controversial recognition of Croatia and Slovenia by the European Community a few months earlier, and Kinkel was left to face the aftershocks, including an escalating war in Bosnia, the enforcement of sanctions against former Yugoslavia, and the siege of Sarajevo.

High emotions surrounding the war in former Yugoslavia finally pushed the out-of-area debate toward its initial resolution. The government decided to assist the United Nations by having the Bundeswehr participate in air transports to Sarajevo and in the naval enforcement of the UN embargo against Serbia and Montenegro (on July 4th and 15th, respectively). This second action infuriated the Social Democrats, who saw a fait accompli in the government's decision to participate in military actions without resolving the constitutional issue. The SPD brought suit against the government, a high-profile attack which was tempered the next day when the parliament voted to approve the military action after the fact. Yet public support for the government's position was solid enough, and the SPD was divided enough, so that the following months saw a considerable weakening of their hardline parliamentary position. In August, the party declared that it was no longer opposed to any uses of the Bundeswehr under the command of the United Nations, although they explicitly rejected missions of a nature similar to the Gulf War—an ambiguous categorization in itself.

Despite this seeming narrowing of differences, consensus on out-of-area issues proved even more elusive. In December of 1992 the government offered to send 1500 soldiers to Somalia to support the UN humanitarian mission. Three weeks after this offer, UN Secretary General Boutros-Ghali visited Bonn to argue for the unlimited (*uneingeschränkte*) participation of the Bundeswehr in United Nations missions. His plea overjoyed advocates of out-of-area missions and confounded critics, who found themselves in the unenviable position of opposing the direct wishes of the Secretary General.

Emboldened perhaps by Boutros-Ghali's entreaty, the federal government created two Defense Ministry organs to better run out-of-area missions and simultaneously stepped up the participation of the Bundeswehr in the UN Bosnia mission. On February ninth the Defense Ministry created a "Coordination Staff for Mission (*Einsatz*) Tasks," followed on April first by a "Bundeswehr Mission Command (*Einsatzführung Bundeswehr*) for centralized control over "less than war" situations. Depending on one's perspective, these developments were either practical steps to deal with very real exigencies, or uncomfortable echoes of a German general staff and preparations for unconstitutional activities.

Meanwhile, on March 24, the government decided to send German air force transport planes to participate in the humanitarian mission to Bosnia. Two days later the United Nations Security Council made an important ruling empowering UN troops in Somalia to use coercive force to improve the anarchic situation there. While no German troops were in Somalia yet, the shift from distributing food to combating warlords significantly illuminated the potential perils of peacekeeping. On the heels of this development followed a highly-charged month of intense action and reaction in Bonn, starting with the decision to establish the Bundeswehr Mission Command on April first and then, on April second, by a major showdown in parliament.

At issue that day was the participation of German soldiers in AWACs surveillance planes monitoring the no fly zone over Bosnia. The risk of an AWAC being shot down was extraordinarily minimal, but since AWACs identified possible Serb targets and guided NATO fighter planes navigation, soldiers aboard the aircraft bore responsibility for the eventual loss of life on both sides. Thus while no German fighter pilots would participate directly in combat, the implication of the AWACs soldiers engaging in any hostile action was not overlooked in a country where the question of responsibility by association is almost a participant sport. It was therefore incontrovertible that this mission would constitute the first combat mission for German soldiers since the Second World War. Not insignificantly, the theater of operations also happened to be one where German Wehrmacht soldiers had wreaked havoc fifty years earlier.

This precedent-setting decision was approved by the parliament, but only because of the majority held by the CDU/CSU. There was a general feeling that the government had gone too far. The decision to involve the Bundeswehr in a combat mission had been pushed through on a partisan vote with the constitutional issue unresolved, peppered with grave doubts about the wisdom of the effort (there was fear that German participation would only provoke the Serbs), and was infused with an historical uneasiness. In an unprecedented move, the junior partner in the governing coalition, the FDP, joined the SPD in pressing suit against the government for violating the constitution and requested a cease and desist order against the existing decision.

The request to cease and desist was quickly refused on April 8, with the justification that such action could create a serious loss of confidence in Germany by their allies. This decision, however, was not officially to be read as an answer to the constitutionality issue. Despite the lawsuits the Bundeswehr was thus able to continue with its deployment, and the precedent was set, even if it stood the chance of later being ruled unconstitutional. The government achieved the support of the courts to continue as it saw fit until such a time when they reached a decision.

Four days after the court's refusal to suspend the parliament's decision, Boutros-Ghali wrote the government asking for a Bundeswehr contingent for Somalia, a belated answer to the German government's previous December offer of 1500 troops. Although the situation had since changed dramatically from a humanitarian mission to a peace-enforcing nightmare, the parliament eventually voted on April 21st to send supply and transport units to Somalia. While not as controversial as Bosnia, this deployment solidified a shift toward riskier missions. Like the others, it succeeded in parliament because of the CDU/CSU majority over bitter opposition. When the government decided to transfer more military to Somalia in early June the SPD once again took the government to court for constitutional violation, and once again asked for a suspension of the decision. As expected, the Court again refused the suspension, tossing that issue back to the parliament and considered the main suit as part of the earlier suit filed by together with the FDP. On July 2 the parliament gave its partisan approval to the transfer.

From this point until the Court's decision nearly a year later no more deployment decisions were made. Quite the contrary: the Cambodian and Somalian missions came to an end; the former on schedule, the latter early and on a farcical note, when the Indian troops, whose supply was the original reason for the Bundeswehr's participation, failed to appear after nearly half a year, and the German government got tired of waiting. This successful completion of the missions, however, was nearly as important as their beginnings -- with two missions under their belts the government could dismiss as alarmist the dire scenarios presented in parliamentary debates and enjoy the emotional and political benefits of having successfully taken a historical risk.

It was during this year that the Kohl Administration, through the mouthpiece of the Foreign Minister, articulated in a new way its intention to institutionalize Germany's status as a partner in leadership. On the first of July, 1993, the government made officially known for the first time its willingness (and thereby signaled its desire) to hold a permanent seat in the UN Security Council. This announcement was followed by much rhetoric as to the importance of the permanent seat for Germany's responsibility and ways in which other countries could also gain permanent seats, notably Japan, and also India and Brazil. The image of a permanent member of the Security Council is that of a great power both willing and able to undertake military action, and consequently this request met with considerable opposition from the same camp which opposed use of the German military for peacekeeping. There was some attraction, however, to thinking of a permanent German seat as a way to reform the military emphasis of the Security Council and push the UN toward more conflict prevention rather than conflict management. How one views this issue depends in part on whether the UN Security Council is perceived as a hegemonic expression of great power politics seeking to legitimize itself through coopting new members, or whether the UNSC represents an institution capable and willing to seek change and reform through expanding its membership.

While the Security Council itself has not acted definitively on the question of its enlargement, the United States Senate gave its own interesting reply to those who hoped for reconciling a permanent seat with a non-military domestic stance. In a resolution from January 28, 1994, the Senate declared that they would not support a German or Japanese permanent seat *as long as* these countries could not promise to participate in UN peace-creating missions without limitations. This resolution played well with the German supporters of out-of-area missions, who could use it as proof of the importance of "normalizing" the German military in the service of "internationally responsible" action.

When the final court decision came on July 12, 1994 its effect was both astonishing and anti-climactic. In a decision that covered all previous suits on the matter, the court found that the German military participation in multilateral peacekeeping missions was not incompatible with the Basic Law. From this it followed that the government was not acting unconstitutionally, nor was any amendment to the constitution necessary to allow out-of-area missions. This was anti-climactic in the sense that the status quo, such as it existed after the AWACs debate, was legally uncontroversial. It was astonishing in how the CDU/CSU-led government's policies had been so completely vindicated. While the finding that out-of-area missions are compatible with the Basic Law is not identical with support for out-of-area missions *per se*, it was clear that the highest court in the land agreed with the basic argumentation of the Kohl government. The court did find procedural fault with the federal government, ruling that it violated the priority of the parliament by making decisions on missions that went beyond purely humanitarian aid before seeking parliamentary approval. This reprimand about the means, however, was all but invisible behind the court's exoneration of the ends.

Discourses in Action: Responsibility and Normalcy in the Government Narrative

It is an analyst's temptation to view a given historical process in terms of its outcome. Since the out-of-area debate was constitutionally resolved in favor of military involvement, it is not difficult to think that out-of-area involvement is indeed the norm from which Germany, due to its postwar division, merely deviated until now. Even the above cursory treatment of the main events in the debate could be read from that perspective. The normalcy discourse would clearly support such a reading. Yet a discourse does much more than merely support an interpretation, it constructs the possibilities for the acceptance of a particular historical posture as a given. Chapter four investigated the lineage of the normalcy discourse, its scholarly influence and its relevance for the current period. In this section the normalcy discourse returns in a different context: that of the official government positions, primarily through policy addresses.

The major policy speeches of prominent politicians are particularly salient vehicles for discourse analysis. Policy speeches are *not* the best indicators of the policy *process*, for their rhetoric bluster merely hints at the behind-the-scenes feuds from which policy emerges. But speeches are more than a fulfillment of the quotidian chores of high office. Their non-specific nature allows for the transmission of axiomatic ideas in unusually condensed form. Their repetitiveness allows for the discerning of patterns, for the parsing out of fundamentals from flourish. Most clearly, major policy speeches convey the logic of the government as they wish to express it. While the audiences of particular speeches differ, often the message must stay essentially the same in order to avoid the impression of prevarication. There is no question that an official speech can contain half-truths, double-speak, and outright lies. President Johnson's Gulf of Tonkin speech is one of the most well-known examples of such deception. But whether or not the government actually believes its own speech does not detract from its significance as such, for the government wants the audience–which due to media coverage must always include the general public–to believe.

The search for deception, however, is not the task of this discourse analysis. My perception, based on personal interviews, interactions, and observations, is that most all purveyors of the normalcy discourse, whether politicians or scholars, are sincere in their stated positions. Whether or not these positions are "correct" is also not the point of discourse analysis. Rather, what is interesting is *how* these official statements create a context which legitimize certain forms of thinking and, by implication, denigrate others. Through an analysis of these speeches we can see how the terms of the debate are set not by facts alone (as interested parties like to think), but by interpretations and contextualization, by implication and insinuation. The normalist and liberal discourse both aim for hegemony, and to do that they must create the environment for their own success. It is too much to claim that either discourse alone creates the objects of which they speak, for each is firmly embedded in meta-narratives of modernity. But especially in the realm of constructing national identity, these discourses delineate the "normal" nation from the "abnormal," and as such create the nation of which they speak.

The out-of-area debate differs from previous foreign policy debates in the Federal Republic because it is premised on a rupture with the "security-political consensus" which governed foreign policy since the early 80s. This consensus held that out-of-area uses of the Bundeswehr were "fundamentally out of the question."[4] The CDU/CSU broke with this consensus in 1991 with their call to amend the constitution. This break is significant not only for its policy relevance, but because, as Siedschlag understands it, with the push for a more active foreign policy role "there *cannot* be domestic political consensus, since the issue is no longer about the step by step rehabilitation of German foreign policy as an objective, non-partisan common interest, but rather which interests German foreign policy represents or should represent, and in which way these [interests] should be carried out."[5] In this sense, German foreign policy became an arena for contesting interpretations of "Germany."

If the foreign policy debate is no longer a matter of tactics within a set framework, but a debate about the framework itself, then a hegemony-seeking discourse which not only reifies but also constructs a way of looking at the world is paramount for success. A new paradigm, if you will, must be established. This paradigm does not require complete agreement within its ranks, only agreement on the framework in which the debate is to take place. Thus Kohl, Kinkel, and Rühe can and do disagree, sometimes seriously, about the nature of out-of-area missions, the best international organization to lead them, the threshold of threat necessary to provoke action, and so on. But they all seem to agree on a world-view which reflects the discourses we have explored.

---

4 The Federal Security Council's statement from November 1982 states clearly that "Der Einsatz der Bw [Bundeswehr], und zwar im Ausland, ist verfassumgsrechtlich immer dann zulässig, wenn die Bundesrepublik Deutschland selbst Angegriffen wird und sich mithin im Zustand der Ausübung des individuellen Selbstverteidigungsrechts befindet, sei es allein oder sei es gemeinsam mit anderen gleichzeitig angegriffenen Staaten. ... [M]ilitarische Einsätze der Bw außerhalb des NATO-Bereiches [kommen] grundsätzlich nicht in Frage, es sei denn, es läge ein Konflikt zugrunde, der sich gleichzeitig als ein völkerrechtswidriger Angriff auf die Bundesrepublik darstellt." Quoted by Siedschlag in Ibid.: 35.
5 Ibid.: 50.

The images to which Kohl, Kinkel, Rühe, and other government ministers appeal in their rhetoric fall under two main operative terms which are already familiar to us from the normalist and liberal discourses: responsibility and normalcy. The sub-discourse of responsibility presents itself as both a moral and practical imperative.

RESPONSIBILITY AS A MORAL IMPERATIVE

The moral imperative of responsibility can be broken down into two main categories. First, the primary responsibility is to support the perceived progression of the international system in its journey from tribalism through rival nation-states to a world of democratic states. These states are bound by a "community of destiny" (*Schicksalsgemeinschaft*), empowered by economic interdependence and regulated by international institutions. "The day has come," declares Chancellor Kohl, "in which for the first time in history the whole of Germany finds its permanent place in the circle of Western democracies."[6] This circle of democracies represents the highest stage yet attained, but it is not the end of the road. The task, as Kinkel explains, is that "While our free Western societal system has won the conflict with unfreedom (*Unfreiheit*), we must now *prove* that our economic system and our lifestyle can secure long-term sustainable development in the East and South of our earth.[7] This can only be proven if the Western nations understand themselves as a *Schicksalsgemeinschaft*, a community of destiny, a term used by Kinkel among others to describe the European Union. The EU forms a particular community of destiny, bound by geographical propinquity and historical incestuousness, but it is a regional expression of a larger community of destiny, the European-US relationship, which Kinkel refers to as a "civilizational community."[8]

The benefits of living in an economically prosperous, politically stable world of democracies would seem reason enough to strive for this ideal. Yet beyond this, Germany is portrayed as having a particular moral responsibility

---

6 Kohl, *Außenpolitik der Bundesrepublik Deutschland* hereafter: ABD, 722. The original reads: "Der Tag ist gekommen, an dem zum ersten Mal in der Geschichte das ganze Deutschland seinen dauerhaften Platz im Kreis der westlichen Demokratien findet."

7 Kinkel, ABD: 910. The original reads: "Unser freies westliches Gesellschaftssytem hat zwar die Auseinandersetzung mit der Unfreiheit gewonnen, jetzt müssen wir jedoch beweisen, daß unsere Wirtschaftsweise, unsere Lebensstil eine langfristige tragfähige Entwicklung auch im Osten und im Süden unserer Erde sichern können." Emphasis added.

8 On the EU as a *Schicksalsgemeinschaft* See Kinkel, ABD: 1083. See also "Die Außenpolitik der Bundesrepublik Deutschland nach der Wiedervereinigung" in *Europäische Sicherheit*, 1/93: 15. On the US-European alliance as a civilizational community see *Das Auswärtige Amt Informiert* (hereafter: *AA Informiert*), February 4, 1995: 8.

to support and construct this world. This special responsibility stems most clearly from Germany's culpability for the twentieth century's two world wars and the related mass murder of European Jewry. "We should bear in mind," intones Kinkel,

> the horrors of the past. A special responsibility lies especially on us from this past to participate in the restoration of peace, non-violence, and human rights.[9] ... Germany, who has brought much suffering in this century to others and to itself, carries here [in uniting Europe] a special historical responsibility. ... We especially must use all our strength so that this community presents a mature self to deal with the expectations of a new world situation.[10]... Our task remains to make good the terrible injustice of the Nazi period.[11]

Adenauer's postwar proclamation that Germany after the war must be committed to peace has become literally enshrined in the constitution whose preamble states that Germany will serve world peace. Kohl underscores Adenauer, assuring that "With our re-won (*wiedergewonnen*) national unity our country wants to serve peace in the world and expedite European unification: that is the task of the Basic Law, our tested constitution, which is also valid for united Germany. ... In the future only peace will issue forth from German soil."[12]

Beyond the moral obligation for atonement, an obligation is also presented toward those countries and governments which helped West Germany rise from a villainous and vanquished ruin to its current position at the top of the global economic ladder. This obligation extends beyond gratitude and reciprocity, it entails shouldering burdens together and accepting common risks. "We do not have the moral right," states Kohl, "to expect more from those re-

---

9 Kinkel, ABD: 894. The original reads: "Wir sollten bedenken was an Schrecklichem in der Vergangenheit war. Aber gerade uns kommt aus dieser Vergangenheit eine besondere Verantwortung zu an der Wiederherstellung von Frieden, Gewaltlosigkeit, und Menschenrechten mitzuwirken."

10 Kinkel, ABD: 906. The original reads: "Deutschland, das in diesem Jahrhundert viel Leid über andere und sich selbst gebracht hat, trägt hier [uniting Europe] eine besondere geschichtliche Verantwortung. ... Gerade wir müssen alles in unseren Kräften Stehende tun, damit diese Gemeinschaft sich auch in einer neuen Weltlage diesen Erwartunen gewachsen zeigt."

11 Kinkel, AA *Informiert*, 16 Jan 95: 1. The original reads: "Das schlimme Unrecht der Nazizeit wieder gutzumachen, bleibt unsere Aufgabe."

12 Kohl, In ABD: 718-719. The original reads: "Unser Land will mit seiner wiedergewonnenen nationalen Einheit dem Frieden in der Welt dienen und die Einigung Europas voranbringen: Das ist der Auftrag des Grundgesetzes, unserer bewährten Verfassung, die auch für das vereinte Deutschland gilt. ... Von deutschem Boden wird in Zukunft nur Frieden ausgehen."

sponsible in other countries than we expect from ourselves."[13]In the same vein Kinkel beseeches Parliament in one of many debates on the out-of-area issue:

How long can and will Germany still allow itself to merely look on while other peoples send their soldiers, with all the consequences, to secure peace?[14] ... The notion, that the economically strongest and most populous state in the middle of Europe can withdraw itself into some sort of snail shell after the fall of the wall and the iron curtain does not match reality.[15]

The German government seeks fervently to avoid the impression of being a free rider on allied military nations. "For us Germans" intones Kohl, "there is no niche in world politics, and there is no refuge for Germany from its responsibilities."[16] President Herzog drives this message home: "The end of free riding is at hand. Germany belongs to the concert of great democracies whether it wants to or not."[17] Representative of such statements is the joke about the German support for the UN mission to Bosnia which goes "We will fight until the last Frenchman." The obvious implications, that Germany could be viewed as willing to sacrifice others while enjoying a privileged position, forms the cornerstone for the moral obligation of *solidarity*.

The second source of the moral imperative lies within the brute effect of Germany's existence on others. "As an 80-million strong people," worries Kinkel, "as the economically strongest country in the middle of Europe, we are a Saint Bernard in the living room, who every time he wags his tail threatens the coffee settings. This means we carry–alone because of our weight–a special responsibility whether it fits us or not."[18] This image plainly expresses

---

13 Kohl, *Bulletin* 4 Feb. 94 12: 106. The original reads: "Wir haben nicht das moralische Recht, von den Verantwortlichen anderer Länder mehr zu verlangen, als wir selbst tun."

14 Kinkel, ABD: 897. The original reads: "Wie lange kann und will sich Deutschland noch erlauben, nur zuzusehen, das andere Völker ihre Soldaten zur Friedenssicherung mit allen Konsequenzen einsetzen?"

15 Kinkel, ABD: 916. The original reads: [D]ie Vorstellung, der wirtschaftsstärkste und jetzt Bevölkerungsreichste Staat in der Mitte Europas könne sich nach dem Fall dem Mauer und Eisernem Vorhang in eine Art Schneckenhaus zurückziehen, während unsere Partner für uns die Kastanien aus dem Feuer holen, hält doch der Realität nicht stand.

16 Kohl, ABD: 788. The original reads: "Es gibt für uns Deutsche keine Nische in der Weltpolitik, und es darf für Deutschland keine Flucht aus der Verantwortung geben."

17 Herzog, in the *Frankfurter Rundschau*, "Herzog betont Deutschlands Gewicht" March 14, 1995. "Das Ende des Trittbrettfahrens ist erreicht." The quote is continued in Schönbohm 1995: "Deutschland gehört zum Konzert der großen Demokratien, ob es will oder nicht."

18 Kinkel, *Bulletin*, 3 March, 1993, Nr.18: 142. The original reads: Als Achtzig-Millionen-Volk, als wirtschaftsstärkstes Land in der Mitte Europas, sind wir wie ein Bernhardiner im Wohnzimmer, der jedesmal, wenn er mit dem Schwanz wedelt, das Kaffeegeschirr bedroht. Das heißt, wir tragen, ob uns das paßt oder nicht, allein auf Grund unseres Gewichts eine besondere Verantwortung."

the latent fear that Germany left alone will deviate from the international norm and come into conflict with its neighbors. The "special responsibility" here is thus to harness this unwieldy power, to change the geopolitically dangerous *Mittellage* to a place in "the middle of a politically and economically uniting Europe."[19] The responsibility, however, extends beyond Germany's European environment to include global interests: "Germany is, as a leading industry, trade and cultural nation, specially dependent on its world-wide connections. For this reason we cannot remain apart from the crises and conflicts in this world." Kohl states German responsibility for others clearly: "Only in worldwide responsibility can we find a just balance between the concerns of economics and ecology. As one of the great industrial nations *we have a special responsibility to all peoples on our earth.*"[20]

This responsibility to all peoples takes the primary form of expanding stability and prosperity within the framework of supporting human rights. Human rights is a cornerstone of German foreign policy, contained in the first article of the Basic Law. "This," according to Kohl, "is the decisive moral drive for the policies of unified Germany."[21] What the incorporation of human rights into policymaking means is given more concrete form by Kinkel: "Presently we are moving from a prohibition on intervention in the name of state sovereignty to a dictate of intervention in the name of human rights and humanitarian aid."[22] This is a significant statement, for its summarizes succinctly both the perceived change in world politics since the cold war and the corollary change in German policy. Kinkel does not mean that state sovereignty as such is overcome, rather it is diminished to the extent that "interference in internal affairs" is no longer taboo for those regional and international organizations who support human rights along with democracy and the free market. Here we see the liberal discourse at work, for the world becomes divided into "zones of peace and zones of turmoil."[23] "We must engage [*aufbi-*

---

19 Kinkel, *Bulletin* March 5, 1995, Nr. 40: 350. The full German quote reads: "Unser Platz ist vielmehr in der Mitte eines sich politisch und wirtschaftlich vereinigenden Europas."

20 Kohl, New Years Address in Bulletin, December 31, 1989: 2. Emphasis added.

21 Kohl, ABD: 733. The original reads: "Dies ist der entscheidende moralische Antrieb für die Politik des vereinten Deutschlands."

22 Kinkel, ABD: 910. The original reads: "Gegenwärtig bewegen wir uns vom Interventionsverbot im Namen Staatlicher Souveränität hin zum Interventiongebot im Namen der Menschenwürde und humanitäre Hilfe."

23 These "zones" are terms from Singer and Wildavsky 1993.

eten] all our might," pleads Kinkel, "to bind as many countries as possible to the stability zone of the industrial states."[24]

Human rights does not exist in an economic or political vacuum. Hence the necessity not only to prevent or halt atrocities, but to instill democratic and free market systems as a method of prevention. This approach relies on the democratic peace theory, which holds that democracies do not fight each other, and that economic and political liberalism are necessarily co-extensive. Thus Kohl can maintain that "Free markets are an act of humanity for the third world. Global free trade is truly help in the form of self-help, and therefore *more important than* development aid."[25]

RESPONSIBILITY AS A PRACTICAL IMPERATIVE

Responsibility as a practical imperative draws on variations of the moral claims. There are three main categories of practical responsibility. First is a responsibility to make the international system (the basis of the first moral imperative) succeed. To this end, Germany must inspire and influence those organizations from which the new international order emanates. This translates into active leadership in the EU, NATO, UN, OSCE, WTO (formerly GATT) and related organizations. Exerting influence means not being singled out, not existing in a "niche of world politics." Realizing the sheer potential as a leader implicit in Germany's economic and geographic weight is viewed as a practical responsibility to the international system. International organizations are the only game in town: "With all the present imperfections in the efficiency of these organizations," says Kinkel, "they alone are capable of preventing the world from falling back into nationalist power-

---

24 Kinkel, *AA Informiert*, 16 January 95: 7. The original reads: "Wir müssen alle Kräfte aufbieten, um möglichst viele Länder an die Stabilitätszone der Industriestaaten anzubinden."

25 Kohl, "Deutsch-amerikanische Parnterschaft für Frieden, Freiheit, und Wohlstand." *Bulletin*, September 16, 1994, Nr. 84: 782. The original reads: "Als weltweit größte Exportnation haben wir ein gemeinsames Interesse an der Sicherung des freien Welthandels und der eigenen Wettbewerbsfähigkeit. ... Offene Märkte sind ein Akt der Menschlichkeit gegenüber der Dritten Welt. Der freie Welthandel ist für Entwicklungsländer wirkliche Hilfe und Selbst-hilfe und daher wichtiger als Entwicklungshilfge." Emphasis added. It is questionable whether this form of responsibility toward others would be equally welcomed by the designated other, since global free trade can also create structural patterns which disadvantage weaker parties. See cites on the disadvantages of global free trade.

politics."[26]Accordingly, German engagement in these organizations is an imperative, a form of duty:

> With its expanded influence Germany must help support and strengthen the
> United Nations in her responsibilities.[27] ... Germany is, as an industrial state
> with world-wide connections, in its geostrategical middle-position in
> Europe, as a member of the UN, as participant in the OSCE, as a member of
> NATO, the EU, and the WEU, continuously affected by regional and global
> developments. From this and from our specific past emerges a duty for co-
> responsibility (*Mitgestaltung*).[28]

Blanket restraints on German out-of-area military operations is considered a major obstacle to meeting this responsibility, and accordingly a source of embarrassment and a needless delay of the natural course of events.

A second practical imperative concerns the definition and projection of national "interests." Most specifically this refers to enhancing and protecting German export markets through a spirited defense of free trade. "As the world-wide largest export nation we have a common interest in securing global free trade and our own competitiveness" notes Kohl. Since prosperity is the handmaiden of stability and democracy, safeguarding Germany's achievements in economic growth cannot be left solely to the economics ministry and private sector, and is thus openly a foreign policy priority. "Our welfare rests to a high degree (*hochgradig*) on free and unhindered foreign trade....It remains the first priority (*Gebot*) in securing the future to place a great amount of energy on strengthening our position in the world market."[29] Free trade is the "geo-economic challenge for the now-larger Germany" which must be pursued "with our full weight."[30] Given Kohl's pronounce-

---

26 Kinkel, ABD: 908. The original reads: "Bei aller noch vorhandenen Unvollkommenheit in der Effizienz dieser Organisationen sind allein sie in der Lage, die Welt vor einem Rückfall in nationalistische Machtpolitik und gewalt zu bewahren."

27 Lamers and Ruck, In *Politik für den Frieden*, 1993:74-75. The original reads: "Mit seinem gestiegenen Einfluß muß Deutschland mithelfen, die Vereinten Nationen in ihrer Verantwortung[en] ... zu unterstützen und zu stärken."

28 Schönbohm, 1995: 9. The original reads: "Deutschland ist als Industrestaat mit weltweiten Verflechtungen, in seiner geostrategischen Mittellage in Europa, als Mitglied der VN, als Teilnehmer der OSZE, als Mitglied der NATO, der EU, und der WEU stets von regionalen und globalen Entwicklungen betroffen. Daraus und aus unserer spezifischen Vergangenheit ergibt sich eine Pflicht zur Mitgestaltung."

29 Kinkel, ABD: 905-906. The original reads: "Unser Wohlstand beruht hochgradig auf freiem und ungehindertem Außenhandel. ... Eine große Kraftanstrengung zur Stärkung unserer Stellung auf dem Weltmarkt bleibt erstes Gebot unserer Zukunftsicherung."

30 Kinkel, ABD: 1085. The full original quote reads: "[Free trade is the] geo-ökonomische Herausforderung für das größer gewordener Deutschland: Wir müssen mit unserem vollen Gewicht – gerade innerhalb der EU – dafür eintreten, daß das

ments about free trade as a humanitarian act, and the link between economic growth and peace, Germany's interest in free trade (as the world's largest exporter per capita) fits conveniently into the particular neo-liberal world-view being constructed by the government's narrative.

The third practical imperative of responsibility centers around the concept of *"Bündnisfähigkeit,"* being a reliable and capable ally. One of the strongest criticisms leveled against the Social Democrats by the governing coalition is that a SPD-led government would be unable to garner trust and reliability in foreign policy, and thus endanger the alliances which form the bedrock of Germany's security guarantees. "If we leave these partners [NATO and UN allies] in the lurch now with the new tasks of peace-securing and peacemaking," warns Kinkel gravely, "we will, in the end, be an incapable ally *(bündnisunfähig)*."[31]Being an incapable ally is not only a shameful situation for Germany, but, far worse, it endangers the entire system:

> Without the participation of the armed forces of the most populous country, that is without the German armed forces, a European security identity in the framework of the European Union could not ensue. For this reason Germany cannot allow its position to diverge from its partners in questions of security and long-term defense. Even the renewal of NATO will hardly succeed if we do not participate fully in its new tasks within the CSCE-realm.[32]

This passage particularly highlights the marriage of necessity and responsibility inherent in Kinkel's claims. Refusal to participate is an act of *bündnisunfähigkeit*, an irresponsible act which will once again present Germany as the weak link in the political and military integration of Europe and the peacekeeping endeavors of the international community. NATO's "new tasks in the CSCE-realm" is short-hand for out-of-area operations, linked here to NATO's renewal and hence survival. To even insinuate that Germany could be responsible for an eventual failure of NATO ("out-of-area or out of business") is to raise all the fears of a united Germany undermining the very order which it pledged to preserve.

---

internationale Handels- und Finanzsystem in Richtung freier Wettbewerb und nicht Protektionismus weiterentwickelt wird."

31 Kinkel, ABD: 916. The original reads: "Wenn wir diese Partner nun bei den neu hinzugekommenen Aufgaben der Friedenssicherung und Friedensschaffung im Stich lassen, dann werden wir letztlich bündnisunfähig."

32 Kinkel, ABD: 979. The original reads: "Ohne die Beteiligung der Streitkräfte des bevölkerungsreichsten Landes, also ohne die deutschen Streitkräfte, könnte eine europäische Sicherheitsindentität im Rahmen der Europäischen Union nicht entstehen. Deshalb darf Deutschland auch bei Sicherheit und Verteidigung auf Dauer keine von sienen Partnern abweichende Haltung einnehmen. Auch die Erneurung der NATO würde wohl kaum gelingen, wenn wir uns an ihren neuen Aufgaben im KSZE-Raum nicht voll beteiligten."

This fear of being regarded as an unreliable partner is deep, driven in part by the historical fickleness of Germany's *Mittellage*, cold-war allied apprehension that Germany could cut a separate peace with the Soviet Union, and post-wall variations of the ghost of the Rappalo treaty. Accordingly, significant energy is devoted to underscoring Germany's reliability in the past: "The Germans have been a calculable, reliable and respected partner"[33] stresses Kohl –and in the future–"Germany remains a reliable partner."[34] Kinkel's entreaties to Parliament in favor of out-of-area peacekeeping missions are couched in the language of reliability: "Let us make our country into an action-capable (*handlungsfähigen*) partner conscious of our responsibility (*verantwortungsbewußt*), which the world community and ourselves wish to see in us!"[35] "This is neither striving for great-power status (*Grossmachtstreben*), nor is this a 'militarization of foreign policy.'" notes Schönbohm, "All of this revolves around the central question, to what extent Germany – as a sovereign state in the heart of Europe – is prepared to stand up to its international duties."[36]

Kinkel is fond of the sports metaphor of a "team player" for highlighting Germany's "reliable and successful" performance during the Cold War. Now Germany must learn to play a different and more important position on the team, as it were, to make best use of its newly gained weight.[37]Germany's size and world-view means it is no longer merely any player, but, as Kinkel delicately tried to phrase it, "a good team player ... without the captain's armband – but, say, as a player with special responsibility."[38]

While the issues of moral and practical responsibility are usually made separately, despite their intimate connection, in one speech Kinkel bundled them together into three unusually concise sentences: "Not least because of

33 Kohl, ABD: 724. The original reads: "Die Deutschen sind berechenbare, zuverlässige und geachtete Partner geworden."
34 Kohl, Bulletin 16 Sept. 84: 783. The original reads: "Deutschland bleibt ein verläßlicher Bündnispartner."
35 Kinkel, ABD: 912, 919. The original reads: "Machen wir unser Land zu einem handlungsfähigen und verantwortungsbewußten Partner, den die Weltgemeinschaft und wir selber in uns sehen wollen!"
36 Schönbohm 1995: 10. The original reads: "Dies ist weder "Großmachtstreben" noch handelt es sich um eine "Militarisierung der Außenpolitik." Es geht einzig um die zentrale Frage, in welchem Umfang Deutschland – als souveräner Staat im Herzen Europas – bereit ist, international zu seine Pflichten zu stehen."
37 Kinkel, *Bulletin*, August 29, 1994, Nr. 76: 713.
38 Kinkel, *Bulletin*, August 29, 1994, Nr, 76: 715. The original reads in full: "Vier Jahre danach [after unification] wird man uns zugestehen müssen, daß wir versucht haben, ein guter Mannschaftsspieler zu bleiben. Und bei dieser Rolle wollen wir es auch in Zukunft belassen – ohne Kapitänsbinde – aber sagen wir mal als Spieler mit besonderer Verantwortung."

our historical past Germany is morally bound to participate in the defense of peace. Without readiness for this, Germany would be incapable of alliance and action (*bündnis- und handlungsunfähig*). Our vital interests in the world as an economic, trade, and cultural nation would be damaged."[39]

THE DISCOURSE OF NORMALCY

Both the moral and the practical imperatives of responsibility follow from the need to adapt to a geopolitical "reality" which appears as a historical necessity: "The essential characteristic of the political changes in Europe is the rebirth of the European middle" according to Schönbohm. "Now Middle-Europe (*Mitteleuropa*) can become the anchor of stability for the continent."[40] Within this new geopolitical reality, "Germany must," explains Kinkel, "assume the role which befits an industrial state of our size in the safeguarding of global and regional stability, free trade and sustainable development."[41] This role is nothing less than what is "normal" for a country with Germany's characteristics. Furthermore, the potential for this role always existed, only it was proscribed historically by dangerous experimentation with "special paths" and, later, the peculiar constraints of the Cold War. Thus responsibility is primarily conceived of as responsibility *to be normal.*

The sub-discourse of normalcy, then, exists in a circular relation to the concept of responsibility. Being normal involves a dialectical process between "internal" and "external" normalcy. Kinkel is the politician most visibly concerned with normalcy:

> What do I mean by normalization? For foreign policy, it has to do among other things with the assumption of world-wide peace tasks by the Bundeswehr under the cover of the United Nations and with the consent of the parliament. Domestically, public consciousness must first be raised that the international community expects a German contribution to peace at a global

---

39 Kinkel, ABD: 1057. The original reads: "Nicht zuletzt aufgrund unserer geschichtlichen Vergangenheit ist Deutschland moralisch verpflichtet, sich an der Verteidigung des Friedens zu beteiligen. Ohne die Bereitschaft dazu wäre Deutschland bündnis- und handlungsunfähig. Auch unsere vitalen Interssen als Wirtschafts-, Handels- und Kulturnation in der Welt würden Schaden nehmen."

40 Schönbohm, 1995. The original reads: "Das wesentliche Merkmal der politischen Veränderungen in Europa aber ist die Wiedergeburt der europäischen Mitte. ... Jetzt kann Mitteleuropa zum Stabilitätsanker des Kontinents werden...."

41 Kinkel, *Bulletin* No. 18, August 29, 1994: 713. In the original the role which "befits" actually "comes to" Germany *zukommen*. The original reads: "Deutschland muß bei der Sicherung globaler und regionaler Stabilität, des freien Welthandels und einer tragfähigen Entwicklung den Part übernehmen, der einem führendem Industriestaat unserer Größenordnung zukommt."

level, a contribution which, if we really want to enjoy recognition, rejects any special role.[42]

Internal normalcy is thus a form of recognition of moral responsibility that allows for the realization of external normalcy, which is the application of practical responsibility.

Internal Normalcy

Internal normalcy consists of three main elements. First is a national consciousness as a prerequisite to functioning "normally" in an international environment of other nation-states. This national consciousness would allow for consensus on German foreign policy issues. Here internal normalcy hinges on working backwards from the international system–seeing how other nation-states function, and fitting "Germany" into its character as a self-confident nation-state among others. "We Germans," speaks the always-eloquent former President Richard von Weizsäcker, "work with diligence on our unity. If we succeed in a humane manner, then we will have found our place in the world community. Then the search for the lost normalcy can be completed."[43] "Together we must have the courage," pleads Kinkel somewhat less articulately in the out-of-area debate, "to accept the normalization of our situation as a nation and to draw the resulting consequences for our international capability to act (*Handlungsfähigkeit*)."[44]

The second element consists of recognizing the expectations placed on Germany by others. These perceived expectations must be met to insure responsibility. Accepting Germany's role in the world "will be rightfully expected of us–and we must rightly meet these expectations."[45]Schönbohm brings in the sense of duty: "Our partners in the world expect a strong German contribution. We are historically, morally and politically bound to this."[46] It is questionable to what extent these expectations accurately mirror opinions

---

42 Kinkel, *Bulletin*, October 7, 1992, Nr. 109: 1013.

43 von Weizsäcker, *Bulletin* 109: 1206. The original reads: "Wir Deutschen arbeiten nach Kräften an unserer Einheit. Wenn sie menschlich gelingt, dann werden wir unseren Platz in der Weltgemeinschaft gefunden haben. Dann wird die Suche nach der verlorenen Normalität eingestellt werden können."

44 Kinkel, *Bulletin* Oct. 7, 92, 109: 1014. The original reads: "Wir müssen gemeinsam den Mut haben, die Normalisierung unserer Lage als Nation anzunehmen und daraus für unsere internationale Handlungsfähigkeit die Konsequenzen ziehen!"

45 Kohl, ABD: 788. The original reads: "Es [accepting Germany's role in the world] wird zu Recht von uns erwartet – und dieser Erwartungen müssen wir gerecht werden."

46 Schönbohm 1995: 22. The original reads: "Unsere Partner in der Welt erwarten einen stärkeren deutschen Beitrag. Wir sind dazu historisch, moralisch und politisch verpflichtet."

abroad.[47] Nonetheless, the aforementioned US response to a German permanent seat in the UN Security Council – that they would support it only if all constraints on German military were lifted – certainly adds credence to the German perception of high expectations from abroad.

Recognizing Germany's role in the international "community of destiny" (*Schicksalsgemeinschaft*), and responsibly fulfilling expectations produces the third element of internal normalcy: rejection of any special path or attempts to go it alone. In the government's construction, the slope toward a special path begins with restrictions on foreign policy which other countries of similar stature do not have. This means, above all, restrictions on the use of the military for out-of-area operations, and not the popular German pledge to forsake all nuclear, chemical, and biological weapons. While the same logic would seem to apply, these two areas are differentiated by the issue of non-proliferation, which the German government champions as a foreign policy priority. The interpretation of what constitutes a special path – deviation from postwar principles of pseudo-pacifism or deviation from international norm of subordinating one's military for political purposes including peacekeeping or peace-enforcing – is a point of contentious debate, although the government clearly wishes to emphasize the latter. "I find," says Kinkel,

> that history teaches us a clear lesson: never again diverge from the community of Western peoples, never again pursue a special path, not even the path of moral superiority and the ethics of our convictions![48] ... We cannot allow ourselves to misunderstand our increased political weight as a call for national solos (*Alleingänge*). On the contrary: we stand today, more than before and more than others, responsible for all of Europe.[49]

External Normalcy

These then are the elements of internal normalcy: consciousness as a nation-state, recognition of the importance of other's expectations and needs, and rejection of any special path. External normalcy is a combination of the means and the ends which internal normalcy is to serve. Above all, external normalcy is determined by willingness to participate in global peace-keeping tasks. Participation in every mission is not called for, but as Kinkel argues, it

---

47 See Hacker, 1995.

48 Kinkel, ABD: 916. The original reads: "Ich finde, daß eine Lehre aus dieser Geschichte wirklich nur lauten kann: Nie wieder aus der Gemeinschaft westlicher Völker ausscheren, nie wieder Sonderwege, auch nicht den der moralischen Besserwisserei und der Gesinnungsethik!"

49 Kinkel, ABD: 1058: "[W]ir dürfen unser gestiegenes politisches Gewicht nicht als Aufforderung zu nationalen Alleingängen mißverstehen. Im Gegenteil: Wir stehen heute, ungleich mehr als früher und mehr als andere, in der Verantwortung für ganz Europa."

is easier to say no to a request after first saying yes, and after all "in order not to fight, one has to be able to fight."[50] Capability and legal clarity for peacekeeping actions are therefore paramount. Secondly, a permanent seat in the UN Security Council is viewed as an unavoidable accouterment of normalcy. Given the delicateness of this issue, permanent membership is presented not as a prerequisite, but as a logical extension of German responsibility. Kinkel, the most tireless advocate for permanent membership, maintains that "We must now place our ability for inner and outer normalcy under proof, if we do not want to be severely damaged politically. A German permanent seat in the UN Security Council belongs to this normalization."[51]

Thirdly, external normalcy is to be achieved by paying more attention to defining and implementing national "interests." During the Cold War the notion of national interest was particularly subordinated to European and Allied interests to dampen latent fears of German nationalism. The sovereign status of unified Germany, however, carries the implication that a normal state requires national interests. Although Germany does have to be specially sensitive to others, Kinkel says, "this does not mean that we in the Union–as well as others–may not represent our national interests. These will exist, as long as nation-states exist."[52]

Despite calls for more emphasis on national interests, the government continues to rhetorically define national interests in terms of European interests: "Our national interest is identical (*Deckungsgleich*) with responsibility for all of Europe," says Kinkel, echoing Kohl's stump phrase that "the unification of Germany is inseparably bound with that of Europe"[53] National interests, as such, are presented as European interests for which Germany has a particular responsibility or is disproportionately affected by, for example, reforms in Eastern Europe.[54] "We are also predestined, on the basis of our *Mittellage*

---

50 Kinkel, "Das Konzept der 'Erweiterten Sicherheit,'" *Frankfurter Rundschau*, 16 December, 1993. The original reads: "Um nicht kämpfen zu müssen, muß man kämpfen können."

51 Kinkel, ABD: 908. The original reads: "Wir müssen jetzt unsrere Fähigkeit zur Normalität nach innen und außen unter Beweis stellen, wenn wir politisch nicht schwer Schaden nehmen wollen. Zu dieser Normalisierung gehört auch ein deutscher ständiger Sitz im Weltsicherheitsrat...."

52 Kinkel, *Bulletin* 3 March 1993, 18: 142 . The original reads: "Although we have to be specially sensitive to others, "Dies heißt nicht, daß wir in der Gemeinschaft nicht – so wie andere auch – unsere nationalen Interessen vertreten dürften. Diese wird es geben, solange es Nationalstaaten gibt."

53 Kinkel, ABD: 1058. The original reads: "Unser nationales Interesse ist deckungsgleich mit der gesamteuropäischen Verantwortung." Kohl, ABD: 719. The original reads: "Die Einigung Deutschalnds ist untrennbar verbunden mit der Europas."

54 See Bach, 1996.

(geographic position in the middle), our size and our traditional relations to Central (*Mittel*) and Eastern Europe, to draw the main advantage from the return of these states to Europe"[55] says Kinkel. Accordingly, he states unequivocally that "Germany will remain the advocate of our Eastern neighbors in the [European] Community."[56]

As should be apparent from this overview of the official narrative, the terms responsibility, normalcy, *Bündnisfähigkeit*, and *Sonderweg* are metonymically connected, that is, each term exists only as part of the others. Being normal means being responsible in the sense of being *"bündnisfähig,"* and all of these mean avoiding any special paths (*Sonderwege*). Thus in speeches by Kinkel, Kohl, and other government officials, the terms become interchangeable such that all these speeches reify unspoken assumptions about the nature of sovereignty and the world. Because of the authority of the persons making these speeches, authoritative legitimacy is given to the concepts. Keeping in mind that "words, expressions, propositions, etc., change their meaning according to the positions held by those who use them,"[57]and the corollary logic of discourses as hegemony-seeking, it is not surprising that the government narrative strives to monopolize the meanings of the above terms.

It is only an illusion, however, that the dominance-seeking discourse sets its own terms. This is not only because the terms themselves are located in larger metanarratives, but because the government narrative is also shaped by the discourse it is opposing. It tries to construct its subjects (both in the philosophical and legal sense) by prescribing roles into which their identity should grow. In a way similar to how Pecheaux sees subjects being constructed by ideology, the dominant discourse offers an image with the false alternatives of either conforming freely, and thus being a "good subject," or rejecting the image and being a "bad subject"–a "troublemaker," as Macdonell puts it. The troublemakers here are the SPD and other opponents of out-of-area missions whom the foreign minister addresses as obstacles, blind to the self-evident (for what is more self-evident than "normalcy", for "normal" people?). "I hope" he says, "...that despite the resistance of the SPD so far, [they] will join in making the necessary step toward normalcy in foreign and security pol-

---

55 Kinkel, "Verantwortung, Realismus, und Zukunftssicherung - Deutsche Außenpolitik in einer sich neu ordnenden Welt" originally in the *Frankfurter Allgemeine Zeitung*, March 19, 1993, reprinted in *Außenpolitik der Bundesrepublik Deutschland*: 905. The original reads: "Wir sind aufgrund unserer Mittellage, unserer Größe und unserer traditionallen Beziehungen zu Mittel- und Osteuropa auch dazu prädestiniert, den Hauptvorteil aus der Rückkehr dieser Staaten nach Europa zu ziehen."
56 Kinkel, ABD: 907. The original reads: "Deutschland wird der Anwalt unserer östlichen Nachbarn und Freunde in der Gemeinschaft bleiben...."
57 Pecheux in Macdonell, 1986: 24.

icy."[58] But the troublemakers develop their own "counter-identification" in which the terms claimed by the government narrative are given a different meaning. Responsibility, normalcy, and *Sonderweg* are metonymically linked, but their assumptions to which they are bound differ.

OPPOSITION TO THE GOVERNMENT NARRATIVE

It has almost become an Orwellian maxim that when the military speaks of "peace" the opposition interprets it as "war." Approximately half of the Social Democratic Party (SPD), most all of the Green Party, all of the Party of Democratic Socialism (PDS), and the loose organizational network known as the peace movement (*Friedensbewegung*) accuse the government of, at best, misguided interpretations of Germany's role and, at worse, deception and hidden nationalistic aims. In an inverse of the claims of the governing coalition, responsibility to others requires being different, yearning for similitude. This difference results from sensitivity to Germany's responsibility, one that exists in the double sense–*for* the war and the Holocaust and *to* Europe and the world to never again create the conditions for German aggression. Of course at the level of oratory, the coalition concurs, and is confident that its approach actually resolves the tension between responsibility *for* and responsibility *to*, effectively restoring "normalcy." Kohl, as quoted earlier, exhorts that peace alone shall henceforth emanate from German soil.

The opposition usually does not question the sincerity of Kohl and other conservative's desire for peace. They question the means. The basic issue is structural: which conditions are most conducive for preventing involvement in war and the possibility of future aggression.

This counter-discourse consists of two main elements. First, Germany should not engage in combat, even under the aegis of UN peacekeeping. This does not mean that Germany cannot support UN actions, nor that it must forfeit its leading role in international organizations and the construction of a European "security identity." Rather, Germany's history and constitution should be so interpreted as precluding such a "normal" role given the excesses of the past, the tenuous separation of peacekeeping from combat missions, and latent Germanophobia. This basic posture keeps Germany true to its principles of peace, and by being true to itself it is being true to others, since "being true to oneself" is a universal imperative which all must respect.

---

58 Kinkel, *Bulletin* 3 March, 1993, 18: 141. The original reads: "Ich hoffe es ... trotz der bisherigen Weigerung der SPD, den notwendigen Schritt in die außen- und sicherheitspolitische Normalität mitzumachen." See also the article "Kinkel sorgt sich um das Deutschlandbild," *FAZ* 19 May 1994, where he implies that a constitutional amendment is inevitable and is being held up "unbearably" by the SPD.

This is essentially the corollary of the official discourse's "moral responsibility."

The second element is the corollary to the official discourse's "practical responsibility." Germany can only be truly responsible if it does not use its historical legacy as an excuse to turn inward and smug. The opposition largely agrees that Germany has a special mission to be a force for change in the world. They disagree, of course, about military use to achieve this change. The peaceful resolution of conflicts through economic and political means is the main task of German foreign policy. The current focus on the military detracts from these efforts.

Here the opposition discourse adopts the Czempiel/Senghaas version of World Domestic Policy (*Weltinnenpolitik*) as presented in Chapter 5. Historical progress is achieved by overcoming the "military impulse" and accentuating the "civilizing impulse," as evidenced through the societal world. The primary difference with the official discourse here lies in the disjunction between the military and civilizing impulses. While the official discourse often rejects the "normalizing" agenda as militarist, it does see a concrete role for the military, both because of realist constraints on international relations and because of the necessity for credible enforcement of peace in conflict-laden regions.

The issues of internal and external normalcy are not as pronounced among the opposition discourse. They are, nonetheless, hidden in the assumptions of *Weltinnenpolitik* and the societal world. Internal normalcy is akin to a just, stable, and tolerant domestic order within a state. States in the liberal discourse are still the containers for identity and autonomy, although decreasingly so. This rather Rawlsian approach to what a state should be–a set of procedures for channeling competing moral perspectives into meaningful and peaceful coexistence–is a microcosm of what the international system should strive for. Thus internal normalcy essentially amounts to extending the concept of "model Germany."

This internal perfection of democracy and justice forms the basis for the opposition discourse's equivalent of external normalcy. External normalcy is actually a misnomer here, since it is not so much compliance with existing external norms (as it is in the official discourse) as a normative program for extending the logic of the societal world. The "normalcy" of the government approach is seen as little more than a static reaction to the dynamic process of progress. Thus the concept of "normalcy" is rarely used in the oppositional discourse, because of its intimations of protecting the status quo at the expense of seizing the opportunity for global change.

6. A Discursive Analysis of the Bundestag Debate on Deploying German Troops to the Former Yugoslavia

Wars in the Balkans provide the bloody book-ends of the twentieth century, and historical irony invites historical analogy. The Balkan wars of 1912-13 sharpened the imperial rivalries which converged in the convoluted catastrophe of World War One. The 1991-95 wars in ex-Yugoslavia revived ghosts of old alliances, but the West chose to play down differences and put a more optimistic spin on an otherwise disastrous failure of conflict resolution. They emphasized the war in former Yugoslavia as a learning opportunity for international institutions who are cutting their teeth on conflict prevention after the Cold War. Thus while "would have, could have, should have" was a sentiment in all camps, the Dayton Peace agreement of November 1995 which ended–for now–the war in Bosnia, is widely regarded as a serious litmus test for the UN and NATO's peacekeeping ability. This aspect highlights the Bosnian War's importance for the credibility of international institutions and, by implication, for the post Cold War order. Every Western country's stake in the post-Cold War order thus rests to some degree on events in Bosnia.

For Germany, Bosnia is important in ways which it is not for most other countries involved. The Dayton agreement presented Germany with the first request to send ground troops to a peacekeeping mission with combat potential. To make matters more difficult, ex-Yugoslavia is a most historically–and hence politically–uncomfortable destination for German soldiers. The decision to send troops in support of the Dayton Agreement thus forced a debate on the fundamental nature of German foreign policy.

This chapter examines the Bundestag debates on sending 4,000 German troops to the international force (IFOR) tasked with enforcing the Dayton peace accords in former Yugoslavia (henceforth the "Dayton debates"). The debates occurred over two days, November 30, and December 6, 1995. The debate on December 6 preceded a final vote on this issue, while November 30th was a "pre-debate" on the government's motion in the form of a governmental declaration on German participation in IFOR and various motions from the opposition.[1]

---

1 The texts used are the stenographic reports from the German *Bundestag* for Thursday, November 30th, 1995 13th electoral period, 74th session, and Wednesday, December 6th, 1995, 13th electoral period, 76th session. All page numbers for quotes from the debates refer to these consecutively numbered reports unless otherwise noted.

While there have been other debates on sending troops "out-of-area," only two of them occurred after the constitutional legitimacy of German participation in peacekeeping missions was clarified by the high court's June 1994 decision.[2] The first of these two debates focused on the sending of fighter jets of the type ECR (Electronic Combat Reconnaissance) Tornados to the existing UN mission in former Yugoslavia.[3] The second was the Dayton debates. We focus only on Dayton for two reasons: First, while the Tornado debate was the first "out-of-area" debate since the court decision, the Dayton debates are the first to focus on ground troops, a significant distinction. Second, the background for the Tornado debate was not a peace agreement, but the enforcement of a no-fly zone and later plans for the possible withdrawal of the rather hapless UN mission. The Dayton debates represent the first action of this kind of in support of a peace treaty at the explicit invitation of the warring parties. Dayton is therefore not only historic in its military aspects, but also in its capacity as a post-Cold War conflict resolution success (thus far).

Discourse analysis is the method employed here for analyzing the debates because of its focus on the linguistic construction of knowledge. This allows for an analysis of social reproduction; words, phrases, and terms are viewed here as constitutive of meaning rather than conduits for pre-existing intentional stances.[4] It is part of a broader constructivist approach which seeks to "explain the continuity and discontinuity of historical structures."[5]Social reproduction undergirds historical structures; it is the process by which ideas and historical interpretation combine with situations, resulting in certain practices, which themselves reinforce certain ideas and historical interpretations.[6] One need not focus exclusively, however, on sweeping historical studies. Banerjee writes "There is an intimate relationship between long-term structural history and what one might call microhistory – the detailed reconstruction of critical episodes. Microhistorical analysis shows the recurrence of discourses, cognitions, and practices in a way which explains their continuity."[7] The following analysis of the Dayton debates are in this sense "microhistorical analysis," focusing on the discourses which are reproduced and stabilized through their reproduction.

---

2 For an overview of German peacekeeping activity, see Ehrhart, 1996.

3 See Heinrich, 1995.

4 The linguistic construction of knowledge is an epistemological stance *not* to be confused with naive or radical relativism: yes, reality can be material.

5 Sanjoy Banerjee, 1996: 1.

6 Sanjoy Banerjee, Ibid. writes that "Social reproduction is a process in which certain practices, discourses, and cognitions cause each other to reiterate." On the the relation between discourse analysis, cognitive science, and the study of social reproduction see Banerjee, 1996.

7 Ibid.

This reproduction and stabilization is a function of one discourse achieving "linguistic dominance." [8] Linguistic dominance enables a discourse to perpetuate itself through establishing a dominant perception of reality, a metanarrative in which the meanings of terms are defined by their relative space in the dominant story, the discursive economy. A discursive economy legitimizes assumptions, filters perceptions through these assumptions, and establishes the paths of reference between terms by institutionalizing binary oppositions (dualisms). The level at which a discursive economy operates is ontological, whereas the choice and success or failure of a particular discursive strategy operates at the epistemological level.[9]

The struggle for linguistic dominance in Germany focuses intently on control of the meaning of the past. Foreign policy functions as a means for absolution and adaptation within the international framework of Western values, allowing Germany's past to be both accounted for, negated, and transcended, in short, *aufgehoben* through participation in the post-Cold War world order. When we look at the parliamentary debates surrounding Dayton, we are thus entering an ongoing conversation about identity, special paths, geopolitics, and morality which goes back at least as far as 1871. In the last decade the conversation has been continued most prominently through the peace movement, the *Historikerstreit*, unification, and German foreign policy.[10]

The Dayton debates reflect the two discourses which characterize the most recent incarnation of this conversation: the discourses of normalization and liberalism.[11] These discourses exist in an antagonistic relationship. This antagonism is intrinsic to a competition for linguistic dominance, which results from claims of correctly perceiving reality – what Michael Shapiro called once "ownership of the means of enunciation." Whether all discourses must have a metanarrative impulse, that is, be hegemony-seeking, is part of the debate about the meaning of postmodernism. If we accept the view of postmodernism as the destruction of metanarratives, incommensurable truths may coexist as minor narratives.[12] Without wading too deeply here into this contentious quagmire, German foreign policy discourse is not postmodern in this sense, since it relies heavily on modernist metanarratives which are hegemony-seeking in their claim to represent reality.[13] Rather, there is a connection here between discourses and ideology, where, reminiscent of the lordship-

---

8 Townson, 1992.
9 These themes are discussed in greater detail in chapter two.
10 See chapter one.
11 See chapters three and four.
12 Lyotard, 1989.
13 Though this should not be interpreted as a refutation of either the possibility of postmodernism or the consideration of alternate interpretations of the term, which abound.

bondage dialectic, discourses, like ideologies are "formed as a means of domination and resistance, [they] are never simply free to set their own terms but are marked by what they are opposing."[14] This is the opposition of prevailing discourse and counter-discourse. The respective explication of each is the focus of the next section.

Prevailing and Counter-Discourses

THE PREVAILING DISCOURSE

The prevailing discourse in German foreign policy is most clearly associated with the center-right political spectrum, although the majority of the Social Democrats and even some Greens have also come to accept its logic. It is essentially an adaptation of normalization tempered with liberal notions of multilateral civilizatory progress.[15] A pastiche created from speakers in favor of the government's resolution (to send 4,000 troops to ex-Yugoslavia) illustrates the narrative at work in the debates.

The nature of discourse lies in its production in a variety of settings. Each representative has her or his own story and agenda. The point is exactly that they all represent, legitimize, and vindicate a particular world-view. A world-view does *not* mean that everyone agrees, but rather that notions expressed through a discursive economy lay claim to the vocabulary available for interpreting events. Within this economy there is plenty of room for debate (for example: whether ECR Tornados are militarily necessary to enforce the no-fly zone in Bosnia). That all the speakers represented here differ individually in many ways from their colleagues is taken for granted. What interests us here is how a specific discourse suffuses and constrains the very parameters of agreement and disagreement and comes to prevail.

The prevailing discourse begins by acknowledging that in the Second World War German soldiers committed atrocities under the leadership of the criminal Hitler dictatorship, occupying and destroying neighboring countries and eventually itself. This was an example of the "use of armed force...for the oppression of people."[16] "German soldiers have been misused in the past by a criminal regime to break international law and destroy peace."[17]

---

14 Macdonell, 1986: 34.

15 That realism and liberalism are two sides of the same coin rather than opposing approaches has recently gained much recognition. For a treatement of this subject see RBJ Walker, 1993. See also Jim George, 1994.

16 "Einsatz bewaffneter Gewalt ... zur Unterdrückung von Menschen." Voigt, 6457.

17 "Deutsche Soldaten sind in der Vergangenheit von einem verbrecherischen Regime dazu mißbraucht worden, das internationale Recht zu brechen und den Frieden zu zerstören." Irmer, 6645.

German liberation by victors who became occupiers, then allies (in the West) serves as a normative guide for the future: "We are all aware that Germany was liberated...from this ensues *the right and the duty to liberate others or to bring others to freedom.*"[18] That the allies first waged a liberatory, and later risked a nuclear, war to help (West) Germany imbues Germany with the "self-evident duty of a people after the experience of two world wars, above all after the collapse at the end of the Second World War, and after the tremendous experience of being helped by others in our reconstruction."[19] "We Germans could rely on our partners in the hardest of times during the division of Germany and Berlin. Now we want to and must demonstrate solidarity."[20] "Let us not forget: since more than four decades our friends in NATO protect the freedom and peace of our land."[21]

The historical lesson has been learned. This mission to ex-Yugoslavia will show "that here a different Germany will be active, a Germany which has learned from its history."[22] Germany has become "adult enough" to "enter into fully natural international (*völkerrechtliche*) obligations.[23] Her new maturity has secured acceptance back into the world of states. The mission in ex-Yugoslavia is a perfect opportunity "to prove that there is a chance to learn from history."[24] This opportunity takes two general forms corresponding to the categories of moral and practical responsibility explored in the previous chapter.

As a moral imperative, learning from history means atoning for past crimes: "Especially because German soldiers were *forced* in the past to break the law creates today an obligation for us–as a democratic state under the rule of law–

---

18 "Uns allen ist doch bewußt, daß Deutschland befreit worden ist. ... Daraus ergibt sich auch das Recht und die Pflicht, andere zu befreien oder anderen Freiheit zu bringen.." Schulz: 6665. Emphasis added.

19 "Selbstverständliche Pflicht eines Volkes nach den Erfahrungen von zwei Weltkriegen, vor allem nach dem Zusammenbruch am Ende des Zweiten Weltkrieges und nach der großartigen Erfahrung der Hilfe durch andere, die uns bei Wiederaufbau geholfen haben." Kohl: 6633.

20 "Wir Deutsche konnten uns in schwierigsten Zeiten der Teilung Deutschlands und Berlins auf unsere Partner und Freunde verlassen. Jetzt wollen und müssen wir auch Solidarität zeigen." Kinkel: 6431.

21 "Vergessen wir nicht: Seit über vier Jahrzehnten schützen unsere Freunde in der NATO die Freiheit und den Frieden unseres Landes." Waigel: 6654.

22 "...daß hier ein anderes Deutschland tätig wird, ein Deutschland, das aus seiner Geschichte gelernt hat...." Verheugen: 6666.

23 "...erwachsen genug" her "ganz natürliche völkerrechtliche Verpflichtungen einzugehen." Gerhardt: 6441.

24 "...[zu] beweisen, daß es doch eine Chance gibt, aus der Geschichte zu lernen." B. Schulte: 6653.

to engage ourselves internationally for the preservation of peace."[25]"We have the unique chance to give a country a spark of hope with German soldiers, where once before German soldiers brought no hope. In addition, this is also a chance for our country if we package it cleverly and openly represent our presence there."[26] "Will Germany, under whom all the peoples of Yugoslavia had to suffer in the Second World War, possess the power to become a partner and friend to all the peoples of former Yugoslavia through the peace process? ... The goal of this peace mission is the antithesis to the war goals of Hitler. In the appeal to the UN mandate we seek a synthesis with the norms of peace and international law which were formulated after the Second World War as an answer to Hitler's barbarism."[27]

The link between moral and practical responsibility lies in viewing peacekeeping actions as a response to Hitlerian barbarism. This is the practical imperative both of solidarity and of a sober realism: "One must not build only on good will. Humanity is–unfortunately–not so. Rather one must be capable of making the use of military power seem fruitless. This is the actual core of securing peace. ... He who is not prepared to fight will not secure peace."[28]This reformulation of basic deterrence theory acquires its moral edge because it is assumed that the target of such peacekeeping is always an evil Serb-like aggressor, barbaric like Hitler, who must be constrained by the civilized world, whose forces are fighting not for "the defense of one's own country," but to "help further those values and fundamental ideas of coexistence which are a distinctive feature of our country."[29] "We will only be able

---

25 "Gerade daraus, daß deutsche Soldaten in der Vergangenheit gezwungen waren, Recht zu brechen, erwächst für uns eine Verpflichtung, uns heute als rechtsstaatliche Demokratie auch international für die Friedenswahrung einzusetzen." Irmer: 6645. Emphasis added.

26 "Wir haben die einzigartige Chance, auch mit deutschen Soldaten einem Land einen Funken Hoffnung zu geben, in dem früher einmal deutsche Soldaten waren, die keine Hoffnung für dieses Land waren. Auch dies ist im übrigen eine Chance für unser Land, wenn wir sie klug anpacken und unsere Anwesenheit dort offen vertreten." Gerhardt: 6440.

27 "Wird Deutschland, unter dem im Zweitem Weltkrieg alle Völker Jugoslawiens leiden mußten...die Kraft besitzen, im Friedensprozeß zum Partner und Freund aller Völker des ehemaligen Jugoslawien zu werden? ... Die Ziele dieses Friedenseinsatzes sind eine Antithese zu den Kriegszielen Hitlers. In der Berufung auf ein Mandat der Vereinten Nationen suchen wir die Synthese mit den Friedens- und Völkerrechtsnormen, die nach dem Zweiten Weltkrieg als Antwort auf die Hitler-Barbarei formuliert wurden."Voigt: 6448: 9.

28 "Man darf nicht nur auf den guten Willen bauen. Die Menschen sind–leider–nicht so. Vielmehr muß man notfalls in der Lage sein, den Einsatz militärischer Gewalt nicht lohnend erscheinen zu lassen. Das ist der eigentliche Kern der Friedenssicherung. ...Wer nicht bereit ist, zu kämpfen, wird den Frieden nicht sichern." Schäuble: 6639.

29 Scharping: 6634: 5.

to secure peace, now and in the future, if every aggressor who wants to use force to attain his goals must reckon with the decisive and superior resistance of the *civilized world*."[30]

This practical responsibility requires a complete rethinking of what the military is. Germany as a "peace power" (*Friedensmacht*) with a "readiness for responsibility"[31] means recognizing that "he who wants peace in the Balkans must also want the peace-troops."[32] These soldiers "are not solders of war, rather they are police in an international order of peace and law."[33] The image of soldiers as war-fighting actors is old-fashioned, here "their task is not war and fighting, their task is the protection and the implementation of peace."[34] This redefinition does not apply solely to the situation in ex-Yugoslavia, but to the role of the Bundeswehr as a whole: "[You must] understand that noone could live in peace if the Bundeswehr soldiers did not provide their services for our peace."[35] Today it is "a wholly different German army which is being sent to former-Yugoslav soil."[36] This "wholly different army" did not occur overnight: "The Bundeswehr has been a peace army for forty years long, and it remains such.... I regard as highly symbolic the situation where the first large mission undertaken by the Bundeswehr serves the ending of a persistent war and the erection of peace."[37]

Indeed, the transformation of the military into a force for peace is presented as a natural extension of West German foreign policy: "German foreign policy in the postwar period was clearly oriented toward two concepts, namely integration and cooperation. From integration in the Western alliance arose the possibility of cooperation with all who were prepared to share the demo-

---

30 "Wir werden auch in Zukunft Frieden nur sichern können, wenn jeder Aggressor, der zum Durchsetzung seiner Ziele Gewalt anwenden will, mit dem entscheidenen und überlegenen Widerstand *der zivilisierten Welt* rechnen muß." Seiters: 6435. Emphasis added.

31 "Verantwortungsbereitschaft" Gerhardt: 6441.

32 "Wer Frieden auf dem Balkan will, der muß auch die Friedenstruppe wollen." Rühe: 6446.

33 "sind nicht Soldaten des Krieges, sondern sie sind Polizisten einer internationalen Frieden- und Rechtsordnung." Voigt: 6448.

34 "ihre Aufgabe ist nicht Krieg und Kampf; ihre Aufgabe ist der Schutz und die Durchsetzung von Frieden." Scharping: 6634.

35 "Begreift, daß keiner in Frieden leben könnte, wenn die Soldaten der Bundeswehr...ihren Dienst für unseren Frieden nicht leisteten." Schäuble: 6640.

36 "...eine ganz andere deutsche Armee, die auf ehemals jugoslawischem Boden zum Einsatz kommt." Verheugen: 6666.

37 "Die Bundeswehr ist 40 Jahre lang eine Friedensarmee gewesen, und sie bleibt es....Ich halte es für einen Vorgang von hoher Symbolik, daß der erste größere Einsatz, den die Bundeswehr leisten muß, der Beendigung eines langandaurnden Krieges und der Herstellung von Frieden gilt." Irmer: 6644.

cratic values of the Western Occident (sic)."[38] This cooperation, under the rubrics of solidarity and morality, leads Germany to partake in the peacekeeping missions of the United Nations. In retrospect, the direction of past decisions "to defend freedom and peace, to put solidarity on the proof stand" shows a teleological progression: "It was yes to the Bundeswehr. It was yes to European defense. It was yes to NATO, yes to the NATO two-track decision, and it is now yes to international solidarity in Bosnia."[39]

Thus today, with a decision to support sending troops to Bosnia, legally supported by the Constitutional Court's decision of June 12, 1994, the Bundestag is finally making good on "the expectations of the world community for unified Germany to make our contribution for the securing of peace in Europe."[40] With what Michael Stürmer once called the four "G"s – Geographie, Größe, Gewicht, und Geschichte (geography, size, weight, and history)[41] – together with full sovereignty and constitutional clarity, no one can deny "the larger significance of Germany's role and the special responsibility to which it is bound," which makes it impossible for Germany "to retreat to solely European or other contexts if the issue concerns securing long-term peace with civil means."[42]

In short, "Germany has achieved, with this contribution to the international peace troops, a level of normalcy in the international activities of foreign and security policy."[43]In this way does Germany become "a reliable, full European and transatlantic partner," which is what "we must be and want to be,

---

38 "Die deutsche Außenpolitik der Nachkriegszeit war völlig klar auf zwei Begriffe ausgerichtet, nämlich auf Integration und auf Kooperation. Es war die Integration in das westliche Bündnis, und von dort aus bestand die Möglichkeit der Kooperation, mit all denjenigen, die dazu bereit waren, die demokratischen Werte des westlichen Abendlandes zu teilen." Breuer: 6659.

39 "...um Freiheit und Frieden zu verteidigen, um Solidarität unter Beweis zu stellen.... Es war das Ja zur Bundeswehr. Es war das Ja zur europäische Verteidigung. Es war das Ja zur NATO, das Ja zum NATO-Doppelbeschluß und ist jetzt das Ja zur internationalen Solidarität in Bosnien." Waigel: 6655.

40 "Die Erwartungen der Völkergemeinschaft an das wiedervereinte Deutschland ...[which is] unseren Beitrag für die Sicherung des Friedens in Europa [zu] leisten." Kohl: 6632.

41 See Stürmer, 1992.

42 "...die gewachsene Bedeutung der Rolle Deutschlands und die damit verbundene besondere Verantwortung... allein auf europäische oder andere Zussamenhänge zurückzuziehen, wenn es um die langfristige Sicherung des Friedens mit zivilen Mitteln geht." Scharping: 6637.

43 "...mit diesem Beitrag zur internationalen Friedenstruppe [hat Deutschland] einen Grad der Normalität im internationen Umgang in der Außen- und Sicherheitspolitik erreicht....Deutschland praktiziert Verantwortung und Mitverantwortung." Kinkel: 6650: 51.

also in the arena of peace-securing."[44] There is "no militarization in the Federal Republic of Germany," for "we don't want any show of muscle, we don't want any 'great power' feeling, no gun-boat politics, rather we want to make our contribution in complete modesty and without hurrah–nothing more and nothing less." [45] The "level of normalcy" means that Germany has, in a sense, finally become the peer of the allies who nurtured West Germany: "I ask you, why should we express ourselves any differently than the American President?"[46] Thus does this narrative, which began with Germany's nadir of shame and destruction, division and debilitation, end optimistically with a united Germany possessing the moral and the constitutional right, the duty and the ability, the stature and the desire, the expectance and the perseverance to use its military to help its allies enforce a world order of peace and justice.

THE COUNTER-DISCOURSE

As with the prevailing discourse, the starting point of this counter-narrative is the Second World War, where Germany's aggression and genocidal crimes mark Germany as unique within (though not separate from) the "civilized" world. This lamentable uniqueness is not something which successful rehabilitation can or should erase. Germany must certainly "make our contribution based on history," but here history leads to the conclusion that one can "not agree with the mission of the Bundeswehr in former Yugoslavia," since "war and army...belong inextricably together.[47]

Germany's contribution must consist of non-violent means for two reasons which mirror the prevailing discourse's categories of moral and practical responsibility. First is Germany's responsibility to itself and its past – "After the war we said: Never, never do we want to bear arms, never, never do we want war again, let those at the top slug it out among themselves, we simply will

---

44 "...ein zuverlässiger, vollwertiger europäischer und transatlantischer Partner," which is what "wir müssen und wollen auch im Bereich der Friedenssicherung...sein."Kinkel: 6426.

45 "...keine Militisierung... in der Bundesrepublik Deutschland. ... Wir wollen keine Muskelspiele; wir wollen keine Großmachtgefühle, keine Kanonenpolitik, sonder wir wollen ganz bescheiden und ohne Hurra unseren Beitrag leisten – nicht mehr und nicht weniger." Pflüger: 6664.

46 "Ich frage Sie: Warum sollten wir uns weniger differenziert äußern als der amerikanischer Präsident?" Rühe: 6669. He makes this remark after quoting Clinton's address to US troops on their mission in Bosnia.

47 "...aus der Geschichte heraus dazu unseren Beitrag leisten. ... dem Einsatz der Bundeswehr im früheren Jugoslawien nicht zustimmen," since "Krieg und Armee...gehören unauflösbar zusammen." E. Altmann: 6670.

not participate!"[48] Germany's past, rather than providing a moral imperative to *use* its military for peaceful purposes in the Balkans, demands that German military *abstain*: "The arguments which refer to the historical responsibility of Germany remain as valid as ever. German soldiers have no business in the Balkans."[49] "One German soldier–any German soldier–in Yugoslavia is not a part of the solution, but a part of the problem."[50]

Secondly, non-violent means are ultimately the only viable approach for changing the world: "Military power has historically ended in a dead end, this is crystal clear. It is...our [the Green's] task to make this understood in politics and to turn [this insight] into *Realpolitik*."[51] "History teaches us that the attempt to defend peace with violent means is accompanied by streams of blood, reducing millions and billions of valuable resources in the end to scrap metal and misery."[52] "Only civil means of creating peace...conflict research, and catastrophe assistance can protect people in the end from further senseless murder and destruction through war and the military."[53] Germany's moral and practical responsibility, to itself and to others, therefore demands an exclusively non-violent approach to solving conflicts: "The Bundeswehr has no business in foreign missions, regardless of which helmets they wear."[54]

---

48 "Wir haben damals nach dem Krieg gesagt: Nie, nie wollen wir Waffen tragen, nie, nie wollen wir wieder Krieg, laßt doch die oben sich alleine schlagen, wir machen einfach nicht mehr mit!" Heuer: 6672.

49 "Die Argumente, die auf historische Verantwortung Deutschlands verweisen, sind nach wie vor gültig. Deutsche Soldaten haben auf dem Balkan nichts zu suchen." Lederer: 6443.

50 "Ein deutscher Soldat – jeder deutsche Soldat – in Jugoslawien ist keine Lösung, sonder ein Teil des Problems." Zwerenz: 6457.

51 "[M]ilitärische Gewalt [ist] historisch in eine Sackgasse geraten, ganz klar. Es ist...unsere [den Grünen] Aufgabe, das in die Politik einzupflanzen und in Realpolitik umzusetzen." Nickels: 6649.

52 "[D]ie Geschichte uns lehrt, das der Versuch, Frieden mit gewaltsamen Mitteln zu verteidigen, davon begleitet ist, daß Ströme von Blut geflossen sind, Millionen und Milliarden von Werten letzten Endes zu Schrott und Leid geworden sind. Diese gewaltsamen Mittel, im Übermaß angehauft, haben zu Unterdrückung, zu entsetzlichen Völkermorden und Kriegen geführt....Es ist historisch endlich angesagt, gewaltfreie Optionen zu fördern und als Mittel der Politik einzusetzen." Nickels: 6642: 43. On p. 6642 she continues in a similar vein: "Diese Entwicklung hat ihren schrecklichen Höhepunkt in der Entwicklung der Atombombe gefunden....Daran wird deutlich, daß letzten Endes der Versuch, mit gewaltsamen Mitteln Frieden zu schaffen, zu sichern und zu erhalten, auch die Vernichtung dessen beinhalten kann, was man eigentlich verteidigen will."

53 "Nur zivile Friedensmaßnahmen..., Konfliktforschung und Katastrophenhilfe schützen letztendlich die Menschen vor weiterem sinnlosen Morden und Zerstörung durch Krieg und Militär." E. Altmann: 6671.

54 "Die Bundeswehr hat bei Auslandseinsätzen nichts zu suchen, egal unter welchen Helmen." Lederer: 6443.

The privileging of military over non-violent means occurs in the service of a perceived "remilitarization of German foreign policy." This is most clearly presented be a criticism of a perceived favoritism towards NATO rather than the OSCE or the UN. "Following the collapse of the Eastern Bloc it would have been possible to expand the OSCE in every respect. Instead, NATO has become far greater than this conference [the OSCE]. This is visible in the budget allocations and also in the small tasks of the OSCE....The OSCE is seriously weakened. Yet it would have been exactly the appropriate all-European conference to have had a chance at conflict prevention and conflict resolution."[55] Not only is the OSCE given a relatively slim role in Bosnia compared to the resources lavished on NATO, but placing the mission in the hands of NATO rather than the UN is also a source of concern. "The whole point has been to increase the weight of NATO at the expense of the UN."[56] The use of NATO troops is seen as a step "away from the UN and toward NATO,"[57] supported by policies which see "the NATO mandate [as] more important than the strength of the UN."[58]

The concern that the governing coalition is privileging military over non-military means of assistance and action connects the center-left/left, otherwise divided over support for the Bundeswehr mission. Thus even supporters of sending troops warn that "We notice with a certain concern, Mr. Chancellor, that programs and financial decisions for non-military, for civil securing of the peace, lag behind the military means presented here."[59] "For the OSCE is this a test which it can only pass if it receives the necessary outfitting for the fulfillment of its tasks....It must transcend its role as a neglected orphan....The sending of international peace troops under NATO command as a solution for the Bosnia conflict is not suitable as a model for the future."[60] "We Social

---

55 "[N]ach dem Zusammenbruch des Ostblocks [es hatte] die möglichkeit gegeben, den OSZE-Prozeß in jeder Hinsicht auszubauen. Statt dessen ist die NATO wesentlich wichtiger geworden als diese Konferenz. Das sieht man auch an der Verteilung der Haushaltsmittel und daran, daß die Aufgaben der OSZE sehr klein sind....Die OSZE ist stark geschwächt worden. Dabei wäre genau das die gesamteuropäische Konferenz gewesen, die die Chance gehabt hätte, konfliktvorbeugend und konfliktbeseitigend zu wirken." Gysi: 6647: 46.
56 "Zweck des Ganzen ist, das Gewicht der NATO gegenüber und zu Lasten der UNO zu verstärken." Lederer: 6443.
57 "[W]eg von der UNO, hin zur NATO," Fischer Joschka: 6657.
58 "...das Mandat der NATO [als] wichtiger als die Stärke der UNO." Nickels: 6642.
59 "Wir beobachten, Herr Bundeskanzler, mit einer gewissen Sorge, daß Programme und Finanzierungsentscheidungen zur nichtmilitärischen, zur zivilen Absicherung des Friedens hinter den vorgelegten militärischen Maßnahmen herhinken." Scharping: 6637.
60 "Für die OSZE ist das eine Bewährungsprobe, die sie aber nur bestehen kann, wenn sie auch die nötige Ausstattung zur Erfüllung ihres Auftrages erhhält....Sie muß aus der Rolle eines vernachlässigten Waisenkindes heraus. ... Die für den Bosnien-Konflikt

Democrats...demand that more money be spent for reconstruction than for soldiers."[61]

The perceived neglect of non-violent alternatives fits the logic of "remilitarization," perceived as part of a larger process to move Germany away from its postwar pacifist principles. "We have experienced a process in which we bit by bit become used to international Bundeswehr missions and the militarization of foreign policy. We are supposed to become comfortable with...the use of military missions to underscore the great power role of Germany."[62] "Step by step the path to war is being trodden, not so loud, but softly, through different steps: Kampuchea, Somalia–you know them all."[63]

The logic of these "salami tactics" reaches their contemporary apogee in the mission to ex-Yugoslavia. "This until-now largest and riskiest foreign Bundeswehr mission [is] a further decisive step in the expansion of the Bundeswehr to a force for world-wide combat missions."[64] This is the image which most frightens the opposition. One can see "...preparation for missions in the whole world in the 1995 and 1996 combat missions facing the Bundeswehr in former Yugoslavia."[65] The Dayton mission, thus signifies the opening of a door "which you will never get closed again."[66]

This door is the way to the military support of "vital security interests" to which belong, according to the Defense Minster, "maintenance of free global trade and unhindered access to markets and natural resources in the whole world in the framework of a just economic order."[67] In light of this larger

---

gefundene Lösung einer internationalen Friedenstruppe unter Leitung der NATO wird als Modell für die Zukunft nicht taugen." Verheugen: 6432: 33.

61 "Wir Sozialdemokraten...verlangen, daß mehr Geld für den Wiederaufbau als für die Soldaten ausgegeben wird." Voigt: 6448.

62 "Wir haben einen Prozeß erlebt, in dem wir scheibchenweise an den internationalen Einsatz der Bundeswehr und auch an die Militarisierung der Außenpolitik gewöhnt wurden. Wir sollten uns daran gewöhnen..., daß die Großmachtrolle Deutschlands auch durch Militäreinsätze unterstrichen werden muß." Gysi: 6647.

63 "Schritt für Schritt der Weg zum Krieg beschritten wird, nicht so laut, aber leise, über verschiedene Schritte: Kampuchea, Somalia – Sie wissen das alle." Heuer: 6672.

64 "[D]ieser bisher größte und riskanteste Auslandseinsatz der Bundeswehr [ist] ein weiterer entscheidender Schritt beim Ausbau der Bundeswehr zu einer Truppe für weltweite Kampfeinsätze." Nachtwei: 6671.

65 "...in den, 1995 und, 1996 anstehenden Kampfeinsätzen der Bundeswehr im früheren Jugoslawien eine Vorbereitung zu Einsätzen in der ganzen Welt." E. Altmann: 6670: 71.

66 "...die Sie nie wieder zubekommen."Gysi: 6649.

67 "vitale Sicherheitsinteressen, " to which belong   "Aufrechterhaltung des freien Welthandels und des ungehinderten Zugangs zu Märkten und Rohstoffen in aller Welt im Rahmen einer gerechten Wirtschaftsordnung." Defense Minister Volker Rühe, Vital Security Interests number 8, in Verteidigungspolitischen Richtlinien, November 26, 1992, quoted in the debates by Gysi: 6649.

context, "I fear that we will always find new and always different justifications for such [military] actions...The reference has already been made today that...[security policy] concerns itself with access to markets and natural resources in the whole world. The Defense Minister once declared: [security policy] concerns the protection of the family of free nations and the export of democracy and security. So at issue here is much more [than just Dayton]: at issue is a long-term...process."[68]

Thus for the counter-discourse, the military is inextricably linked with militarism, and German responsibility is linked to anti-militarism. Consequently, even though *no* speaker condones the war in Bosnia, use of the German military *per se* (other than for self-defense) is a slippery slope to reversing the morally important position of Germany as the only quasi-pacifist great power (with the possible exception of Japan). This role is important because, to loosely borrow a formulation from Marx, agents make their own history but within a structure directly given and transmitted from the past. The tradition of all the war-oriented generations weighs like a nightmare on the brain of those who see it as their historical role (*Aufgabe*) to promote non-violence.[69] Use of the military to further political goals (in general, and thus also in the specific case of Bosnia *despite* the obvious injustice there), would reify a wrong approach to world politics. It would turn Germany away from being the one state in Europe with both the power and the historical purpose for ushering the world-system from its reliance on military solutions to non-violence.

Discursive Struggles

As mentioned in the introduction, the prevailing discourse acquires its form by the discourse it opposes. It tries to construct its subjects (both in the philosophical and legal sense) by prescribing roles which their identity should grow into. The dominant discourse offers an image with the false alternatives of either conforming freely, and thus being a "good subject," or rejecting the

---

68 "Ich fürchte, daß wir immer neue und immer andere Begründungen für solche [military] Aktionen finden werden....Es ist heute schon darauf hingewiesen worden, daß...[security policy] gehe um den Zugang zu Märkten und Rohstoffen in aller Welt. Der Bundesverteidigungsminister hat einmal erklärt: Es geht um den Schutz der Familie freier Nationen und um den Export von Demokratie und Sicherheit. Es geht also um sehr viel mehr [than just Dayton]: Es geht um einen langfristigen...Prozeß."Nachtwei: 6672: 3.

69 In the Eighteenth Brumaire Marx wrote: "Men make their own history, but they do not make it just as they please; they do not make it under circumstances chosen by themselves, but under circumstancs directly found, given, and transmitted from the past. The tradition of all the dead generations weighs like a nightmare on the brain of the living."

image and being a "bad subject," a "troublemaker," as Macdonell puts it.[70] The troublemakers here in the Dayton debates are clearly opponents of out-of-area missions. Troublemaker is an especially appropriate term, for the opponents of the prevailing narrative are generally presented as pests, persons who know better but who persist in making what should be a straightforward affair antagonistic and embarrassing.

Discourse analysis is useful in highlighting the dualisms inherent but often hidden in the relation between the narratives. The dualisms are most clear when the two discourses intersect directly, that is, during the attempt of one to set the public image of the other. This happens both through openly addressing the other, as well as by implication. The basic oppositions at stake in the Dayton debates are the terms moral/immoral, responsible/irresponsible, mature (the ability to learn from history)/childish (an inability or refusal to learn), and normal/abnormal. Each side offers different interpretations of these metonymically-linked concepts. Metonymical linking means that each term exists only as part of the others.[71]The terms become interchangeable such that, as we will see, the speakers in the debate reify unspoken assumptions carried through the narrative about the nature of sovereignty and world order.

For the prevailing discourse, morality, responsibility, and maturity are linked to normalcy, and normalcy is synonymous with solidarity (a form of sameness) with the allies. For the counter-discourse, morality and responsibility can mean differing from the allies, where differing is not a lack of solidarity but can be an example of maturity. Each discourse, however, claims the positively-charged version of each term for its own. In the ensuing struggle over discursive dominance, certain words appear briefly ambiguous, they appear as "the stake," (as Althusser once wrote), "in a decisive but undecided battle."[72]Of course the ambiguity is relative to the strengths of the discourses, because the prevailing discourse can enlist the situated force of its utterances where words accrue authority through the position and power of the speaker. Several particular issues dominate the debates and thereby appear as sites where particular terms can be observed in the process of being normalized. Five discursive sites of struggle stand out: "morality" (who is moral); "peace" (who can speak for "peace"); "military" (what the military represents); the "mission" (what the nature of the mission is); and what the "real" point of debate is.

70 Macdonell, 1986: 39.
71 See Macdonell, 1986.
72 Quoted in Macdonell, 1986: 51.

WHO IS MORAL?

About halfway through the November 30th debate Defense Minister Rühe mounted the podium and began an address on the European nature of the mission to Bosnia, garnering favorable trans-partisan response. After explaining the nuts and bolts of the troops duties, he stated that s/he who wants peace must say yes to the "peace troops," adding that "anything else would be immoral." After applause from the governing coalition, he continued:

> After the experiences of the first half of this century – Auschwitz among others – if the sentence: "it can be very immoral not to counter injustice by sending troops" ever possessed real meaning, then it is now, where a peace treaty, peace troops, and unified international will exists to counter human rights violations and crimes. And this is worthy not only of political support. Anything else would be immoral. It would be simply immoral to refuse to do this. This must be clearly said.[73]

This claim of immorality naturally struck the Greens and the PDS as crassly unjustified, and they demanded that he retract his assertion. Rühe, however, stood his ground, claiming that morality "is always concrete. ... It can be very immoral to send in soldiers. There are God knows enough examples in this century. But in this concrete situation...it would be immoral, to refuse [to send soldiers].[74]

Rühe's logic is deceptively simple. He is saying that what may be immoral in one setting (e.g. *Wehrmacht* soldiers in Yugoslavia in 1943) can be moral in another (e.g. *Bundeswehr* soldiers in Yugoslavia in 1996). But if events acquire morality only in concrete situations, how can one define morality across situations? To answer this requires separating concrete from abstract morality. At an *abstract level* morals appear as a form of natural law, e.g. people in need must be helped; peace is better than war. The invocation of this abstract morality results from inductive interpretations of like occurrences– shelling civilians remains immoral whether or not intervention to stop it is contemplated. The shelling thus becomes a concrete instantiation of the abstract moral principle. In this way *moral judgment* is possible.

---

73 "Alles andere wäre unmoralisch. ... Wenn der Satz "Es kann sehr unmoralisch sein, sich dem Unrecht nicht entgegenzusetzen durch den Einsatz von Soldaten" nach den Ereignissen in der ersten Hälfte dieses Jahrhunderts – Auschwitz und anderes – jemals eine Bedeutung gehabt hat, dann jetzt, wo es einen Friedensvertrag, eine Friedenstruppe und den gescholssenen internationalen Willen gibt, sich Menschenrechtsverletzungen und Verbrechen entgegenzustellen. Da heißt es nicht nur, dies politische zu unterstützen. Alles andere wäre unmoralisch. Es wäre schlicht unmoralisch, sich hier zu verweigern. Das muß man ganz deutlich sagen." Rühe: 6447.

74 Rühe: 6447, 6450.

Rühe, however, is not merely passing moral judgment on the situation in Bosnia, he is making a normative claim about *moral action*. To transform moral judgment into moral action requires a set of decision rules. In this case a set of practical requirements – Rühe cites the request for help from the afflicted countries, the legal legitimization of NATO troops through a peace treaty, and a consensus among other countries involved[75]–function as conditions which empower moral judgment to express itself through action. In this way a heuristic emerges: if the "law" of abstract morality is invoked then moral judgment can be passed, and if moral judgment is passed and the practical requirements for translating judgment into action are met, then action is possible.

This goes part of the way to answering the question posed by the opposition as to why the government decided on action in this concrete case, and not in other concrete cases (e.g. Rwanda, Burundi, Afghanistan): "If one justifies this military mission on purely moral grounds because of genocide and human rights violation, then the question arises: why here, and why not other places?"[76]The ability to apply decision rules makes it possible to distinguish between moral judgments which require specific action and those which do not. Of course one can then argue passionately over the nature of decision rules and about whether the decision rules are adequate. Viewed in this light, the argument need not be one of morality/immorality, since both the government and the opposition clearly agree on moral condemnation of the war in Bosnia, but rather debate about the decision rules which allow moral judgment to become moral action.

The above description of "concrete morality" could correspond with Rühe's assumptions. He nonetheless chooses to distinctly frame the debate in terms of morality/immorality. Since the above excursus on moral action suggests that this dichotomy is not necessary for debating the issue, Rühe's utterances can be relocated in the search for control over the associative and denotative meanings of the competing discourses' rhetorical arsenal. Morality is thence linked to accepting the prevailing discourse and its implications.

Numerous other utterances in the debates support this linguistic strategy of transforming dissenting views into immoral views. Addressing Joschka Fischer, the leader of the Green party, one coalition speaker asserted that Fischer "lacks the ethical dimension of international responsibility in [his] core, and therewith a part of the capacity to fundamentally orient German for-

---

75 Ibid.

76 "Wenn man rein moralisch diesen Militäreinsatz mit Völkermord und der Verletzung von Menschenrechten begründet, dann entsteht doch die Frage: Warum hier, und warum woanders nicht?" Gysi: 6665. See also Gysi: 6648.

eign policy, which is what this country needs."[77] "Is this country adult enough," asks the same speaker, "to...accept fully natural international duties?"[78]By making the "duties" "natural", it is implied that only immature persons would oppose them. The Defense Minister drives home this point by stating that "You [the Greens] are not only isolated, but there is *absolutely no-one in the whole world* who does not support peace troops."[79]

In the prevailing discourse the opposition appears immature, silly, immoral, and removed from reality. Fischer's difficult personal decision to support sending troops to Bosnia is described as "connection to reality," whereas those who do not support sending troops have no connection to reality.[80]Furthermore, "The peace movement *has contributed nothing* to the solution of the problems. The peace movement has abdicated, because they have proven that they only demonstrate for something when it goes against the USA."[81] Especially given the extraordinary support for the US in the context of Dayton (e.g. "the incontrovertible and indispensable leadership role of the United States of America"[82]) this charge presents the opposition as not only useless, but knee-jerk anti-American, and therefore unserious. It is bad enough to be useless, it is worse to be unserious, but it is worst of all to be obstructionist, and thereby immoral:

> Freedom, equality, resisting aggression, solidarity with the helpless, saving human lives – all of this is surrendered by some in the Greens with appeal to a higher moral and the principle of non-violence. This is an ethically and politically untenable position. He who holds freedom for less valuable than peace obeys a bent moral compass-needle. He who does not help, although he could, acts immorally and makes himself guilty.[83]

---

77 "...Ihnen im Kern die ethische Dimension internationaler Verantwortung und damit ein Stück fähigkeit zur Grundorientierung der deutschen Außenpolitik fehlt, die dieses Land braucht." Gerhardt: 6441.

78 Ibid.

79 "Sie sind nicht nur isoliert, sondern es gibt überhaupt niemanden auf der ganzen Welt, der nicht zu der Friedenstruppe steht." Rühe: 6446. Emphasis added.

80 "Anschluß an die Realität" Schaetzer: 6455.

81 C. Schmidt Fürth: 6462. Emphasis added.

82 Scharping: 6636.

83 Finance Minister Waigel: 6654. "Wer die Freiheit, Gerechtigkeit, Aggressionsabwehr, Solidarität mit den Schutzlosen, Menschenleben retten – all das wird von einem Teil der Grünen mit der Berufung auf eine höhere Moral und das Prinzip der Gewaltlosigkeit presgegeben. Dies ist eine ethisch wie politisch unhaltbare Position. Wer die Freiheit für geringwertiger hält als den Frieden, gehorcht einer verborgenen moralischen Kompaßnadel. Wer nicht hilft, obwohl er es könnte, handelt unsittlich und macht sich mitschuldig."

Following the opposition's ideas, consequently, would lead Germany to disaster. Germany would be "Europe-incapable" (*Europaunfähig*) and "alliance-incapable" (*Bündnisunfähig*) and their decisions would damage the alliance.[84]

Interestingly, the immediate opposition reaction to Rühe's charge of immorality was to assume he equates "immorality" with "inaction:" "I resist...your branding us with the label "immoral" and thereby equate this with doing nothing. The Peace Movement has done unceasingly much in this conflict. [A long list of activities follows]... You cannot stick the Peace Movement with the label 'passive,' 'standing to the side,' and 'immoral'."[85] This is an attempt to indirectly state that they both share the same morality while differing on how to best be responsible to it, but the prevailing discourse does not allow this move.

Rather than sharing the same morals, the prevailing discourse paints the opposition as claiming morality for itself at the expense of the other (which, of course, is exactly what the prevailing discourse is doing): "I hold as deeply immoral the claim to sole representation for peace politics which you [Nickels] and others in your party [the Greens] raise, because this claim excludes all others in this parliament."[86] Attempting to extend the opposition criticism about German responsibility to universal statements about war and peace, another speaker asks whether the actions of the allies are equivalent to "waging war and thereby morally less valuable and more reprehensible than our contribution?"[87]

WHO CAN SPEAK FOR PEACE?

The question then shifts from 'who is moral' to 'who can speak for peace'? This is a roundabout way of making the same moral argument: moral is s/he who can speak for peace. If the only way to support peace is by sending German soldiers, and if the Peace Movement opposes sending German soldiers, then the Peace Movement is modus tollens opposed to peace.[88] This contra-

---

84 Seiters: 6436: 7.
85 Nickels: 6449: 50. "Ich wehre mich...dagegen, daß sie uns mit dem Etikett "umoralisch" belegen und dies damit gleichsetzen, wir würden nichts tun. Die Friedensbewegung hat in diesem Konflikt unendlich viel getan. ... Sie können der Friednesbewegung nichg das Etikett "untätig," "abseitsstehen" und "unmoralisch" aufkleben."
86 Kossendey: 6466. "Den Alleinvertretungsanspruch auf Friedenspolitik, den Sie [Nickels] und manche andere in Ihrer Partei [Die Grünen] erheben, halte ich für zutiefst unmoralisch, weil er alle anderen in diesem Parlament ausgrenzt."
87 Hornhues: 6458. "Aber ist denn das, was unsere Verbündeten tun,...für Sie Kriegführung, und damit moralisch minderwertiger und verwerflicher als unser Beitrag?"
88 To differentiate between historical German peace movement, a loose collection of grassroots organizations represented in Parliament primarily by the Greens, and the

dictory sounding logic is then employed to "unmask" the Peace Movement as an ideological front. The fact that the historically-burdened PDS also opposes the sending of German troops makes this approach easier: if the Russians are satisfied with this decision, Rühe half-jesting tells PDS Representative Lederer, so should you be.[89]

The opposition itself tends to swing between avoiding the prevailing discourse's tactics and playing directly into them. The Green Party leader Fischer's explanation of his decision to vote in support of sending the troops most clearly tries to deflate the prevailing discourse's moral dichotomizing:

> I respect, even when I do not share your politics, your conviction as much as you should respect my conviction. I think you have an interest in recognizing the basis for our decision today. ... For me our roots [non-violence and the Peace Movement] remain as valid as ever. Only we are engaged in a real conflict of basic values: on the one side is non-violence as a vision for a world in which conflicts are solved through reason, through law and through majority decisions, through constitutional means and no longer through naked violence. The renunciation of military violence serves the goal of creating structures so this is no longer necessary. On the other side of this cursed dilemma, is a situation where only the dispatching of the military will help people to survive. Between solidarity for survival and the obligation to non-violence – that is the contradiction which faces us in this decision.[90]

The raising of this dilemma is itself presented as an important contribution to the debate, not as a false claim to morality:

> We know, that it is a very difficult undertaking to turn non-violent and civil means of defense...into strategic options....Because of this we remain the absolute minority in everyday politics. But this is an important historical task which no-one besides us is doing. We are not arrogant, and we don't find

---

coalition's claim to also be a peace movement, I use proper nouns to refer to the former the Peace Movement and lower case for the latter the peace movement.

89 Rühe: 6446.

90 Fischer: 6656. "Ich respektiere, auch wenn ich Ihre Politik nicht mitteile, Ihre Überzeugung genauso, wie Sie meine Überzeugung respektieren sollten. Ich denke mir, Sie haben ein Interesse daran, die Grundlage für unsere heutige Entscheidung zur Kenntnis zu nehme....Für mich sind diese Wurzeln nach wie vor gültig. Nur sind wir in einem echten Grundwertekonflikt: auf der einen Seite Gewaltfreiheit als Vision einer Welt, in der Konflikte durch Vernunft, durch Recht und durch Mehrheitsentscheidungen, durch Verfassungstaat und nicht mehr durch nakte Gewalt gelöst werden, der Verzicht auf militärische Gewalt, das Ziel, Strukturen zu schaffen, damit diese nicht mehr notwendig ist; auf der anderen Seite das verfuchte Dilemma, Menschen zum Überleben nur noch durch die Entsendung von Militär helfen zu können. Zwischen der Solidarität zum Überleben und der Verpflichtung zur Gewaltfreiheit – das ist unser Widerspruch auch in dieser Entscheidung."

this wonderful (*toll*). This is a heavy burden, and this is our founding impulse.[91]

Yet some of the opposition (primarily from the PDS) cannot resist tossing the prevailing discourse's claims to moral superiority back at them more directly, thereby deepening competing and seemingly incommensurable claims to truth: since Germany is one of the world's largest arms exporters, does this not undermine the governments claims to negotiate disarmament in Bosnia?[92] Why assume that the government, who was politically unable to end the conflict, be assumed to be militarily capable of ending the conflict?[93] How dare a government claim moral high ground when it has done such things as invite a former Nazi as an expert to a hearing (unrelated to this debate)?[94]

SENDING SOLDIERS OFF TO... PEACE?

Rühe's designation of the opposition as immoral colored the first debate. The tone of the second debate was set by Wolfgang Schäuble's criticism of the Greens for tolerating the unfurling of a banner at a party event stating "Soldiers are murderers." The quote itself stems from Kurt Tucholsky, a sharp-tongued and widely-admired political satirist of the interwar period, whose outrage against militarism forced him into exile to Sweden under the national socialists, where he killed himself in despair in 1935. The interjection of this contentious phrase into the debate is notable because it is the direct tie to the struggle over what the military means today. Schäuble's criticism has two main effects: 1. it presents the Greens again as radicals whose actions set them outside the accepted norms for parliamentary credibility and 2. it underscores the new humanitarian image of the military.

The last section detailed the presentation of the Greens as radical and immoral. The struggle for defining the military was noted in the narrative descriptions, but this discursive site merits a closer look. In a country where militarism twice brought ruin and misery, redefining the military as a humanitarian tool ("peace troops") allows the associative and denotative meanings of military deployment to be positively rather than negatively weighted.

---

91 Nickels: 6642. "Wir wissen, daß es ein sehr schweres Unterfangen ist, gewaltfreie und zivile Mittel der Verteidigung...in strategische Optionen umzusetzen.... Damit sind wir im politischen Alltag nach wie vor in der absoluten Minderheit. Das ist aber eine historisch wichtige Aufgabe, die niemand außer uns leistet. Wir sind nicht arrogant, wir finden das nicht toll. Das ist eine schwere Last, und das ist unser Grund-gründungsimpuls."

92 Lederer: 6442-3. See also Gysi: 6661, Pflüger's reaction on 6663-4 and Gysi's response: 6664.

93 Gysi: 6649.

94 Fischer: 6657. He says: "Welche bodenlose heuchelei ist es...wenn [die CDU: CSU]...einen ehemaligen Kriegsrichter der Hitler-Wehrmacht als Experten zu einer Anhörung einlädt, den Vertreter einer mörderischen Justiz!"

To gain support for sending the German military on peacekeeping missions, the German public must change their default association of military with destruction.

During the Cold War the Bundeswehr and NATO were positively weighted insofar as their purpose was self-defense. Yet despite support for self-defense, there was consensus that hostilities between NATO and the Warsaw Pact would wreak fathomless destruction. Deterrence, therefore, was the primary purpose for the Bundeswehr's existence. As Hans-Georg Ehrhart writes, a crisis-reaction type force is "incompatible with the 'citizen in uniform' ideal which ... legitimizes military forces solely for defending the country against an aggressor. The guiding principle [has been] 'being able to fight in order not to be forced to fight.'"[95] Accordingly, a fundamental change in public perception is necessary to support German troop deployment out of the NATO area, especially if these troops risk combat. To avoid them being seen as destruction-causing troops, reminiscent of the world wars and the cold war, they must be presented in a different light. Thus statements that these soldiers are really policemen for peace; or that the Bundeswehr is a "peace army" (as opposed, presumably, to a "war army"); that the soldier's task is not war but peace; that "peace troops" are a sign of normalcy and solidarity, and the like, is part of a discursive process to change the perception of the military. If the soldiers are going to create peace, then they can't be going to war, despite a combat situation.

WHAT KIND OF MISSION IS THIS, ANYWAY?

Due to this shifting of perceptions, the definition of what kind of deployment this actually is becomes an important discursive site of struggle. Terminological unclarity reigns throughout both debates. German soldiers "protect human lives and help people in need,"[96] according to one coalition member, but an opposition speaker claims this doesn't change the nature of the mission: "This is about a combat mission."[97]Well, prevaricates the Defense Minister, "this is in fact a military operation, but of course not (*doch nicht*) for military goals, rather for civil goals, for political goals...how can one speak here of militarization? These are military means to achieve civil and political goals, which we all strive for."[98] "Unambiguously," reformulates an opposition speaker, it

---

95 Ehrhart, 1996: 48.
96 Gerhardt: 6440. "Sie schützen Menschenleben und helfen notleidenden Menschen."
97 "Es handelt sich um einen Kampfeinsatz." Lederer: 6443.
98 "...das ist zwar eine militärische Operation, aber doch nicht für militärische Ziele, sondern für zivile Ziele, für politische Ziele...Wie kann man da von einer Militarisierung sprechen? Es sind militärische Mittel, um zivile und politische Ziele zu erreichen, die wir alle anstreben." Rühe: 6445.

is a "military combat mission."[99] Perhaps, adds a colleague, but what is important is whether the military is in the service of militarism or, as is the case here, anti-militarism.[100]

The whole debate about whether this is a combat mission or not Schäuble considers "misleading and superfluous," since "naturally it is the task of all forces–this is of course completely clear–to secure peace and to see the peace through."[101] As a "peace mission," it is not a "NATO-deployment" but a "UN-deployment."[102] This is important because the UN is more "peaceful" in purpose than NATO, a military alliance. But whether this is indeed the case is questioned by the opposition: this "[I]s a NATO action...." and after all, "NATO is a military pact...."[103] NATO is acting at the behest of the UN, that is true, but it is not a "blue-helmet" peacekeeping operation like other UN missions, rather it is a "green-helmet" "peace-keeping (*Friedensbewahrung*)"[104] mission, which makes it in the end effect a NATO mission. Does this mean it is not a mission in the sense of Chapter VI of the UN Charter ("Pacific Settlement of Disputes"), and a mission in the sense of Chapter VII ("Action with Respect to Threats to the Peace, Breaches of the Peace, and Acts of Aggression")? Or is it a blurring of both, as Fischer claims, making it an exceptional situation?

Tired of this terminological confusion, a coalition speaker tries to set it straight once and for all:

> Legally this is a mission according to chapter eight of the UN Charter. Legally speaking, it is a combat mission. The task itself, from a military viewpoint, is a mission to support combat troops. But it does not matter whether there must be combat or just support [for combat troops]: it [this mission] serves the securing of peace.[105]

But the Defense Minister just said it was "not a combat mission," objects a colleague, asking which one it is then, and adding his personal view that it is "a mission to secure peace."[106] Exasperated, the coalition member tries again: "We emphasize (*Wir stellen fest*): First, it is a mission to secure peace, second it is, seen legally, a combat mission according to chapter eight of the UN

---

99 "militärische Kampfauftrag" Volmer: 6454.
100 Voigt: 6457.
101 Kinkel: 6650.
102 Gansel: 6655.
103 Lederer: 6443.
104 "Friedensbewahrung" Fischer: 6657.
105 Rechtlich gesehen ist das ein Einsatz nach Kapitel VII der UN Charta. Es ist, rechtlich gesehen, ein Kampfeinsatz. Vom direkten Auftrag her ist das ein Einsatz, der Kampftruppen unterstützt, militärisch betrachtet. Aber egal, ob gekämpft werden muß oder unterstützt wird: Es dient der Friedensicherung...."Breuer: 6659.
106 "ein Einsatz zur Friedenssicherung." Urbaniak: 6659.

Charter, and third it is, as regards the German military task, not the deployment of combat troops. I think," he adds, "we should make a common effort to make perfectly clear, that Germany's contribution is a contribution to securing the peace."[107]

By now, however, the nature of the mission is far from perfectly clear: a "combat mission" without the "deployment of combat troops?" Sympathetic Social Democrats try to improve on their coalition colleague's attempt: "This is a task of peace," states an SPD supporter of the mission, "and to this task of peace belongs the readiness to fight (*Kampfbereitschaft*)."[108] So is "readiness to fight (*Kampfbereitschaft*)" the same as a "combat mission (*Kampfauftrag*)?" It would seem so, but please don't tell the soldiers that:

> It was not necessary for the motivation of the soldiers to speak of a combat mission [as General Inspector Naumann had previously done]. It would have been correct to say that the use of military power is allowed under very certain conditions for this peace-securing mission.[109]

"No one speaks of war anymore," sighs an older opposition speaker at the very end, "They only build words which contain the word peace."[110]

The confusion and contortions over what sort of deployment this is belies a deep concern to avoid at all costs the appearance of sending German troops to fight a war. At a deeper level, though, we see here a struggle over what counts as war and what counts as peace. If peacekeeping (or peace-enforcing) entails combat, is it war? Are soldiers acting as police no longer soldiers? Does calling a combat situation a "peace task" make it less war-like, and if a situation is war-like, is it then war? The risk of double-speak seems great here, although perhaps unavoidable. Historically in the United States, calling a war by another name did not make it any less a war: officially both the Korean and Vietnam wars were not wars but "police actions." Local Honor Rolls (war

---

107 "Wir stellen fest: Erstens ist es ein Einsatz zur Friedenssicherung, zweitens ist es rechtlich gesehen ein Kampfeinsatz nach Kapitel VII der UN-Charta, und drittens ist es, was den deutschen militärischen Auftrag angeht, nicht der Einsatz von Kampftruppen. Ich denke," he adds "wir sollten uns gemeinsam darum bemühen,...völlig klarzustellen, daß das, was Deutschland beiträgt, ein Beitrag zur Friedenssicherung ist." Breuer: 6659.

108 "Dies ist ein Friedensauftrag, ... zu diesem Friedensauftrag gehört die Kampfbereitschaft." Duve: 6660.

109 "Es war zur Motivation der Soldaten nicht notwendig, von 'Kampfauftrag' zu reden [as General Inspector Naumann did]. Richtig wäre gewesen, davon zu reden, daß bei diesem friedenssichernden Einsatz die Anwendung von militärischer Gewalt unter ganz bestimmten Bedingungen erlaubt ist." Verheugen: 6666.

110 "Es wird nie mehr vom Krieg geredet. Es werden immer nur Worte gebildet, die mit Frieden zusammengesetzt worden sind." Heuer: 6673.

memorials listing the names of those who served) call the wars "conflicts."[111]
The UN/NATO mission to Bosnia is not comparable to Vietnam, and only
marginally to Korea (because of the UN involvement) and the wisdom of
sending troops to Bosnia may be convincing even without a clear name for
the mission. Yet there is an underlying concern that missions which are difficult to define can develop a destructive dynamic of their own, a dynamic
known in the United States military as "mission creep."

The United States is presented in the prevailing discourse as a forceful advocate for deploying troops. It is thus ironic that the reasoning of a PDS Representative for his opposition to deployment is in fact very similar to US Con-
gressional opposition about peacekeeping missions in general. Uwe-Jens
Heuer states:

> I am not saying that today's decision means war, but with this vote we are
> leaving the decision about peace and war in other's hands. The troops there
> stand, as you all know, under NATO command, they stand under the com-
> mand of a US General. It no longer lies in the hands of this parliament
> whether war will be fought. For this reason I am not able to give my support
> to today's resolution.[112]

WHAT ARE WE REALLY DEBATING, ANYWAY?

Not only is the mission itself difficult to define, indeed, it is not even so clear
from some of the speakers what the whole debate is about. It seems obvious
that the debate is technically a procedure which precedes a vote on the government's decision to send 4,000 troops to former Yugoslavia. Some of the
opposition, however, consider it an *ex post facto* legitimization of decisions
already taken. Echoing the concern that decisions for the German mission are
being made by NATO, a Green colleague asks "Which possibilities does the
parliament actually still have for influence? Why are we having this discussion? The Constitutional Court requires it, but where in substance is the possibility for participation (*Mitbestimmungsmöglichkeiten*) of the opposition?"
The parliament is not debating the Dayton Peace Accord, he continues, rather
the government is asking for approval for their "cabinet's draft (*Kabi-*

---

111 For example the Honor Roll in Skaneatles, NY, lists the Great War, the Second
World War, the Korea *Conflict*, and the Vietnam *Conflict*.

112 "Ich sage nicht, daß die heutige Entscheidung Krieg bedeutet, aber wir geben mit
dieser Abstimmung die Entscheidung über Krieg und Frieden in andere Hände. Die
Truppen dort stehen, wie Sie wissen, unter dem Befehl der NATO, sie stehen unter dem
Befehl eines USA-Generals. Es liegt nicht mehr in der Hand dieses Parlaments, ob dort
Krieg geführt wird. Deshalb bin ich nicht in der Lage, diesem heutigen Beschluß meine
Zustimmung zu geben." Heuer: 6673.

nettsvorlage)" about how to shape the German contribution. "These are," he says, "two fundamentally different questions."[113]

In one sense, he is merely stating the obvious. Of course the parliament is not debating the Dayton Accords, only the German contribution. The debate that followed his statement, however, supports his implication that criticism of the government plan becomes rhetorically equivalent with criticism of Dayton. This is because of the metonymical linkage between support for this particular motion, and support for German normalcy, as described above. Must the debate, however, follow the war-like rules of linguistic dominance? And what are the criteria by which one discourse prevails over the other?

Linguistic Dominance in the Dayton Debates

WHY LINGUISTIC DOMINANCE MATTERS IN POLITICS

Strategies of linguistic dominance appear necessary for fixing "*the* truth" in a world which offers competing truths. Laclau and Mouffe, as Roxanne Doty points out, "suggest that any discourse is constituted as an attempt to arrest the infinite flow of difference and construct a center, a foundation that gives rise to meaning."[114] Fundamental conflicts over meaning are, as Michael Townson puts it, ""resolved" by certain constructs of reality with their attendant systems of beliefs and values achieving dominance and establishing dominant discourses."[115]

For example, the complete answer to "what makes me American" can be: "born in the United States." A corresponding answer is not acceptable in Germany; "being German" is linked to lineal ("blood") descent, in addition to other criteria (language, geographical location, appearance, etc). The use of *ius sanguinus* in Germany versus *ius soli* in the United States is the result of historical experiences as reflected in the debates in both countries about multiculturalism and what it means to be, or not be, an "immigration country." Changing *ius sanguinus* in Germany would, effectively, change the metonymical links associated with "being German," as in "you don't look German." Of course, in the United States the *ius soli* was a reaction to the then-solely European face of immigration, and did not apply to African slaves, Native Americans, or Chinese workers. Emancipation and the changing nature of immigration *combined* with *ius soli*, however, made a broadening of the concept of "who is American" unavoidable in the same way that a broadening of the concept of "who is German" *is* avoidable as long as *ius san-*

---

113 "Das sind zwei grundsätzlich unterschiedliche Fragestellungen." Volmer: 6454.
114 Doty, 1993: 19. See chapter 2.
115 Townson, 1992: 22.

guinus reinforces the ethnic essence of "Germanness." This latter, it should be noted, does not preclude a tolerant society. The point here is to demonstrate how a state's linguistic action (the law of *ius soli* or *ius sanguinus*) creates a "reality" by resolving a conflict through appeal to self-evident truths; it seems "obvious" that Germans–or Hungarians, or Greeks–are defined by their ethnicity, or that Americans can be white or black.

But self-evident truths are rarely self-evident. The process, paraphrasing Townson, starts with *linguistic action* establishing dominant perceptions of reality and defining and creating group identity.[116] These perceptions of reality and identities draw on systems of beliefs and values which have material bases, though the conceptual framework for the interpretation and orientation of these systems are primarily linguistic. A subset of linguistic action is *political action* which works linguistically in three ways, by: 1. regulating (e.g. passing laws on citizenship), 2. persuading (e.g. forbidding hiring "illegals," or arguing court cases), and 3. bonding (e.g. creating a group with a status in common; legal, illegal, citizen, *Ausländer*, etc.).[117]

Political action is thus a way to solve conflicts and simultaneously create and recreate the standards by which conflicts can be solved. In the verbal act of denying a particular citizenship claim, for instance, both the immediate conflict is solved and the "reality" of group identity (legal/illegal) is reinscribed. Political action does not exist for its own sake; it serves the respective system of beliefs and values in a variety of practical and ideological ways. To have the power necessary to be effective, politics must operate on the basis of self-evident truths, and these self-evident truths are acquired through linguistic domination.

Following Townson, linguistic domination is constituted through three acts: naming, referencing, and signifying.[118] In the Dayton debates, both discourses attempt to establish this dominance.

"Naming" refers to the establishment of terminology, such as the government's term "peace troops," or the opposition's term "re-militarisation," helping each discourse create favorable presuppositions.[119]

While naming entails constructing new terms with clear indications of their ideological role, "referencing" seeks to lay claim to previously-existing terms which are positively weighted but ideologically unbound. In the Dayton debates, "peace," "morality," "responsibility," and "solidarity" are among the positive terms to which both discourses lay claim, and which then *per se* are

---

116 In the following paragraphs I adopt Townson's theoretical approach as presented in pages 25-33.
117 Townson, 1992: 32.
118 Ibid.: 25-26.
119 Ibid.: 25.

unusable for the other side. In addition to claiming positively-weighted terms, referencing also negatively burdens the terms and associates them with the opposition, such as *"Europaunfähig"* and *"Bündnisunfähig."*

"Signifying" refers to the respective discourse's claim to the "sole possession of the 'true' meaning of a word, and that the opponent is 'misrepresenting' or 'abusing' the 'true' meaning." When Joschka Fischer described the Greens as a "non-violent" (*gewaltfreie*) party, a CDU colleague yelled out "Are we a *violence* party?"[120] exposing the implicit reference in Fischer's claim to possessing the 'true' meaning of the word "non-violent." Signifying can also involve adopting the other discourse's favored terms with the intention of either deflating them –the rhetorical question "Are we a violence party?" obviously implies the contrary. A "non-violence" party thus appears at best nonsensical or, at worse, trying to unjustly declare moral high ground. Signifying can also co-opt the other side's terminology, as with adaptation of the word "peace" to describe all manner of military activities.[121]

If one discourse is able to dominate the naming, referencing, and signification in the debate, then that discourse has solidified control over the denotative and associative meanings of the words which define the debate, and thereby the debate itself. The meaning of a concept such as "normalcy" becomes a self-evident truth; for example: a "normal" country (especially a normal great power) sends troops to participate in UN peacekeeping missions. This power to control denotative and associative meanings, Townson notes, "is a significant factor both in the exercise of political control and the creation of solidarity."[122]

Controlling meaning can be essential to implementing otherwise unpalatable policies. While all Germans desire to see the Bosnian war end, it remained a relatively marginal parliamentary issue between the recognition debates in 1991 and the Tornado debates in 1995. The use of German troops "out-of-area" was a singularly unpopular idea and sending the German military into a possible combat zone in former Yugoslavia would have been a very hard sell just months before Dayton, even with a cease-fire in effect. The "non-linguistic background" of sending German troops to Bosnia was politically undefined territory. To make matters more difficult, the government *had*

---

120 Fischer and Hornung: 6656.
121 Referencing and signifying, as Towson notes, "can be viewed as complementary aspects of the process of 'ascribing meaning.'" Towson: 25.
122 Townson: 28.

partially defined this issue before Dayton by stating categorically that German troops would *not* be sent to Bosnia.[123]

As Townson points out, until a non-linguistic background is structured by linguistic action the issue remains "undefined, perceptually amorphous....By the process of linguistic constitution, [the non-linguistic background] [can] be categorized and thus politically activated in such a way that further consequences [can] ensue."[124] The prevailing discourse's strategy for linguistic dominance successfully categorized the mission to Bosnia as the most responsible and moral option, and thereby politically enabled German soldiers to be sent with overwhelming political support, despite the historical and political taboo on exactly such missions.

WHAT MAKES A DISCOURSE PREVAIL?

Explaining the workings of discourse in this political debate, however, does not explain *why* one particular strategy is successful. This enters the realm of theory choice. Let us briefly consider three possibilities:

1. The prevailing discourse best reflects the values and beliefs of the actors involved. 1.This means that, rhetorical strategy aside, the dominant discourse corresponds most closely to experience and other indicators of "truth." To the extent that objectivity can be assumed, the prevailing discourse is objectively true, is recognized as such, and is therefore. This assumes that discourses are competing on a level epistemological playing field; that is, were the other discourse to correspond better to the truth, it then would prevail.[125]

2. The prevailing discourse relies on interests that are powerful enough to rig the debate. The outcome of the debate is preordained and serves certain political interests. Here, political discourse does not take place on a level playing field, but on a terrain already controlled by one faction. Sophistry, not "truth," helps the discourse prevail.[126]

---

123 "[T]he Federal Government rejects the direct participation of German troops in peace missions in the former Yugoslavia." Kinkel in October, 1994, quoted in Ehrhart, 1996: 40.

124 Townson: 234.

125 This position corresponds to the liberal view of politics as the marketplace of ideas. Rationality, or at least bounded rationality, a correspondence theory of truth, and equal opportunity set the guidelines.

126 This position corresponds to several different strains of political theory. If this position sees the powerful interests distorting a truth which can be known through other means, then we are in the realm of Marxian critique. If this position sees truth as a social construction again: this does not mean "nothing is real", then we are in the realm of agonistic postmodernism, a la Lyotard.

3. The prevailing discourse prevails because it contains elements of "truth" (of a correspondence nature), elements of power, and, most importantly, is situated in a larger metanarrative.

This third option is best suited to understanding why a certain discourse prevails. The element of truth in the Dayton debates was the effect that the material deployment of troops had on stopping the fighting in Bosnia. To the extent that ending the war in Bosnia took priority over the finer points of policy formation, the government was able to count on support even from traditional opponents. Yet favoring deployment clearly supported factional interests: the coalition validated its long-standing position on using the *Bundeswehr* for peace-keeping missions, and by association its general foreign policy outlook. The mission helped redefine NATO's responsibilities–not an uncontroversial issue–and Germany's role in a redefined NATO.

As mentioned earlier, however, these debates are anchored in larger metanarratives of German and European history and the respective ontologies which inform the idea of history. The prevailing discourse gains immeasurable benefit from being part of the metanarrative of Germany as a great power, with links to realist and nationalist narratives. The related metanarrative of liberal democracy as a historically peaceful and progressive movement, with links to the teleology of European integration, are also suffused in the debates. There is not a direct fit between the normalist and liberal discourses of German foreign policy and the prevailing counter-discourses of the out-of-area debates. Narrative coherence and logical consistency are not synonymous. For example, "Normalcy" in the prevailing discourse most closely corresponds to the metanarrative of national identity where the nation-state appears as discrete and homogeneous. Yet the signifier of "normalcy" is participation in international organizations, which challenge the conventional image of the nation-state. This does not undermine the respective discourses of normalcy and liberalism, but rather indicates real-world contradictions that complicate their "pure" perpetuation. Furthermore, it denotes assumptions common to both discourses despite their differences. These contradictions and common assumptions are the focus of the next and last chapter.

7. Situating Germany

Germany's "Postmodern" Predicament

The search for a salient German identity to serve as the basis for policy is in one sense more difficult following the "second" national unification than the first: the first could more earnestly hold the nation-state ideal as the telos which legitimated the primacy of foreign policy. In the 1990s there is no clear choice between the primacy of foreign or domestic policy. In the context of economic interdependence and political integration it is increasingly difficult to clearly distinguish foreign from domestic policy, above all in the areas of economic policy. This is one reason why those areas of foreign policy which can still support a "clearer" inside/outside distinction, namely the use of military force, are caged in the language of national identity. The difficulty of separating the domestic from the foreign also points out the situated character of the German identity crisis in the larger context of crisis of the nation-state as a domestic ordering principle.

It is difficult to settle on an analytical term for the current postunification era. The uncertain space between the primacy of sovereignty and the project of integration–the discursively disordered terrain of Germany in the 1990s–is a form of vacuum calling out for assignation. Contenders for an adequate term include the oft-invoked terms "post-Cold War," "the new world order," and "postmodern." "Post-Cold War" is merely temporally descriptive, and while it echoes the hope of the postwar era, it contains few normative guidelines. George Bush's erstwhile "new world order" indicated an era of peace and prosperity, premised on the hegemony of an enlightened and internationalist United States and its allies. In the dust of the Gulf War this term lost its glitter, however, and, with the violent disintegration of Yugoslavia and war in Central Africa, the optimistic term fell into disuse, engendering parodies about the "new world disorder." The term "postmodern" has had more lasting resonance, although it is often employed with little regard for its theoretical heritage. Yet it is perhaps best suited to capture Germany's situation, despite, or perhaps because of, its inherent ambiguity and theoretical entanglements. Before arguing for its potential relevance, however, let us cast a glance at a problematic deployment of the term "postmodern" within in the foreign policy community.

CZEMPIELIAN "POSTMODERNISM" AS GLORIFIED MODERNISM

The German foreign policy community's casual use of the word postmodern is a serious misnomer. By "post-modernism" Czempiel, Janning and others mean nothing more than modernity *pur*.[1] The postmodern world, for Czempiel, is identical with the societal world, defined by the advanced interactions of the OECD states, their interdependence and democracy. Contained within are all the ingredients which define modernity: a clear teleology associated with progress stemming from the socially and economically advanced core outward. "The post-modern world which is clearly emerging within the OECD...is spreading to those countries which still form part of the 'modern world.'"[2] Here postmodernity appears as the successful sublimation of the barbarism which Adorno saw inherent in modernity by the triumph of the good parts of modernism. It is spatially and temporally hierarchical, narratively cohesive, and socially normative. The common usage of "the postmodern world" in the Czempielian sense is *as* a metanarrative.

Though irony and paradox are staples of postmodern thought, viewing postmodernity unreflectively as a metanarrative of progress denies the very assumptions from whence it emerges. Lyotard's controversial definition of postmodernism as the death of metanarratives is neither the first nor the last word, but it does convey a clear sense of what postmodernism is *not*; it is *not* a more advanced stage of modernity, an improved metanarrative, a normative framework for resolving contradictions.[3] Critics of Lyotard, above all Frederic Jameson, contest the ascendancy of minor narratives, arguing instead that the metanarratives have not gone the way to dusty death but have descended into the political unconscious.[4] Here postmodernism is viewed critically as the "logic of late capitalism," effectively undermining opposition to the workings of capital through a dizzying cornucopia of consumerism.[5] But even here postmodernism is a distraction from metanarrative, its very essence lies in articulating fragmentation, dissonance, the world unraveled (if one can speak of a postmodern essence!). This is why even though both Jameson and Czempiel use postmodernism as a sobriquet for particular forms of social interaction within the industrialized West, Czempiel's use remains theoretically impoverished—he seeks continuity with the past by construing postmodernism as a modernist teleology. This forces him to treat the normative claims inherent in his "descriptive" term as categorical imperatives (i.e. the role of the societal world in civilizing the tribal world).

---

1 For example see Czempiel, 1996b, and Joffe, 1995, who writes on: 45 "Regarding foreign policy we live in a postmodern era whose main principle is 'anything goes.'" "Auch außenpolitisch leben wir im Zeitalter der Postmoderne, und deren Hauptprinzip besagt: 'anything goes.'" For an example where German political science does deal with postmodernism as critique in the philosophical sense see Albert, 1994.

2 Czempiel, Ibid.: 213.

3 Lyotard, 1989.

4 See Jameson, 1981.

5 See Jameson, 1984.

Postmodernist theories recognize, and often celebrate, the following: contingency, the indeterminacy of meaning, the confutation of Kantian reason, the refutation of romanticism and scientism, the authenticity of the subaltern, of alterity, of minor narratives and the richness of the margins. No matter what one's interpretation of Nietzsche, it would be a stretch to consider him a Cartesian rationalist. Likewise, while still admitting that postmodernism is necessarily open to vast interpretation (like any other philosophical approach), a Czempielian definition of postmodern as a new and improved modernist metanarrative is at best seriously misguided.

POSTMODERNISM, OR UNITARY NARRATIVES LOST

Because of its proximity to theories of deconstruction and because of its rejection of certain approaches to scientific method, postmodernism is invariably viewed in critical theory as the negative moment of the dialectic, or (from a more Popperian view) as the surrender of reason to authority. An emerging literature contests such interpretations, envisioning postmodernism as an ethical posture.[6] The articulation of a postmodern ethics hinges in part on addressing the aporia between recognizing difference and recognizing the constitutive role of the other in the self. This is a rearticulation of the problematic relationship of universalism and particularism, and addresses the question of how particularisms are to relate to each other if not in a purely hierarchical power position or in a naively relativistic way (with implications of "separate but equal").

The tension between universalism and particularism is central to the discursive disorder stemming from the end of the Cold War and the rise of globalization. But neither discursive disorder nor the ensuing tension between universalism and particularism are inherently postmodern conditions. The revolutions of 1789, or 1848, may well have disordered the dominant discourses even more than the revolutions of 1989. What makes this round of disorder arguably "postmodern" are the historical conditions which seem to deny access to the solutions of the past. These conditions fall into two general categories.

First are the changing economic relations, including globalization of trade, which leads to the most commonly perceived "erosion" of state sovereignty.[7] These could be described as "external" conditions, because regardless of world view negatively affected individuals directly experience unease and

---

6 See, among others, Haber, 1994, Albert, 1994b, and the works of Michael Shapiro and William Connolly.

7 This includes the global sinking of wages as capital enjoys unprecedented mobility while labor suffers from its lack of the same. See Hirst and Thompson, 1996 and Robinson, 1996.

discomfort when their factory moves or their wages and benefits are cut. The increasing ineffectiveness of local and national solutions to economic problems is disorienting and questions the role of the sovereign state in fundamentally new ways.

The second historical condition is less easy to characterize with one word. It is in a sense the "internal" corollary to the external condition, for it stems from reactions to modern events which fundamentally unsettled the ethical basis of Western society. Auschwitz, Hiroshima and the Holocaust radically put the character of Western civilization into question; the Vietnam war challenged the righteousness of the American mission; the Civil Rights movement in the United States exposed the hypocrisy of democracy based on active discrimination; decolonialization provided a new lens by which to view old actions; and the nuclear arms race deeply unsettled long-established beliefs about war and war-fighting. A critique of dominant interpretations grew out of these events and manifested itself *inter alia* through multiculturalism, political correctness, post-colonialist literature, women's studies as an accepted academic field, and challenges to the Western literary and philosophical canon. Whatever one's opinion of aspects on these critiques, they represent an attempt to change, expose and undermine dominant narratives which became identified with oppression and coercion. While not always consistent, they reject existing master narratives and are not necessarily primarily concerned with replacing them, leaving a highly variegated range of responses with no stated common agenda.

This lack of focus on confronting the dominant metanarratives with a coherent front has been attacked as a counter-productive lack of solidarity on the left, allowing representatives of the dominant narratives to exploit the cacophony of difference for their own ends. This argument must be taken seriously, though it risks glossing over precisely that point which makes the condition of postmodernity different than, say, worker's discontent in the first half of the twentieth century. Starting perhaps with Kuhn in the philosophy of science, the turn away from behaviorism in the social sciences (with Berger and Luckman), deconstruction and Foucauldian genealogy in the humanities, and the critical legacy of the Frankfurt School, a philosophical basis has arisen which, while encompassing severe methodological diversity, creates an epistemological base which entails the questioning of metanarratives (paradigms, discourse communities, etc.). Epistemology itself is in ongoing foment, both mirroring and a mirror of the wariness of metanarratives.

Parallel to the critiques of metanarratives there is a growing literature on the narrative structure of the self (as discussed in chapter 2). Such an approach underscores the inescapability of some form of social narrative. Just as personal identities are a function of the social narratives into which they are born, so social narratives also exist in a wider context of interacting narratives. The question of universalism and particularism in a narrative context is thus necessarily also a question of hermeneutics, of how encounters with others shape and reshape selves. And this leads back to a crux of the postmodern condition: how can asserting particularism in the face of oppressive universalist narratives maintain particularity without either being re-marginalized or claiming universalism itself?

Let us for the moment limit the implication of a narrative approach to identity to the question of how it affects the postmodern aspects of contemporary discursive disorder. Postmodernism manifests itself, even in its celebratory moments, as recognition of, and a coming to terms with, a loss. The metanarratives which oppressed also gave closure to lives. Postmodernism can perhaps be seen as acknowledging the second great loss of faith, or conversely the attempt to regain faith(s) in the light of loss. The first great "loss" was the move from religion to rational, scientific secularism, which set the conditions for the second "loss"–the loss of appeal to reason as the ultimate arbiter of right and wrong, an extension of Weber's famous "disenchantment of the world" to the problems of multicultural societies in a global economy.[8]

AFTER HISTORY

As indicated above, what is "post" about this crisis of modernity is the perception that the tools of modernity are no longer adequate to solve its own problems–or as Audre Lourde formulates the problem: "the master's tools shall never tear down the master's house." In Lakatosian terms, perpetuating the existing metanarratives only leads to degenerative research programs in defense of an ultimately untenable hard core. New identities, and new relations between identities, are sought–new stories, or more exactly, new histories. Perhaps a useful way to grasp what can be called the postmodernism condition is to consider the once-fashionable term "after history." There are three competing interpretations of this phrase.

First, "after history" can be understood as the end of history (Czempiel echoing Fukuyama echoing Hegel). Here history is understood as a dialectical process with a clear telos, a plateau where the tensions which drove subject-object relations are sublimated by the establishment of a universal class, be it Hegel's bureaucrats, Marx's proletariat, or Czempiel's OECD citizens of the societal world. Secondly, "after history" can be interpreted as "post-histoire" (Gehlen), where history represents the metanarratives which have been frag-

---

8 In disenchantment, however, is of course the possibility for reenchantment. On the subject of enchantment and philosophy of science see Berman, 1981.

mented and disempowered. There is no universal class here, if anything there is a triumph of particularism. This variation is often stereotyped as "relativist" postmodernism, and is the bugaboo of many cultural critics .[9]

Both these interpretations conceive of the "after" in "after history" temporally in the sense of following upon, coming after, ensuing from. Yet "after" also implies pursuit, chasing, a searching for. By incorporating the double meaning of "after" into the definition of "after history" we can express both the sense of displacement (history is no longer a unitary narrative) and the sense of openness (a new history–a new story, is needed to make sense of the world).[10] We are after history in both senses of the word. This is the third way of conceiving the postmodern condition in its effect on the German nation-state: searching for a new identity by searching for a new history. But we know from Heidegger's concept of the "fore-structure of understanding" and Gadamer's subsequent explication of the role of prejudice in understanding that a person (or society's) situatedness restricts the imaginable to the limits of the identity-conferring narratives. More straightforwardly: a new history can only be based on an old history. Since history is open to interpretation and manipulation, however, the truth of the "new history" is to be found not in the "facts" of the past, but in the ethical posture one brings to incorporating the past into the search for new legitimizing stories.

This brings us back to the location of identity in the narrative function of resolving apparent contradictions. The fundamental contradiction remains the base of the self/other divide: the primary contradiction between universalism and particularity. Finally then, we come back to post-unification Germany, whose historical situation lends itself especially to addressing the problem of national identity under postmodern conditions expressed through the de-centering of the narrative of the nation-state as a domestic ordering principle.

GERMANY'S "POSTMODERN" PREDICAMENT

Germany is particularly suited for addressing the problems of identity, not because Germany is in some sense more "advanced" in dealing with issues of identity, but for reasons which hopefully have become clear in the preceding chapters. To briefly recapitulate: the German nation-state is de-centered both from above and from below. From above the logic of European integration implies some significant level of merging national identity into European identity. This challenges the idea of the nation as the *summum bonum*. Yet even if, as government ad campaigns emphasize, Baden (or Bavaria, or Swabia) will remain as distinct within a Europe of regions as it does within a

---

9 See Sokal, 1996; Himmelfarb, 1994.
10 In this sense postmodernism can be both descriptive and normative.

federal Germany, there is an attachment to "Germany" which is threatened by integration. This is true, in its own way, for all countries of the European Union. What makes Germany somewhat different is that European identity was for a long time the positive *ersatz* for a perceived shameful German identity.[11] This difference connects the de-centering from above and below: German national identity is primarily a negative identity. But in a world of nation-states, a negative identity can be seen as a liability, as has become clear in the normalist discourse. The idea of dissolving German identity in a European identity is simultaneously attractive and threatening.

Secondly, as the world's second largest exporter after Japan and the country with the highest cost of labor, Germany is affected by the globalization of the economy perhaps even more directly than other European countries. With the cost of incorporating East Germany dragging the economy down, while unemployment rises and the government tries to scale back social services, Germany is finally facing issues which have dogged Britain and the United States for years. These include an aging population, budget-busting pension and welfare services, outsourcing and the relocation of companies to locations with cheaper labor, and the deregulation of state-run monopolies. An added complication are the austerity measures necessary to reduce the deficit to under 3% of GDP, a requirement for the much-heralded European Monetary Union at the century's end. All this indicates that the social effects of globalization will be felt strongly and will further disorder the narratives of progress and economic growth which are part of (West) Germany's foundational myth.

Thirdly, unification itself challenges the abstract notion of national community (*Volksgemeinschaft*). The cultural gap between East and West is one ingredient—with additional complications from integrating East German history into the legacy of Germany, including coming to terms with the Stasi past.[12] Perhaps most importantly, unification has unsettled narratives which could order the experience of the Third Reich, the interpretation of which, at least since the Historian's Dispute, has re-emerged as the site of battles over German identity. And now the legacy of the Bonn Republic is also coming into question.

Related to this is what we might call the hidden side of Bonn's civic nationalist orientation, or what Lutz Hoffmann calls the "other side of the Bonn medallion." The most prominent side was the fealty to *Westbindung*, while the other side was the conscious preservation of the sense of German as a "Volk" rather than a "peuple" regarding East Germany. Democracy was the operative word to the West, notes Hoffmann, while "German Volk" was the operative

---

11 Markovitz and Reich, 1997.
12 On the relation between dealing with the Stasi and the Nazi past see Pampel, 1995.

term toward the East, where official policy was to grant instant West German citizenship to any ethnic German, from the GDR or any other Eastern country from Poland to the Soviet Union. This civic/ethnic disjuncture was always in danger of open contradiction, but the Cold War enabled its absorption into the repertoire of the normalized contradictions of divided Europe. Writing against a background of increased xenophobia and a growing intellectual right, Hoffmann writes:

> Through the collapse of the communist empire the "German Volk" lost the context which it respectively preserved and relativized for forty years. The basis has disappeared which allowed for compatibility between the unenlightened concept of the "German Volk" and the West-integration of the Bonn Republic. This concept is no longer justified–and thereby no longer held relatively in limits–by claiming that it contributes to the ultimate victory of Western thought. With this the always-existing contradiction between the preservation conception and the relativized idea [of the "German Volk"] rises to the forefront and forces the resolution of the contradiction in one direction or the other.[13]

In sum three metanarratives which defined German identity prior to 1989 have come unraveled: 1. The narrative of the Cold War, which allowed West Germans to define their identity in opposition to the communists (the "double negative" of German identity); 2. the narrative of the Bonn Republic, with its comfortable reputation as a political dwarf and its delicate and important security function on the front line of divided Europe; and 3. the narrative of "model Germany," the economy which was able to have it all–acceptable unemployment, high wages and benefits, low inflation, and high productivity–as a result of the economic miracle of the 1950s, a source of considerable national pride. Ernst Fraenkel's 1963 depiction of modern Germany serves as an example of the early optimism of economic progress:

> Today the external symptoms of the disease which was present between the world wars is almost totally vanished. In the seemingly crisis-proof welfare

---

13 Hoffmann, 1994: 23. The original reads: "Durch den Zusammenbruch des kommunistischen Weltreiches hat das "deutsche Volk" den Kontext verloren, der es vierzig Jahre lang einerseits konservierte und andererseits relativierte. Die Grundlage ist entfallen, die bisher einen unaufgeklärten Begriff des "deutschen Volkes" mit der Westintegration der Bonner Republik kompatibel machte. Er wird nicht mehr gerechtfertigt und damit auch nicht mehr relativierend in Grenzen gehalten von dem Anspruch, dem freiheitlichen Denken des Westens zum Siege zu verhelfen. Damit tritt der immer schon vorhandene innere Widerspruch zwischen der konservierten Vorstellung und den sie relativierenden Ideen offen zutage und drängt darauf, zugunsten der einen oder der anderen überwunden zu werden."

state is, instead of lasting depression, the permanent super-boom, instead of unemployment is a surplus of jobs....[14]

Given the anchoring of the postmodern condition in the fragmentation of metanarratives, it is fair to say that in this respect Germany faces a postmodern predicament, but in quite a different way than envisioned by Czempiel.

Assessing the Foreign Policy Discourse: Synthesis or Historic Bloc?

Chapter 2 introduced foreign policy discourses as one of the ways in which the state tries to reestablish the narrative coherence necessary for its self-understanding. Foreign policy has a clear self-interest in preserving the state system, for it is an appendage of the state. Yet foreign policy also reflects the changing self-understanding of the state, since its rationale depends on defining modes of interaction with "others" in relation to the national "self." The changing self-understanding of the contemporary German state emerges from the above postmodern predicament. Challenges to the nation-state narrative can be seen as variants of the self/other conundrum; in foreign policy they appears as a fundamental contradiction between the universal and the particular. The discourses presented in Chapters 3 and 4 grapple to resolve this contradiction in their quest for narrative coherence. The manner of their respective endeavors, to which we now turn, divulges the boundaries of their discursive abilities.

ASSESSING THE NORMALIST NARRATIVE

The normalist discourse encompasses sincerely divergent views, from staunch Atlanticists to the nominally anti-Western intellectual Right. It is, nonetheless, possible to discern four components common to all variations. The first is an essentially nation*ist* (as opposed to nationalist) assumption that national identity is a thing-in-itself. As such, there is a "true" and a "false" national identity, and the general consensus among normalists is that both National Socialism and the negative nationalism of the postwar era are false identities. Hacke draws quite different conclusions than Kinkel, but both see self-confident national identity as the missing ingredient in the otherwise objectively positive post-Cold War situation. National identity figures in the discourse as something positive but lacking. Yet versions of national identity which are too self-critical are excluded, because the *function* of national identity is the legitimization of Germany as a Great Power similar to other Great Powers, which amounts to being "normal." Self-criticism must be not undermine the self-confidence necessary for "normalcy."

---

14 Fraenkel, 1991: 69.

This leads directly to the second component: the adaptation of classical realist assumptions. Though realists hardly form a single school of thought, there is one common aspect–the essential sameness of international interaction, from the Pelopenesian Wars to the Gulf War. Continuity is emphasized through the intractable and ultimate tragedy of the human condition: man is wolf to man. This axiom is not paralyzing, one *can* learn from history and work to promote cooperation and minimize conflict, but the basic structure of the security dilemma remains the same, even if the source of threat shifts.

The appeal of classical realism as opposed to neo-realism lies not only in its reassurance that the more things change, the more they stay the same, but in its metaphysics. Classical realism was, as Ole Wœver put it, an ethico-philosophical position, making broad claims about the world, drawing on history and the human condition. During the era of behavioralism and bipolarity, neo-realism supplanted its classical precursors by moving from the general to the specific, seeking scientifically testable hypotheses which necessarily consisted of precise statements. Neo-realism came to owe less to the philosophy of history than to the philosophy of science a lá Popper.[15] Recently, without the eminently modelable bipolar confrontation and with the increased questioning of scientific narratives in the social sciences, neo-realism has lost both explanatory power and appeal. In its precision, the theory lost flexibility. Classical realism, however, as a philosophy of history, is particularly suited for a renaissance.[16]

Neo-realism concentrated almost exclusively on the state, but classical realism can also address the nation. By viewing nations as natural and unique, realism admits of a large degree of particularism, and because of respect for state sovereignty, is even willing to tolerate a degree of relativism in the character of nation-states. It *has* to acknowledge difference, otherwise the claim to the uniqueness of a particular nation can hardly be made. Yet the particular is subordinated to the universal rules of state interaction.[17] Foreign policy functions here as the crew of the ship of state, helping the captain (presumably the Chancellor or Foreign Minister) maneuver through the caprice of the sea.

The role of navigator for foreign policy leads us to the third component, a sense of responsibility akin to Max Weber's "ethics of responsibility". Following Agnes Heller and Ferenc Fehér, Weber's ethics of responsibility underscores the amoral quality of politics:

> The highest, and at the same time the only, moral obligation of the politician is to find out the foreseeable consequences of his/her actions and to take re-

---

15 See Wœver, 1997. See also Mouritzen on Waltz in the same volume.
16 See Spegele, 1996, also Buzan, 1996.
17 See Walker, 1993.

sponsibility for them. ... Kantian morality has no place in politics where the realities of the world are frequently at odds with the politician's own beliefs; it thus is incumbent upon the politician to measure his/her actions according to the results they are likely to engender and to be prepared to meet the unintended consequences of any action.[18]

At the domestic level this approach may seem overly cynical (though it does express the tension between representative democracy and a marketplace of ideas). Substitute "state" for "politician," however, and we are dealing with the primary tenets of classical realism. Classical realism recognizes that politician's/state's own beliefs are often at odds with "realities of the world."

The ethics of responsibility, however, are not synonymous with *Realpolitik*, but rather an attempt to create an ethics out of power politics *in opposition to* an "ethic of ultimate ends...in which one would pursue the ultimate end of the 'redemption of mankind' and judge all means deemed necessary to attain this objective as equally legitimate."[19] Such messianistic universalism Weber regarded–and this was before Stalin's purges and National Socialism!–as devastatingly dangerous. Classic realist texts such as E.H. Carr echo this warning.

This fear is well placed, yet as Heller and Fehér point out, Weber eludes his own methodological rigor in positing an ethics of responsibility: The ethic of responsibility itself cannot, and is not supposed to, differentiate between "good" and "bad" consequences. Yet political decisions are to be made on the basis of the ethic. This poses a problem: "[t]aking responsibility for consequences presupposes a *prior* distinction between good and bad consequences and this can only happen on a basis *other* than that of the ethic of responsibility."[20] So the ethic of responsibility is a smoke and mirrors theory, looking to established political principles for normative content while claiming to be the rational force behind politics. This leads to an acceptance of the status quo, wherein resides the respective moral foundations of the "amoral" ethics of responsibility. And taking the status quo for granted leads to envisioning action in primarily negative terms by seeking merely to 'avoid' worst-case scenarios. "Responsibility for any positive outcome of the present world situation in accordance with the wills, needs and desires of nations and regions, is excluded by definition."[21]

The ethics of responsibility helps illuminate the ethos of responsibility in the normalist discourse. Responsibility here means acting in accordance with the forces of history, which are tied more to the fate (or 'objective situation')

---

18 Heller and Fehér, 1988: 61.
19 Ibid.: 62.
20 Ibid.: 63.
21 Ibid.: 66.

of the nation than to responsibility for the "wills, needs and desires" of individuals or communities at any given time. But moral guidelines for "good" and "bad" consequences do reside in the particular principles of the respective nation, and this leads us back to national identity. We find the rationalism of realist assumptions, including the ethic of responsibility, ironically premised on essentially romantic notions of national identity (see Chapter 2). Although oxymoronic, romantic rationalism is perhaps one way of characterizing the epistemological influences of normalism. We can turn to Max Weber again to capture this notion: "For what purpose is Germany unified if not to be a Great Power?"[22] This question, asked in 1895, fits seamlessly into the normalist discourse of 1995.

The normalist discourse resolves the contradictions of the condition we have termed "after history" by a double move. First, the nation becomes *re-historicized*; positive historical connections are re-emphasized in light of the negative nationalism of the Bonn Republic. The German nation is in a sense re-discovered, after decades of being obscured. This re-discovery involves re-learning how to think nationally after the trauma of the Third Reich. Second, the state becomes *dehistoricized*. Here the temporal aporia of being "after history" is resolved by removing the telos from history–by affirming the timelessness of classical realism. A "normal" state exemplifies both moves: it is premised on a firm national identity, and faces responsibilities concomitant with the objective, geopolitical criteria of a Great Power. This is "back to the future" in its least playful sense.

ASSESSING THE LIBERAL NARRATIVE

While the normalist discourse seeks to reestablish a telos of the nation in an incorrigible world of potential conflict, the liberal discourse embeds the nation in a cooperative international telos. As with the normalist discourse, despite variations there are three components which undergird the liberal approach. First, the liberal discourse adopts the insights of (neo)liberal institutionalism on interdependence–the capacity of states to pursue absolute gains rather than relative ones–and establishes thereon a theoretical basis for escaping from the security dilemma without jettisoning the format of an anarchical world of nation-states. Self-help in this system changes from a zero-sum to a positive-sum game. Most importantly for the German discourse, the liberal institutionalist escape from the security dilemma creates the space for the second component: the reintroduction of morality into international politics.

---

22 Cited by Claus Leggewie during a lecture at Cornell on February 22, 1996.

Arguably not all interpretations of liberal institutionalism need admit the relevance of moral concerns merely because absolute gains supplant relative gains in the state's drive for self-preservation. Yet the liberal logic is inherently normative because improving absolute gains necessitates more than a balancing interest in other state's affairs; it needs global economic prosperity to insure both peace (according to democratic peace theorists) and growth. Global economic prosperity requires conditions amicable for capital mobility, and this requires significant standardization of economic systems. The proverbial theoretical wisdom is that free-market economics and democracy are two sides of the same coin. If this is the case, the moral values inherent in the political principles of democracy are necessarily part of any foreign policy strategy of pursuing peace and prosperity through cooperation rather than alliance-based or autarkic balancing. This shift in thinking is highly visible, for example, in the Clinton Administration's reformulation of US foreign and security policy to focus more intently on economic and democratization issues than traditional military security.[23]

For German foreign policy liberals, a liberal institutionalist approach vindicates the orientation of the Bonn Republic while simultaneously allowing Germany to go beyond Bonn. The immorality of the national socialist legacy leaves a moral vacuum which (at least until 1989) normalism qua realism could not fill because neither the nation nor an amoral international system were acceptable responses to the legacy of national socialism. This helps explain the fundamentally neo-liberal character of the West German state as the model "trading state." In this context, European integration and the liberalization of international trade always had a moral component. And this moral component was always tied to the desirability of progress in international cooperation.

This concept of progress leads to the third component, which is essentially *Weltinnenpolitik*. Progress entails a telos, clearly described by the authors examined in chapter 4 as a global version of the relations currently visible in the OECD world (the societal world). The conundrum of being "after history" is neatly resolved by first positing a version of Hegel's end of history in one segment of the globe and, second, creating a temporal hierarchy wherein those parts of the world still in "history" or pre-history are interpreted as stages on the way to the end.

This is hardly a novel way of resolving the contradiction between universalism and particularism--colonialism, imperialism, Marxism, communism, and fascism have all made use of this resolution. Its lack of originality, however, hardly diminishes its narrative appeal. The tenacity of this resolution lies

---

23 See Bach, 1995.

in its exemplification of the modern approach to universalism and particularism: the *canceling* of the distinction by universalizing a particular. Previously the universal was literally incarnated in a segment of society, such as the church or the nobility. In the nineteenth century, however, European culture itself came to be seen as universal. As Ernesto Laclau writes:

> there were no intellectual means of distinguishing between European particularism and the universal functions that it was supposed to incarnate, given that European universalism had constructed its identity precisely through the cancellation of the logic of incarnation and, as a result, of the universalization of its own particularization. So, European imperialist expansion had to be presented in terms of a universal civilizing function, modernization, etc. The resistances of other cultures were, as a result, presented not as struggles between the particular identities and cultures, but as part of an all-embracing and epochal struggle between universality and particularisms–the notion of peoples without history expressing precisely their incapacity to represent the universal.[24]

Laclau notes that while a racist interpretation of this argument is easy, there is also a "progressive" version, "asserting that the civilizing mission of Europe would finish with the establishment of a universally freed society of planetary dimensions."[25] This progressive version most closely mirrors the liberal discourse. Liberals would doubtless be distressed that their call to "civilize" the world could even be construed as racist. That such an interpretation is possible, however, resides in the logic of the liberal resolution of universalism and particularism, which subordinates particularisms to their universal.

As Ashis Nandy attests, debates on core-periphery relations tend to "assume that the impact of political and economic inequality is skin-deep and short-term. Remove the inequality, they say in effect, and you will have healthy individuals and healthy societies all around." [26] Coming from the liberal teleology, however, this assumption entails, "paradoxically," the rejection of "the otherness of the latter [here the periphery] and 'accepting' them as earlier stages of the evolution of the self."[27] What results is the production of a "pecking order of cultures"[28] and a reduction of "all choice to those available within a single culture, the culture affiliated to the dominant global system."[29] This manifests itself in the proselytizing character, the "secular eschatology"

---

24 Laclau, 1996: 48-49.
25 Ibid.
26 Nandy, 1992: 25.
27 Ibid.: 12.
28 Ibid.: 14.
29 Ibid.: 25.

(Laclau[30]) of the German liberal discourse of "world domestic policy" and the societal world.

THE OUT-OF-AREA DEBATES: TOWARD SYNTHESIS?

More than the Gulf War, the war in Bosnia pushed Germany to define itself in post-Cold War Europe vis-à-vis its allies. In the political debates about deploying German troops we see a blurring of the distinctions between the normalist and liberal discourse. We saw in Chapter 6 how the prevailing discourse incorporated both normalist and liberal themes in its successful attempt to linguistically control the debates. Normalist conceptions of national pride and liberal conceptions of international responsibility combined to successfully include German troops in peacekeeping missions with potential combat situations, even in lands which the German army had occupied a half-century ago. Following nearly five decades where the German military's task was defined by self-defense (including defense of its NATO allies), this historic decision enjoyed broad-based support among purveyors of both discourses. Given the differences between the discourses, how was this support possible?

One reason is that the war in Bosnia simultaneously challenged and affirmed both discourses' assumptions. For the normalists the war was proof of the irascibility of human action, and the ever-present threat of ethnic war following the bipolar conflict. For liberals, the war confirmed the perils of nationalist thought and pointed to the need for better mechanisms of conflict prevention. Both discourses drew the conclusion that intervention was necessary, for it served the telos of each respective approach: for the normalists, intervention demonstrated Germany's will to act concomitant with its geopolitical power status. For liberals, intervention demonstrated Germany's commitment to perfecting strategies of peacekeeping and conflict management.

What is striking is how neither discourses' aims are mutually exclusive. The rationale and the emphasis differs—e.g. combat versus non-combat missions, intervention under NATO command versus UN or OSCE command—but the action taken is ultimately acceptable to both. Each discourse "wins," since by taking the all-important taboo-breaking step of deploying German combat troops to a peacekeeping mission in Europe the stage is set to focus on how to best configure future peacekeeping. German participation *per se* was never questioned, the contentious issue was always the manner—specifically the military extent—of participation. The German military is no longer forbidden territory for parliamentary discussion. Given this ground, it is likely that future policy will be able to satisfy both sides by agreeing simultaneously to the

---

30 Laclau, 1985: 54.

necessity of military preparation and increased conflict resolution mechanisms.[31]

We can speak, therefore, of a policy compact in which multilateral intervention in the form of peacekeeping forms an essential part of foreign policy. Several contentious issues are thereby "resolved." First, NATO remains the cornerstone of European security *and*, since European security is redefined as "security *for* Europe" (General Naumann), NATO becomes a legitimate institution for peacekeeping (rather than merely collective defense). While the OSCE has its supporters as an alternative security forum, NATO has become a fait accompli, and even critical voices such as the Hamburg Institute for Peace Research and Security Policy are (understandably) devoting attention to how to make the best of it.[32]

Secondly, the role of the military expands dramatically from, as a 1993 article in *Bundeswehr aktuell* (The Current Federal Army) describes it, "war-preventers to active peace-promotion (*Vom Kriegsverhinderer zum aktiven Friedensförderer*)."[33] As the discursive analysis in Chapter 6 demonstrated, a whole new vocabulary has replaced the military parlance of the past, so that, as Wolfram Wette, drawing on official Defense Ministry literature, writes:

> We Germans must assume "Co-responsibility for the safe-guarding of peace, humanity, and international security," must take part in "peace-protecting" (*friedensbewahrenden*), "peace-maintaining" (*friedenserhalten-den*), "peace-creating" (*friedenschaffenden*), "peace-causing" (*frie-densstiftenden*), and if necessary also in "peace-enforcing" (*friedenserzwin-genden*) missions. ... Military advertisements involve terms such as "humanity," "solidarity," "humanitarian assistance," and refer to a Bundeswehr "for peace and humanity in the world." [34]

Beyond the Orwellian overtones there is a deep irony in the recasting of the military in terms of peace: the normalist discourse complains bitterly about the distorted relationship which Germans have to the military as a result of their allegedly unhealthy obsession with the past. In recasting the military in

---

31 As I hope is obvious, the focus here is not on the particularities of the situation in Bosnia–and therefore not a judgement on intervention in Bosnia overall–but on the justifications for intervention internal to Germany.

32 See IFSH, 1997.

33 Quoted in Wette, 1994: 196.

34 Ibid.:196. The original reads: "Wir Deutschen müßten 'Mitverantwortung für die Wahrung von Frieden, Humanität, und internationaler Sicherheit" übernehmen, müßten uns beteiligen an 'friedensbewahrenden,' 'friedenserhaltenden,' 'friedenschaffenden,' 'friedensstiftenden,' notfalls auch 'friedenserzwingenden' Missionen. ... Weiter ging es in der Militärwerbung um Begriffe wie 'Menschlichkeit,' 'Solidarität,' 'humanitären Beistand,' und um eine Bundeswehr "für Frieden und Menschlichkeit in der Welt."'

concepts reminiscent of the peace movement, the military's image has been vastly improved, yet it is hardly a classical image of the military. To talk about the military in terms of peace is part of the 'normalization' process of German foreign and security policy, but it bears little resemblance to the military discourse in the "normal" models, i.e. the US, UK, and France. Talking comfortably about the German military still requires a special vocabulary to, in effect, de-militarize the military. This, however, might be a price normalists find worth paying.

This is very much in keeping with the liberal discourse's view of military power at the 'end of history'–an era of democratic peace: since democracies are structurally disinclined to fight each other, the only legitimate role for the military lies in its orientation toward the not-yet-societal world (what Singer and Wildavsky called "zones of turmoil" as compared with "zones of peace"). Here the military serves two roles: self-defense against potential threats (terrorism, refugee flows, drugs) and enforcement of peace and democratic principles (especially elections) in the turmoil zones.

The paradox of stopping violence with violence lamented by Joschka Fischer in the last chapter makes sense in this context. "War" has become a separate term from "military action." "War" is what happens in zones of turmoil, "military action" is the intervention of the societal world to stop or prevent wars. Logically, the vocabulary of "troops" or "attacks" can then give way to "crisis reaction forces" (*Krisenreaktionskräfte*) and "crisis management occurrences" (*Krisenbewältigungsfall*) without straining the imagination.[35] Disassociated from war, the military loses its synonymy with militarism, but retains, or regains, a prominent and positive role in society. In this sense the normalist desire for a "normal military" is achieved, albeit in a liberal framework. Rather than a point of conflict, this is point of synthesis, the common agreement on a positive recasting of the military. By accepting some limitations on anarchy moderate normalists can agree with liberals about the nature of the military, though they may disagree about when and where to use it.

Another reason why normalists may find the liberal recasting of the military acceptable is because it allows for another recasting–that of national interests. Unilateral state action remains an option of last resort, and even the "national normalists" concur that international institutions are an unavoidable part of national interest articulation. Once again we see the similarities upon which difference are built: participation in institutions is a source of common ground–the difference lies in whether these institutions are merely the expedient fora for coordinating national interests, or a step toward ultimately dis-

---

35 See Lütkehaus, 1994: 212-213.

solving national interest in supranational bodies. Although a serious disagreement, it still allows common fealty to international institutions. But it
also allows for the appropriation of the rhetoric particular to one discourse to
elide with the intentions of the other, so that 'national interest' and 'multilateralism' do not appear as contradictions.

The Making of a 'Multilateral' Historic Bloc?

A variation on understanding how normalism and liberalism compliment each
other as parts of the prevailing discourse is by viewing them as the expression
of an historic bloc in the Gramscian sense. At one level, normalism and liberalism compliment each other in the pursuit of class interests on a global scale.
Yet the concept of an hegemonic bloc is an analytical concept which goes
considerably beyond the instrumentally economic, because it expresses the
complex relationships through which hegemony is generated and sustained.
The concept of historic bloc, writes Mark Rupert,

> encompasses political, cultural, and economic aspects of a particular social
> formation, uniting these in historically specific ways to form a complex, po-
> litically contestable and dynamic ensemble of social relations. An historic
> bloc articulates a world view, grounded in historically specific socio-
> political conditions and production relations, which lends substance and
> ideological coherence to its social power. It follows then, that hegemonies
> and historic blocs have specific qualities relating to particular social con-
> stellations, their fundamental class forces, and productive relations. They
> can be dominantly bourgeois or proletarian, conservative or transforma-
> tive.[36]

The "multilateral" historic bloc is dominantly conservative in the traditional
liberal meaning of the term, forming global class alliances in the interest of
investment capital, in whose name globalization works to reduce barriers to
trade and production. In such a context, the foreign policy discourses, rather
than presenting truly different approaches to world order, act as "organic intellectuals" who use their common elements (outlined above) to, as Robert
Cox writes, "perform the function of developing and sustaining the mental

---

36 Rupert, 1995: 29-30. Walter Adamson describes historic blocs as having two
dimensions in parallel to hegemony: "Just as hegemony represents a highre stage withi the
political moment of the development of a class, so an historical bloc is in one sense an
effort to infuse this hegemony throughout society, above all by means of class alliances.
Once these horizontal linkages are achieved, an historical bloc, like hegemony-
maintenance, can be understood on a vertical dimenstion as a relatively stable "organic"
relationship between structure and superstructure, between the productive, economic life of
a society and its political and cultural awareness, between its being and its consciousness."
Adamson, 1980: 176.

images, technologies and organizations which bind together the members of a class and of an historic bloc into a common identity."[37]

The foreign policy intellectuals expand the internal hegemony of a dominant social class outward into a world hegemony. This world hegemony is both a desirable and necessary expansion of the dominant social class, for their dominance is based simultaneously on an economic system dependent on a core-periphery dynamic and an ideology of universalism. Modes of production and modes of representation work together to create a global civil society in which inter-state conflict is subordinated to the linking of social classes. This does not eliminate a role for inter-state conflict, but successfully regulates it such that military conflict is tailored to expedient circumstances for pursuing hegemonic interests, rather than unpredictably manifesting itself in untamed explosions of aggression.[38]

The mental images sustained by the discourses are of a state-world divided along a hierarchy of economic, political, cultural, and, ultimately, national maturity. Intelligence, economic, diplomatic and military technologies underscore the ability of mutually beneficial state interaction, while international organizations articulate the universal norms necessary for hegemony. International organizations, following Cox, simultaneously "1. embody the rules which facilitate the expansion of hegemonic world orders; 2. are themselves the product of the hegemonic world order; 3. ideologically legitimate the norms of the world order; 4. co-opt the elites from peripheral countries; and 5. absorb counter-hegemonic ideas."[39] In line with the liberal discourse, mere order among states is not the goal of foreign policy. One can logically view "world domestic policy" as a form of hegemony in the sense of "an order within a world economy with a dominant mode of production which penetrates into all countries and links into other subordinate modes of production. It is also a complex of international social relationships which connect the social classes of the different countries."[40]

From a critical international political economy perspective, then, the "new world order" is an adaptation of the "the endless accumulation of capital [as] the raison d'être and the central activity of capitalist civilization"[41] to conditions of unprecedented financial mobility. This mobility is enabled and encouraged through the gradual loosening of state control over tariffs and trade, the mercantilist hallmarks of sovereignty. Under the name of globalization

---

37 Cox, 1993: 57.
38 See Ibid.: 61.
39 Ibid.: 62.
40 Ibid.
41 Wallerstein, 1995: 142.

arises a hegemonic regime of accumulation, created and legitimated by a historic bloc. In this context, "world-domestic politics" is less a vision of global redemption than a cover for economic interests which remain, despite the creation of a global civil society, anchored in localized class-based interests. In Susanne Peter's critique these class-based interests do not transcend national interests, rather, they use the norm-legitimating structure of international organizations to further both class and national interests.

Peters warns that neo-liberal institutionalism can serve as a moral "mask" for expanding the regime of accumulation. In essence she argues that neo-liberal institutionalism creates an historic bloc in support of "Western" hegemony. Multilateralism is the catch-word which "can be a rhetorical deception used by Western elites to mobilize Western support for power politics."[42] The international organization most effective in legitimating hegemony is NATO, which "is particularly well-suited to securing the continued dominance of the developed world in the current phase of world capitalism."[43]

Citing NATO's expanded notion of security to include "the disruption of the flow of vital resources" Peters sees the application of realist "power politics" hidden under the peace rhetoric. Here is the point of synthesis: the normalist focus on military power as the primary force of international relations merges with the liberal concern for the maintenance of free markets. Since free trade tends to disproportionately benefit those economies which are already industrialized, there is an element of naked self-interest which belies the rhetoric of democratization and actually subordinates democracy to the interests of capital.[44] Building on a world-systems view where core-periphery relations logically preclude the establishment of a global "societal world" (the Czempielian telos), the need arises to stabilize a system of economic relations which structurally disadvantages the Third World. In a post-colonial, post-imperialist (and postmodern?) era a new sort of hegemony is necessary, and the role of the "multilateral" historic bloc is to infuse this hegemony horizontally through societies and, once infused, vertically through stabilization of relations.[45] In this context Peters sees wolves in sheep's clothing:

> The Western states' emphasis on the notion of the "threat from the South"
> as well as the Western public's concern for pacifying the various crises in
> the periphery by "humanitarian intervention" and "peacekeeping operations"
> serves as pretext to restructure their national and regional military forces
> into global power projection forces. ... [M]ilitary forces function as an in-
> strument of the core to prevent the periphery from taking action which

42 Peters, 1996: 161.
43 Ibid.
44 See Wood, 1995.
45 On the vertical and horizontal aspects of the historic bloc see Adamson, 1980.

would violate either the *economic* or the *hierarchical structure* of the world system.[46]

In the context of an historic bloc, discourses of normalism and liberalism reinforce each other's assumptions in the service of securing the economic core of the world system.

On one hand it is self-evident that the industrialized economies are beneficiaries of the current structure of world economy. On the other hand it seems cynical, if not verging on conspiracy, to accord too much intentionality to "Western elites" who appear so clever as to create entire schools of scholarly thought merely to divert attention from their carefully calculated exploitation.[47] Peters' criticisms are important not because she points out a hidden agenda, but precisely because the agenda is not hidden. The dynamics of core-periphery relations become normalized such that it seems unquestionable, for instance, that Europe faces a threat from the South and must shape its military accordingly.[48]

There are also non-economic reasons for using the historic bloc as an analytical concept, reasons which bring us back to linguistic analysis. The normalization of core-periphery relations which Peters' criticizes is not solely based upon class interests. As Roxanne Doty demonstrates, an historic bloc is not necessarily economically deterministic or essentialist, but can be thought of as a form of discourse with no monolithic foundation or issue-bound territory.[49] There are three major advantages to viewing an historic bloc as discourse: first, in moving away from economic determinism it allows the introduction of "identity" as a socio-psychological category in the construction of hegemony. With this we can view the constituent foreign policy discourses not as manichean tools of capital but as variations of the perpetuation function of narratives (see chapter 2). And in fulfilling their function of perpetuation they also struggle honestly with the ontological narrative quest of resolving contradictions–a return to this chapter's theme of the contradictory relation of universalism to particularism.

The second advantage is that as a discourse, an historic bloc resists closure. Historic blocs, writes Doty, are "never fully sutured or closed...like all discourses an historic bloc is inherently incomplete and partial."[50] This is both linguistically necessary (since language is inherently elastic) and politically

---

46 Peters, 1996: 183-4.

47 Lack of intentionality does not imply absolution, however.

48 Peters notes that "some German draftees have learned in their political education classes that their role as soldiers might be to prevent migrants from entering Germany." Peters, 1996: 181.

49 Doty 1993: 18.

50 Ibid.: 19.

desirable, because it allows for the possibility, if not inevitability, of change rather than total hegemony.[51] In addition, the third advantage is the ability to analyze historic blocs discursively, that is, by locating the nodal points which work to "fix" the flow of meaning and thereby normalize particular interpretations. Doty has examined the marginal points of national identity, particularly immigration, where key tensions in the dominant narrative are located. This study has focused on the fixing of nodal points in the center rather than on the margins, but in a center which, for historical reasons, had become decentered. The quasi-Gramscian approach sketched above allows a non-economically deterministic synthesis of normalism and liberalism based on the concept of a historic bloc as a form of discourse. Here the liberal and normalist discourses converge, though not merge, into a policy-oriented posture where German foreign policy-makers no longer view the military as forbidden territory.

Situating Germany in a Post-Wall Cartography

The first German unification in the 19th Century occurred while the concept of the nation-state was ascendant. During this century a tension between universalism and particularism manifested itself through the competing concepts of culture-state versus nation-state. Latest after 1871, when some form of modern German state became an inescapable reality, the controversy over German identity shifted its locus to the relation of the state to *das Volk*, the people. In foreign policy *Weltpolitik* and *Lebensraum* became the new forum for expressing the tension between the universal and the particular. These two concepts were reactions to the geopolitical trap, each ushering in competing interpretations of history and identity in their search to define "Germany." While conceptually different, *Weltpolitik* and *Lebensraum* were eventually more complimentary than the rhetoric of either side would indicate, enabling the tension between the universal and the particular to uneasily co-exist, at least until the 1930s.

The most recent unification of 1990 took place in an environment strongly influenced by the geopolitical trap, but no longer defined by it. With the possible exception of the self-proclaimed "intellectual right," normalists and liberals alike accept that Germany is part of the West. This new geopolitical situation, however, did not eliminate the unresolved tension between the universal and the particular, which has accompanied every incarnation of the German nation-state. As discussed earlier, this tension is both a function of

---

51 In this sense all hegemonic forces are, more technically, always "hegemony-seeking" rather than "hegemonic," since hegemony, as a mode of discursive dominance, always requires fixing flows of meaning.

the nation-state *as such*, and an outgrowth of the historical German dualism between rationality and culture. After fifty years in which foreign policy remained subordinate to the dictates of the Cold War, post-unification foreign policy has again become a site for addressing this tension.

The external context for German foreign policy, however, is no longer shaped by the question of Germany caught between East and West, but by the postmodern predicament sketched at the beginning of this chapter. If *Weltpolitik* and *Lebensraum* clashed over the proper role of Germany in an era when nation-states were paramount, the normalist and liberal narratives struggle over the meaning of Germany in an era when nation-states are undergoing a crisis of legitimacy. The normalist narrative confronts this predicament by reviving images of inside and outside within the comfortable confines of a realist worldview. While not (yet) anachronistic, the exigencies of globalization compels this position to look more closely at its state-centric assumptions in order to remain relevant without becoming reactionary.

The liberal narrative confronts the postmodern predicament of being "after history" by effecting a shift from a spatial concept of inside and outside to a temporal one. A balance of power between territorial sovereign states is no longer decisive or desirable, because the locus of sovereignty has shifted, according to Czempiel, from states to the people. All places—including formal states—who have not yet achieved a certain "civilized" level become potential areas for legitimate intervention by the international community. The traditional concept of sovereignty is not entirely delegitimated here, rather, it applies only to those states who meet the criteria of the civilized world.

This is a profoundly problematic approach, since it implies the need, if not the ability, to "civilize" the non-societal world. Yet it is a response to the very real dilemma of how to go beyond the spatial limits of sovereignty, especially given the new forms of cooperation augured by European integration. The *Bundestag* debates about using German troops in Bosnia showed a willingness among representatives of all parties to agree to the necessity, if not the method, of intervention. It is noteworthy that by the second of the two debates, the term out-of-area was no longer at the center of the discussion. This is because out-of-area relies on spatial understandings stemming from a Cold War cartography. A post-wall cartography is emerging that reflects more closely the liberal temporal shift in its view of international relations. With this shift arises a host of ethical and practical considerations which will test the boundaries of German foreign policy's vocabulary and vision.

Epilogue: From the Geopolitical Trap to Todorov's Paradox Revisited

Do the discourses of German foreign policy aid the construction of political identities which address rather than reify the paradoxes of postunification Germany in a "postmodern" Europe? They do wrestle honestly and earnestly with normative questions, but both get stuck trying to resolve the relationship of the universal to the particular. This relationship is, as Jacques Derrida reminds us in "The Other Heading," the philosophical crux of European identity. Echoing what Laclau said above about how modern Europe inscribes the universal in the particular, Derrida writes that "The self-affirmation of identity always claims to be responding to the call or assignation of the universal:

> National hegemony...claims to justify itself in the name of privilege in responsibility and in the memory of the universal and, thus, of the transnational–indeed of the trans-European–and, finally, of the transcendental or ontological. ... to put it quite dryly: 'I am (we are) all the more national for being European, all the more European for being trans-European and international; no one is more cosmopolitan and authentically universal than the one, than this 'we,' who is speaking to you.[1]

The problem that arises from this is the question of contact with others, unavoidable for any period, but especially so in an era of globalization. The encounter with others is fundamental to "foreign" policy. Foreign policy–in German literally "outside" policy (*Aussen*-politik)–ultimately reflects the projection of a nation-state's resolution of the contradiction between universalism and particularity, or inside and outside.

Germans are known for considering themselves the most "European" of Europe's people, that is to say, the least national. Paradoxically they are the least national precisely because they were the most national. The national is clearly the particular, but what is the universal? Europe? The OECD world? The whole world? The expression of the relation of the national to the universal (vaguely defined) remains the key difference between normalism and liberalism. Yet in their different responses they also show themselves as two sides of the same coin. Their respective expressions conform to the basic

---

1 Derrida, 1992: 72-73; 47-48.

paradox posed by Todorov: the understanding of difference manifests itself either by recognizing difference and translating it into superiority and inferiority, or denying difference and assimilating the other into the self.[2]

This "double movement" is the key to understanding the difficulties posed by either discourse for adequately defining the particular in relation to the universal. Normalism seeks to express national identity by emphasizing particularity, the metaphysical element of "Germanness" which enables participation in a world where success belongs to nation-states with strong national identities. But precisely here there is a strong strain of universalism: only by being more national can Germany be truly international–normalists take seriously the "national" aspect of inter-national relations. What is important is being strong enough (economically, politically, militarily if necessary) to prevail in interactions with other states. The liberal discourse expresses national identity by projecting national characteristics onto the world as a whole–other states are either equals or on their way to being equals (with Germany's help). Difference is summarily recognized, but also assimilated–in the world of world-domestic-politics all non-OECD states are on the way to becoming OECD states. Within the OECD there are obviously differences, but they are differences of degree, not of type. Both discourses present themselves as *saving* Western civilization (from itself and from others), both compare themselves to the United States during periods when isolationism questioned its global mission, and both see a special and indispensable role for Germany, the fulfillment of which will, in the words of President Weizsäcker, restore "lost normalcy."

These are less conscious positions than structural constraints of the respective discourses. As Todorov observes,

> The representatives of Western civilization no longer believe so naively in its superiority, and the movement of assimilation is running down in that quarter, even if the recent or ancient nations of the Third World still want to live like the Europeans. On the ideological level, at least, we are trying to combine what we regard as the better part of both terms of the alternative; we want *equality* without its compelling us to accept identity; but also difference without its degenerating into superiority/inferiority. We aspire to reap the benefits of the egalitarian model *and* of the hierarchic model; we aspire to rediscover the meaning of the social without losing the quality of the individual.[3]

---

2 See Todorov, 1987: 42.

The adherents of both discourses would doubtless agree vigorously with this sentiment. But to experience difference in equality, as Todorov points out, is particularly difficult because we find it hard to conceive of the other in any other way than either as essentially different, and hence either superior or inferior, or essentially the same, and hence "an imperfect state of oneself."[4] The two discourses presented here remain caught in this double movement, perhaps in spite of themselves, and as a result recreate rhetoric evocative of earlier instantiations of German foreign policy and identity—specifically the struggle between *Weltpolitik* and *Lebensraum*. Such a comparison is both prohibited by necessity and necessary because of its prohibition. The raising of these discredited specters from the past is not to imply some form of hidden agenda or complicity, but rather to highlight the difficulties of resolving contradictions in ways which transcend rather than reify the aporia presented by Todorov.

That neither the normalist or liberal discourses do so successfully is not a condemnation of their purveyors–a personal decision to intervene in Bosnia had many estimable aspects, not all of which centered around the considerations of Germany. Furthermore, the necessarily open-ended structure of discourses (see chapter 2) leaves space for exploring this aporia: the normalists nominally recognize difference, the liberals nominally recognize the interrelated basis of existence. Given the institutionalized framework for pursuing self-interest the difference between the two discourses is more a matter of degree than fundamental disagreement. Both discourses try to resolve the contradictions of inside/outside by exporting the inside to the outside. Yet this form of resolution is ultimately unsatisfactory, not only because of philosophical reasons, but because of the process noted by critics of globalization: Exporting the inside to the outside in an era when the "inside" is increasingly diverse results in strengthening the very distinctions *within* societies which used to run *between* societies. This risks becoming counterproductive when the discourses which delimit and perpetuate the master narratives implicitly support world-views which see through a lens of–to oversimplify–friend/enemy, or adult/child.

As Michael Naas writes of Derrida, perhaps surprisingly for those allergic to the often incomprehensible deconstructionist, he "argues for the necessity of working within and from the Enlightenment values of liberal democracy while at the same time recalling that these values are never enough to ensure respect for the other." A European identity is sought which "includes respect

---

3 Ibid.: 249.
4 Ibid.: 42.

for *both* universal values *and* difference–since one without the other will simply repeat without submitting to critique the politics of the example." The task is for an identity to be responsible not just to itself, or to the other, but to "itself as other."[5] But, as Derrida presumably would be among the first to admit, respect for universal values and difference is a real aporia–not least because identity is premised on the tension between unique belonging and universal belonging.

Accordingly, it would be glib and haughty to blame the foreign policy discourses for "failing" to correctly balance the universal and the particular, and thereby "free" German identity from its torturous confrontation with contradiction. Blame is not the issue here at all. I have tried to detail how these discourses, while nominally articulating national interests, seek to resolve contradictions yet perpetuate existing, if unsettled, narratives of identity. That they run up against the paradox of Todorov's double movement provides cause for reflection. The ensuing ambiguity behind the seemingly-straightforward *Bundestag* debates on sending German troops abroad underscores the possibilities and pitfalls in the re-establishment of post-unification narrative coherence.

---

5 Nass in Derrida, 1992: xlvi, xlvii. Emphasis in the original.

References

1986. Sinnstiftung oder Apologetik? Eine Dokumentation mit Kommentar. Heidelberg: Fachschaft Geschichte.

1987. *"Historikerstreit"*. Edited by S. Piper. Original ed, *Aktuell*. Munich: Piper.

1995. Außenpolitik der Bundesrepublik Deutschland: Dokumente 1949-1994. Cologne: Verlag für Wissenschaft und Politik.

Adamson, Walter L. 1980. *Hegemony and Revolution: A Study of Antonio Gramsci's Political and Cultural Theory*. Berkeley: University of California Press.

Agnew, John A. 1994a. The Territorial Trap: The Geographical Assumptions of International Relations Theory. *Review of International Political Economy* 1 (1): 53-80.

—. 1994b. Timeless Space and State-Centrism: The Geographical Assumptions of International Relations Theory. In *The Global Economy as Political Space*, edited by S. J. Rosow, N. Inayatullah and M. Rupert. Boulder: Lynne Rienner.

Agnew, John, and Stuart Corbridge. 1995. *Mastering Space: Hegemony, Territory and International Political Economy*. New York: Routledge.

Albert, Mathias. 1994a. "Postmoderne" und Theorie der internationalen Beziehungen. *Zeitschrift für Internationale Beziehungen* 1 (1): 45-63.

—. 1994b. The Status of Ethics in Postmodern IR Theory: Traces of a Pure Performativity. *Paradigms. Journal of International Relations* 8 (1): 87-105.

Alcoff, Linda Martín. 1996. *Real Knowing: New Versions of the Coherence Theory*. Ithaca: Cornell University Press.

Ash, Timothy Garten. 1993. *In Europe's Name. Germany and the Divided Continent*. New York: Random House.

Ashley, Richard K. 1989. Living on Borderlines: Man, Poststructuralism, and War. In *International/Intertextual Relations*, edited by James Der Derian and Michael Shapiro. New York: Lexington Books.

Asmus, Ronald D. 1992. *Germany in Transition: National Self-Confidence and International Reticence*. Santa Monica: RAND Corporation.

——. 1994. *German Strategy and Public Opinion After the Wall 1990-1993*. Santa Monica: RAND.

Austin, J.L. 1975. *How to Do Things with Words*. Cambridge, MA: Harvard University Press.

Bach, Jonathan P.G. 1994a. Narrative and Political/Social Science: A New Direction for Interdisciplinary Research. *Maxwell Review* II (1): 1-7.

——. 1994b. German Foreign Policy, Neoliberalism, and the Search for the Normal State. Paper presented at the German Studies Association Annual Meeting, October, 1994, at Dallas,TX.

——. 1995. *The Partnership and the Pendulum: The Foreign Policy Debate in the United States and Implications for European Security*. Hamburg: Institue for Peace Research and Security Policy.

——. 1996. Forward into the Past? German Foreign Policy and Eastern Europe. *Maxwell Review* IV (1): 1-7.

Baldwin, James. 1963. *The Fire Next Time*. New York: Dell Publishing.

Banerjee, Sanjoy. 1996. Constructivism in International Studies: Cognitive Science, Interaction, and Narrative Structure. Paper read at InternationalStudies Association, April 16-20, at San Diego, California.

Baring, Arnulf. 1994. Germany, What Now? In *Germany's New Position in Europe*, edited by A. Baring. Oxford: Berg.

Bartelson, Jens. 1995. *A Genealogy of Sovereignty*. New York: Cambridge University Press.

Barthes, Roland. 1986. *The Rustle of Language*. Translated by Richard Howard. New York: Hill and Wang.

Baun, Michael J. 1996. *An Imperfect Union: The Maastricht Treaty and the New Politics of European Integration*. Boulder: Westview Press.

Benoit, Kenneth. 1996. Democracies Really Are More Pacific (in General). *Journal of Conflict Resolution* 40:636-657.

Berman, Morris. 1981. *The Reenchantment of the World*. Ithaca: Cornell University Press.

Biersteker, Thomas J., and Cynthia Weber, eds. 1996. *State Sovereignty as Social Construct*. Cambridge: Cambridge University Press.

Bonham, Matthew G., and Michael J. Shapiro. 1994. Representing Discourses of Nationalism. Paper read at International Studies Association 35th Annual Convention, 1 April, at Washington, D.C.

Booz, Rüdiger Marco. 1995. *"Hallsteinzeit:" deutsche Aussenpolitik 1955-1972*. Bonn: Bouvier Verlag.

Boroujerdi, Mehrzad. 1996. *Iranian Intellectuals and the West: The Tormented Triumph of Nativism*. Syracuse, NY: Syracuse University Press.

Bracher, Karl Dietrich, ed. 1982. *Deutscher Sonderweg–Mythos oder Realität?* Munich.

Brockmann, Stephen. 1996. German Culture at the "Zero Hour". In *Revisiting Zero Hour 1945: The Emergence of Postwar Culture*, edited by S. Brockmann. Washington, D.C.: AICGS.

Bulmer, Simon, and William E. Patterson. 1996. Germany in the European Union: gentle giant or emergent leader? *International Affairs* 72 (1): 9-32.

Buruma, Ian. 1994. *The Wages of Guilt: Memories of War In Germany and Japan*. New York: Farrar, Straus and Giroux.

Buzan, Barry. 1996. The timeless wisdom of realism? In *International Theory: Positivism and Beyond*, edited by S. Smith et. al. Cambridge: Cambridge University Press.

Campbell, David. 1992. *Writing Security: United States Foreign Policy and the Politics of Identity*. Minneapolis: University of Minnesota Press.

Carr, David. 1986. *Time, Narrative, and History*. Bloomington, Indianapolis: Indiana University Press.

Carr, E.H. 1964/1939. *The Twenty Years Crisis*. New York: Harper and Row.

Cassirer, Ernst. 1979. *Symbol, Myth, and Culture*. New Haven: Yale University Press.

Chan, Steve. 1997. In Search of Democratic Peace: Problems and Promise. *Mershon International Studies Review* 41 (1): 59-91.

Clifton, Morgan T. 1993. Democracy and War: Reflections on the Literature. *International Interactions* (18): 197-203.

Connolly, William E. 1989. Identity and Difference in Global Politics. In *International/Intertextual Relations: Postmodern Readings of World*

Politics, edited by J. Der Derian and M. Shapiro. Lexington: Lexington Books.

——. 1991. *Identity\Difference: Democratic Negotiations of Political Paradox.* Ithaca: Cornell University Press.

Cooper, Alice Holmes. 1996. *Paradoxes of Peace: German Peace Movements Since 1945.* Ann Arbor: University of Michigan Press.

Coste, Didier. 1989. *Narrative and Communication.* Minneapolis: University of Minneapolis Press.

Cox, Robert W. 1993. Gramsci, Hegemony, and International Relations: An Essay in Method. In *Gramsci, Historical Materialism and International Relations*, edited by S. Gill. Cambridge: Cambridge University Press.

Czempiel, Ernst-Otto. 1987. Gewaltfreie Intervention zugunsten von Demokratisierungsprozessen. In *Internationale Politik und der Wandel von Regimen*, edited by G. Schwan. Cologne.

——. 1993. *Weltpolitik im Umbruch: Das internationale System nach dem Ende des Ost-West-Konfliktes.* Second Revised Edition Munich: Beck'sche Reihe.

——. 1994. Vergesellschaftete Aussenpolitik. *Merkur* 48 (1): 1-15.

——. 1996a. The Political Necessity and Feasibility of Interventions. In *The Changing European Security Environment*, edited by C. Lotter. and S. Peters. Cologne: Böhlau Verlag.

——. 1996b. The Use of Force in the Post-modern World. In *The Changing European Security Environment*, edited by C. Lotter. and S. Peters. Cologne: Böhlau Verlag.

Dann, Otto. 1994. *Nation und Nationalismus in Deutschland: 1770-1990.* Munich: Beck'sche Reihe.

Danto, Arthur C. 1985. *Narration and Knowledge.* New York: Columbia University Press.

Deleuze, Gilles, and Félix Guattari. 1977. *Anti-Oedipus: Capitalism and Schizophrenia.* Translated by Robert Hurley, Mark Seem and Helen R. Lane. New York: Viking Press.

Derrida, Jacques. 1976. *Of Grammatology.* Translated by G.C. Spivak. Baltimore: Johns Hopkins University Press.

——. 1992. *The Other Heading*. Translated by Pascale-Anne Brault and Michael B. Naas. Bloomington: Indiana University Press.

Dijkink, Gertjan. 1996. *National Identity and Geopolitical Visions: Maps of Pride and Pain*. New York: Routledge.

Diner, Dan. 1995. Wird die Bundesrepublik ein westliches Land? Vom Umgang mit deutschen Zäsuren und Kontinuen. Ein "Blätter"-Gespräch mit Dan Diner. *Blätter für deutsche und internationale Politik* (5): 545-553.

Doty, Roxanne Lynn. 1993a. Foreign Policy as Social Construction: A Post-Postivist Analysis of U.S. Counterinsurgency Policy in the Philippines. *International Studies Quarterly* 37 (3): 297-320.

——. 1993b. Sovereignty and National Identity: Constructing the Nation.

——. 1996a. *Imperial Encounters*. Minneapolis: University of Minnesota Press.

——. 1996b. Sovereignty and the Nation: Construction the Boundaries of National Identity. In *State Sovereignty as Social Construct*, edited by T. J. Biersteker. and C. Weber. New York: Cambridge University Press.

Doyle, Michael. 1983. Kant, Liberal Legacies, and Foreign Affairs. *Philosophy and Public Affairs* 12 (3-4).

Ehrhart, Hans-Georg. 1996. Germany. In *Challenges for the New Peacekeepers*, edited by SIPRI. Stockholm: Stockholm Peace Research Institute.

Eisenstadt, Shmuel Noah. 1991. Die Konstruktion nationaler Identität in vergleichender Perpektive. In *Nationale und kulturelle Identität*, edited by B. Giesen. Frankfurt a.M.: Suhrkamp.

Ely, John. 1995. The Frankfurter Allgemeine Zeitung and Contemporary National Conservatism. *German Politics and Society* 13 (2).

Ferguson, Kennan. 1996. Unmapping and Remapping the World: Foreign Policy as Aesthetic Practice. In *Challenging Boundaries*, edited by M. J. Shapiro. and H. R. Alker. Minneapolis: University of Minnesota Press.

Fest, Joachim. 1994. Europe in a Cul-de-Sac. In *Germany's New Position in Europe*, edited by A. Baring. Oxford: Berg Publishers.

Feyerabend, Paul K. 1993. *Against Method*. Third Edition ed. New York: Verso.

Fischer, Fritz. 1986. *From Kaiserreich to Third Reich: Elements of Continuity in German History, 1871-1945.* Translated by Roger Fletcher. Boston: Allen & Unwin.

Foucault, Michel. 1970. *The Order of Things.* New York: Vintage Books.

——. 1981. *Power/Knowledge: Selected Interviews and Other Writings.* New York: Random House.

——. 1994. The Order of Discourse. In *Language and Politics,* edited by M. J. Shapiro. New York: New York University Press.

Fraenkel, Ernst. 1991. *Deutschland und die westlichen Demokratien.* Frankfurt a.M.: Suhrkamp.

Frederking, Brian. 1992. The Power Politics of Poststructuralism. Masters Thesis, International Relations Program, Syracuse University, Syracuse.

George, Jim. 1994. *Discourses of Global Politics: A Critical (Re)Introduction to International Relations.* Boulder: Lynne Rienner Publishers.

Giesen, Bernhard, ed. 1991. *Nationale und kulturelle Identität.* Frankfurt a.M.: Suhrkamp.

——. 1993. *Die Intellektuellen und die Nation.* Frankfurt a.M.: Suhrkamp.

Giesen, Bernhard, and Kay Junge. 1991. Vom Patriotismus zum Nationalismus. Zur Evolution der "Deutschen Kulturnation." In *Nationale und kulturelle Identität,* edited by B. Giesen. Frankfurt a.M.: Suhrkamp.

Gill, Stephen, ed. 1993. *Gramsci, Historical Materialism, and International Relations.* Cambridge: Cambridge University Press.

Gill, Stephen, and David Law. 1988. *The Global Political Economy.* New York: Harvester.

Gillessen, Günther. 1994. Germany's Position in the Centre of Europe: The Significance if Germany's Position and Misunderstandings about German Interests. In *Germany's New Position in Europe,* edited by A. Baring. Oxford: Berg Publishers.

Gilpin, Robert. 1987. *The Political Economy of International Relations.* Princeton: Princteon University Press.

Glotz, Peter. 1994. *Die falsche Normalisierung.* Frankfurt a.M.: Suhrkamp Verlag.

Goethe, Johann Wolfgang. 1986. *Gedichte.* Berlin and Weimar: Aufbau Verlag.

Goldberg, David Theo. 1993. *Racist Culture: Philosophy and the Politics of Meaning.* Oxford: Blackwell.

Goldhagen, Daniel J. 1996. *Hitler's Willing Executioners: Ordinary Germans and the Holocaust.* New York: Alfred A. Knopf.

Görtemaker, Manfred. 1994. *Unifying Germany 1989-1990.* New York: St. Martin's Press.

Gowan, Peter. 1994. The Return of Carl Schmitt. *Debatte: Review of Contemporary German Affairs* 2 (1): 82-127.

Gramsci, Antonio. 1985. *Selections from the Prison Notebooks.* Translated by Quinton Hoare and Geoffery Nowell Smith. New York: International Publishers.

Grass, Günter. 1990. *Schreiben nach Auschwitz: Frankfurter Poetik-Vorlesung.* Frankfurt a.M.: Luchterhand.

Grebing, H., ed. 1986. *Der 'deutsche Sonderweg' in Europa 1806-1945. Eine Kritik.* Stuttgart.

Greenfeld, Liah. 1992. *Nationalism. Five Roads to Modernity.* Cambridge, MA: Harvard University Press.

Griffith, William E. 1978. *The Ostpolitik of the Federal Republic of Germany.* Cambridge, MA.: MIT Press.

Gruner, Wolf D. 1993. *Die deutsche Frage in Europa 1800 bis 1990.* Munich: Piper.

Günther, Horst. 1990. *Versuche, europäisch zu denken. Deutschland und Frankreich.* Frankfurt a.M.: Suhrkamp.

Gutsche, Willibald. 1972. Mitteleuropaplanungen in der Assenpolitik des deutschen Imperialismus vor 1918 (Central European Planing in German Imperialist Foreign Policy before 1918). *Zeitschrift für Geschichtswissenschaft* XX:533-49.

Haber, Honi Fern. 1994. *Beyond Postmodern Politics.* New York: Routledge.

Haberl, O.N., ed. 1989. *Unfertige Nachbarschaften.* Essen: Reimar Hobbing.

Habermas, Jürgen. 1989. *The New Conservatism. Cultural Criticism and the Historian's Debate.* Cambridge, MA: MIT Press.

—. 1992a. *Autonomy and Solidarity: Interviews with Jürgen Habermas*, edited by Peter Dews. New York: Verso.

—. 1992b. Citizenship and National Identity: Some Reflections on the Future of Europe. *Praxis International* 12 (1).

—. 1995. *Die Normalität einer Berliner Republik*. Frankfurt a.M.: Suhrkamp Verlag.

Hacke, Christian. 1993. *Weltmacht wider Willen: Die Aussenpolitik der Bundesrepublik Deutschland*. Revised and Updated Edition ed. Berlin: Ullstein.

Hacker, Jens. 1995. *Integration und Verantwortung: Deutschland als europäischer Sicherheitspartner*. Bonn: Bouvier Verlag – Kulturstiftung der deutschen Vertriebenen.

Hahn, Hans-Werner. 1984. *Geschichte des Zollvereins*. Göttingen: Kleine Vandenhoeck Reihe.

Hartmann, Geoffrey, ed. 1986. *Bitburg in Moral and Political Perspective*. Bloomington: Indiana University Press.

Hartwich, H.H., ed. 1989. *Macht und Ohnmacht politischer Institutionen*: Opladen.

Hedetoft, Ulf. 1994. The State of Sovereignty in Europe: Political Concept or Cultural Self-Image. In *National Cultures and European Integration*, edited by S. Zetterholm. Oxford: Berg.

—. 1995. *Studies in the Political Semiotics of Self and Other in Contemporary European Nationalism*. Dartmouth: Dartmouth Publishing Co.

Heidelberger-Leonhard, Irene. 1991. Der Literaturstreit--ein Historikerstreit im gesamtdeutschen Kostüm? In *Der deutsch-deutsche Literaturstreit oder "Freunde, es spricht sich schlecht mit gebundener Zunge."* Edited by K. Deiritz. and H. Kraus. Hamburg: Luchterhand.

Heinrich, Arthur. 1995. Unternehmen Tornado: Unvollständige Chronologie einer außenpolitischen Grundsatzentscheidung. *Blätter für deutsche und internationale Politik* (2): 144-155.

Heller, Agnes, and Ferenc Fehér. 1988. *The Postmodern Political Condition*. New York: Columbia University Press.

Helman, Gerald B., and Steven R. Ratner. 1992. Saving Failed States. *Foreign Policy* 89 (Winter): 3-20.

Henningsen, Manfred. 1995. Der deutsche Sonderweg am Ende? *Merkur* 49 (5).

Herzog, Roman. 1995. Globalisierung der deutschen Außenpolitik. Bonn: Deutsche Gesellschaft für Auswärtige Politik.

Hess, Jürgen. 1986. Westdeutsche Suche nach nationaler Identität. In *Die deutsche Frage in der Weltpolitik*, edited by W. Michalka. Stuttgart.

Himmelfarb, Gertrude. 1994. *On Looking into the Abyss: Untimely Thoughts on Culture and Society*. New York: Knopf.

Hinsley, F.H. 1986. *Sovereignty*. Second Edition, Cambridge: Cambridge University Press.

Hirst, Paul, and Grahame Thompson. 1996. *Globalization in Question*. Cambridge: Polity Press/Blackwell Publishers.

Hobsbawm, E.J. 1962. *The Age of Revolution 1789-1848*. New York: Mentor/New American Library.

Hoffmann, Lutz. 1994. *Das deutsche Volk und seine Feinde: die völkische Droge*. Cologne: PapyRossa Verlag.

Huntington, Samuel P. 1991. *The Third Wave: Democratization in the Late Twentieth Century*. Norman: University of Oklahoma Press.

IFSH. 1997. Security in an Undivided Europe: Using NATO's Eastward Expansion as an Opportunity. Hamburg: Institute for Peace Research and Security Policy.

Inayatullah, Naeem. 1996. Beyond the soveriegnty dilemma: quasi-states as social construct. In *State Sovereignty as Social Construct*, edited by T. J. Bierstecker and C. Weber. Cambridge: Cambridge University Press.

Inayatullah, Naeem, and David L. Blaney. 1996. Knowing Encounters: Beyond Parochialism in International Relations Theory. In *The Return of Culture and Identity in IR Theory*, edited by Y. Lapid and F. Kratochwil. Boulder: Lynne Rienner.

Jacobsen, Hans-Adolf. 1979. *Karl Haushofer: Leben und Werk*. 2 vols. Boppard: Boldt.

James, Harold and M. Stone, eds. 1992. *When the Wall Came Down: Reactions to German Unification*. New York: Routledge.

Jameson, Frederic. 1981. *The Political Unconscious.* Ithaca: Cornell University Press.

——. 1984. Postmodernism, or the Cultural Logic of Late Capitalism. *New Left Review* (146): 116-22.

Jarausch, Konrad H. 1988. Removing the Nazi Stain? The Quarrel of the German Historians. *German Studies Review* 11.

Joffe, Josef. 1995. Deutsche Aussenpolitik--postmodern. *Internationale Politik* 1 (1995): 43-45.

Keane, John, ed. 1988. *Civil Society and the State.* New York: Verso Press.

Kennedy, Paul M. 1993. *Preparing for the Twenty-First Century.* New York: Random House.

Keohane, Robert O., and Joseph Nye. 1977. *Power and Interdependence.* Boston: Little Brown.

Kepnes, Steven. 1992. *The Text as Thou: Martin Buber's Dialogical Hermeneutics and Narrative Theology.* Bloomington, IN: Indiana University Press.

Kerby, Anthony Paul. 1991. *Narrative and the Self.* Bloomington: University of Indiana Press.

Kermode, Frank. 1967. *The Sense of an Ending.* New York: Oxford University Press.

Klessmann, Christoph. 1986. *Die doppelte Staatsgründung. Deutsche Geschichte 1945-1955.* Bonn: Bundeszentrale für politische Bildung.

Kögler, Hans Herbert. 1996. *The Power of Dialogue: Critical Hermeneutics After Gadamer and Foucault.* Translated by Paul Hendrickson. Cambridge, MA: MIT Press.

Kohler-Koch, B., ed. 1989. *Regime in den internationalen Beziehungen.* Baden-Baden.

Kohn, Hans. 1949a. Arndt and the Character of German Nationalism. *American Historical Review* LIV:787-803.

——. 1949b. The Paradox of Fichte's Nationalism. *Journal of the History of Ideas* X:319-43.

——, ed. 1965. *Nationalism: It's Meaning and History.* Malabar, FL: Krieger.

Krishna, Sankaran. n.d. *Producing Sri Lanka from Ceylon: J.R. Jayewardene and Sinhala Identity.*

Kuhn, Thomas S. 1970 [1962]. *The Structure of Scientific Revolutions.* Second Edition, Chicago: The University of Chicago Press.

Kühnl, Reinhard. 1987. *Streit um Geschichtsbild: Die "Historiker-Debatte".* Cologne: Puhl & Rugenstein.

—. 1997. The German Sonderweg Reconsidered: Continuities and Discontinuities in Modern German History. In *Rewriting the German Past,* edited by P. Monteath and R. Alter. Atlantic Highlands, N.J.: Humanities Press.

Laclau, Ernesto. 1995. The Question of Identity. In *Identity Question,* edited by J. Rajchman. New York: Routledge.

Laclau, Ernesto, and Chantal Mouffe. 1985. *Hegemony and Socialist Strategy: Towards a Radical Democratic Politics.* New York: Verso.

Lakatos, Imre, and Alan Musgrave, eds. 1970. *Criticism and the Growth of Knowledge.*

Langer, William L. 1971. *The Revolutions of 1848.* New York: Harper & Row.

Lau, Jörg. 1994. Ansichten zur Außenpolitik. *Merkur* 48 (9/10): 910-921.

Lebow, Richard Ned. 1994. The Long Peace, the End of the Cold War, and the Failure of Realism. *International Organization* 48 (Spring): 249-77.

Lemke, Michael. 1992. "Doppelte Alleinvertretung." Die nationalen Wiedervereinigungskonzepte der beiden deutschen Regierungen. *Zeitschrift für Geschichtswissenschaft* (6): 531-543.

Lilla, Mark. 1997. The Enemy of Liberalism. *The New York Review* XLIV (8): 38-44.

Linz, Juan, J. and Alfred Stepan. 1996. *Problems of Democratic Transition and Consolidation: Southern Europe, South America, and Post-Communist Europe.* Baltimore: Johns Hopkins University Press.

List, Friedrich. 1966. *The National System of Political Economy.* New York: A.M. Kelley.

Llobera, Josep R. 1994. *The God of Modernity: The Development of Nationalism in Western Europe.* Oxford: Berg.

Lohmann, Hans-Martin, ed. 1994. *Extremismus der Mitte*. Frankfurt a.M.: Fischer Verlag.

Luhmann, Niklas. 1993. *Risk: A Sociological Theory (Communication and Social Order)*. Translated by Rhodes Barrett. New York: Aldine DeGruyter.

Lukes, Stephen, ed. 1986. *Power*. New York: New York University Press.

Lütkehaus, Ludger. 1994. Deutschland soll endlich wieder Frieden schaffen dürfen. In *Extremismus der Mitte*, edited by H.-M. Lohmann. Frankfurt a.M.: Fischer Verlag.

Lutz, Dieter S. 1993. Endzeit: Alptraum oder Wirklichkeit? *Hamburger Informationen zur Friedensforschung und Sicherheitspolitik* (13): 1-11.

Lyotard, Jean-François. 1989. *The Postmodern Condition: A Report on Knowledge*. Minneapolis: University of Minneapolis Press.

Macdonell, Diane. 1986. *Theories of Discourse*. New York: Basil Blackwell.

Markovits, Andrei S., and Simon Reich. 1993. Should Europe Fear the Germans? In *From Bundesrepublik to Deutschland*, edited by M. G. Huelshof et. al., Ann Arbor: University of Michigan Press.

Markovitz, Andrei, and Simon Reich. 1997. *The German Predicament: Memory and Power in the New Europe*. Ithaca: Cornell University Press.

Mathiopoulos, Margarita. 1995. *Das Ende der Bonner Republik*. Düsseldorf: Econ.

Mayer, Peter et. al. 1993. Regime Theory: State of the Art and Perspectives. In *Regime Theory and International Relations*, edited by V. Rittberger and P. Mayer. Oxford: Oxford University Press.

Mayer-Iswandy, Claudia. 1996. Ästhetik und Macht. Zur diskursiven Unordnung im vereinten Deutschland. *German Studies Review* XIX (3): 501-524.

McCarthy, Thomas. 1995. *Ideals and Illusions: On Reconstruction and Deconstruction in Contemporary Critical Theory*. Cambridge, MA: MIT Press.

McKenzie, Mary. 1996. Competing Conceptions of Normality in the Post-Cold War Era: Germany, Europe, and Foreign Policy Change. *German Politics and Society* 14 (2).

Merkl, Peter H. 1992. A New German Identity. In *Developments in German Politics*, edited by G. Smith et. al., Durham: Duke University Press.

——. (With a Contribution by Gert-Joachim Glaessner). 1993. *German Unification in the European Context*. University Park: The Pennsylvania State University Press.

——, ed. 1995. *The Federal Republic at Forty-Five: Union without Unity*. New York: New York University Press.

Mommsen, Wolfgang J. 1993. *Grossmachtstellung und Weltpolitik*. Berlin: Ullstein Propyläen.

Morgenthau, Hans J. 1954. *Politics among Nations: The Struggle for Power and Peace*. Second Edition. New York: Alfred A. Knopf.

Moses, John A. 1975. *The Politics of Illusion: The Fischer Controversy in German Historiography*. London.

Mosse, George L. 1988. *The Culture of Western Europe*. Boulder, CO: Westview.

Müller, Erwin. 1995. "Weltinnenpolitik–mehr als ein Wort? *Sicherheit und Frieden* 13 (1): 7-13.

Müller, Johann Baptist, ed. 1993. *Deutschland: eine westliche Nation. Konzeptionen und Kontroversen*. Goldbach: Keip Verlag.

Murchadha, Felix ó. 1992. Truth as a Problem for Hermeneutics. *Philosophy Today* (Summer).

Nairn, Tom. 1975. The Modern Janus. *The New Left Review* (94).

Nandy, Ashis. 1983. *The Intimate Enemy*. Dehli: Oxford University Press.

——. 1992. *Traditions, Tyranny, and Utopias*. Dehli: Oxford University Press.

Naumann, Klaus. 1994. "Neuanfang ohne Tabus" Deutscher Sonderweg und politische Semantik. *Blätter für deutsche und internationale Politik* (4): 435-447.

Nelson, Brian, David Roberts, and Walter Veit, eds. 1992. *The Idea of Europe: Problems of National and Transnational Identity*. Oxford: Berg Publishers.

Neocleous, Mark. 1996. Friend or Enemy? Reading Schmitt Politically. *Radical Philosophy* (79): 13-23.

Niethammer, Lutz. 1997. The German Sonderweg After Unification. In *Rewriting the German Past*, edited by P. Monteath and R. Alter, New Jersey: Humanities Press.

Norton, Donald, H. 1968. Karl Haushofer and the German Academy 1925-1945. *Central European History* (I): 80-99.

Onuf, Nicholas Greenwood. 1989. *World of Our Making: Rules and Rule in Social Theory and International Relations*. Columbia, South Carolina: The University of South Carolina Press.

Ormiston, Gayle L., and Raphael Sassower. 1989. *Narrative Experiments. The Discursive Authority of Science and Technology*. Minneapolis: University of Minneapolis Press.

Pampel, Bert. 1995. Was bedeutet "Aufarbeitung der Vergangenheit"? *Aus Politik und Zeitgeschichte* (1-2): 27-38.

Peters, Susanne. 1996. Multilateralism: A Mask for the Militarization of Western European Security? In *The Changing European Security Environment*, edited by C. Lotter and S. Peters. Cologne: Böhlau.

Pinker, Steven. 1994. *The Language Instinct*. New York: Morrow.

Pleßner, Helmuth. 1959. *Die verspätete Nation*. Stuttgart.

Popper, Karl R. 1958. *The Logic of Scientific Discovery*. London: Hutchinson.

Postone, Moishe. 1993. Germany's Future and Its Unmastered Past. In *From Bundesrepublik to Deutschland*, edited by M. G. Huelshoff et. al., Ann Arbor: University of Michigan Press.

Ricoeur, Paul. 1979. The Human Experience of Time and Narrative. *Research in Phenomenology* 9 (25): 17-34.

—. 1983-5. *Time and Narrative*. Translated by Kathleen McLaughlin.

David Pellauer. 3 vols. Chicago: The University of Chicago Press.

Risse-Kappen, Thomas, ed. 1995. *Bringing Transnational Relations Back In: Non-State Actors, Domestic Structures, and International Institutions*. New York: Cambridge University Press.

Rittberger, Volker. 1990. International Regimes in the CSCE Region: From Anarchy to Governance and Stable Peace. *Österreichische Zeitschrift für Politikwissenschaft* (19): 349-64.

—. 1993. Research on Internationalal Regimes in Germany: The Adaptive Internationalization of an American Social Science Concept. In *Regime Theory and International Relations*, edited by V. Rittberger. New York: Oxford University Press.

Rittberger and P. Mayer. Oxford: Oxford University Press.

Robinson, William I. 1996. Globalisation: nine theses on our epoch. *Race and Class* 38 (2): 13-31.

Rouse, Joseph. 1987. *Knowledge and Power: Toward a Political Philosophy of Science*. Ithaca: Cornell University Press.

Rupert, Mark. 1995. *Producing Hegemony*. Cambridge: Cambridge University Press.

—. 1997. Globalization and the Reconstruction of Common Sense in the US. In S. Gill and J. Mittelman, eds., *Innovation and Transformation in International Studies*. Cambridge: Cambridge University Press

Schneider, Theodor, and E. Deuerlein, eds. 1970. *Reichsgründung 1870/71. Tatsachen, Kontroversen, Interpretationen*. Stuttgart.

Schöllgen, Gregor. 1993. *Angst vor der Macht*. Berlin: Ullstein.

—. 1994. National Interest and International Responsibility: Germany's Role in World Affairs. In *Germany's New Position in Europe*, edited by A. Baring. Oxford: Berg Publishers.

Schönbohm, Jörg. 1995. Deutsche Sicherheits- und Verteidigungspolitik vor europäischen und globalen Herausforderungen. Paper read at "Germany's New Foreign Policy" (Conference sponsored by the German Society for Foreign Policy), April 26, at Strausberg.

Schulze, Hagen, ed. 1987. *Nation-Building in Central Europe*. New York: Berg.

Schwan, Alexander. 1987. German Liberalism and the National Question in the Nineteenth Century. In *Nation-Building in Central Europe*, edited by H. Schulze. New York: Berg Publishers.

Schwarz, Hans-Peter. 1985. *Die gezähmten Deutschen. Von der Machtbesessenheit zur Machtvergessenheit*. Stuttgart: Deutsche Verlagsanstalt.

—. 1990. Das Ende der Identitätsneurose. *Rheinische Merkur*, 7 September 1990.

——. 1994. Germany's National and European Interests. *Daedalus* 123 (2): 81-105.

Schweigler, Gebhard. 1973. *Nationalbewusstsein in der BRD und der DDR.* Duesseldorf.

Schweitzer, C.C., and et. al., eds. 1995. *Politics and Government in Germany 1944-1994: Basic Documents.* Providence: Berghahn Books.

Schwilk, Heimo, and Ulrich Schacht, eds. 1994. *Die selbstbewußte Nation. "Anschwellender Bockgesang" und weitere Beiträge zu einer deutschen Debatte.* Berlin: Ullstein.

Searle, John. 1969. *Speech Acts.* Cambridge: Cambridge University Press.

Senghaas, Dieter. 1990. *Europa 2000: Ein Friedensplan.* Frankfurt a.M.: Suhrkamp.

——. 1992. Weltinnenpolitik–Ansätze für ein Konzept. *Europa-Archiv* (22): 643-652.

——. 1994. Global Governance: How could this be conceived? Paper read at Loccum Conference on Peace, at Loccum, Germany.

Shapiro, Michael J. 1991. Sovereignty and Exchange in the Orders of Modernity. *Alternatives* 16 (4).

——. 1989. Textualizing Global Politics. In *International/Intertextual Relations,* edited by J. Der Derian and M. J. Shapiro. New York: Macmillan.

Siedschlag, Alexander. 1995. *Die aktive Beteiligung Deutschlands an militärische Aktionen zur Verwirklichung Kollektiver Sicherheit.* Frankfurt a.M.: Peter Lang.

Singer, Max, and Aaron Wildavsky. 1993. *The Real World Order: Zones of Peace and Zones of Turmoil.* Chatham, N.J.: Chatham House Publishers.

Smith, Anthony. 1983. *Theories of Nationalism.* New York: Holmes and Meier.

Smith, Gordon, William E. Paterson, and Stephen Padgett, eds. 1996. *Developments in German Politics.* Durham, N.C.: Duke University Press.

Smith, Woodruff D. 1986. *The Ideological Origins of Nazi Imperialism.* New York: Oxford University Press.

Sokal, Alan. 1996. Transgressing the Boundaries: An Afterward. *Dissent* 43 (Fall): 93-9.

Sørensen, George. 1992. Kant and Processes of Democratization: Consequences for Neorealist Thought. *Journal of Peace Research* 9:937-414.

Spegele, Roger D. 1996. *Political Realism in International Theory.* New York: Cambridge University Press.

Spero, Joan. 1977. *The Politics of International Economic Relations.* New York: St. Martin's Press.

Stares, Paul B., ed. 1992. *The New Germany and the New Europe.* Washington D.C.: Brookings Institution.

Stürmer, Michael. 1992. *Die Grenzen der Macht: Begegnung der Deutschen mit der Geschichte.* Berlin: Siedler.

—. 1994. Security Policy as seen from Germany. In *Aspects of Security Policy in a New Europe,* edited by K. Gottstein. Starnberg: XIVth ISODARCO Summer Course.

Szabo, Stephen F. 1990. *The Changing Politics of German Security.* New York: St. Martin's Press.

—. 1992. *The Diplomacy of German Unification.* New York: St. Martin's Press.

Todorov, Tzvetan. 1987. *The Conquest of America.* Translated by Richard Howard. New York: Harper Torchbooks.

Townson, Michael. 1992. *Mother-Tongue and Fatherland: Language and politics in German.* Manchester: Manchester University Press/St. Martin's.

Trabant, Jürgen. 1995. Thunder, Girls and Sheep, and Other Origins of Language. Budapest: Collegium Budapest.

Trautmann, Günter, ed. 1991. *Die Häßlichen Deutschen? Deutschland im Spiegel der westlichen und östlichen Nachbarn.* Darmstadt: Wissenschaftliche Buchgesellschaft.

Unger, Frank, and Bradley S. Klein. 1994. Between Globalism and Nationalism in Post-Cold War German Political Economy. In *The Global Economy as Political Space,* edited by S. J. Rosow, N. Inayatullah and M. Rupert. Boulder: Lynne Rienner.

Usher, Roland G. 1913. *Pan-Germanism*. Boston: Houghton Mifflin.

van der Pijl, Kees. 1994. The Reich Resurrected? Continuity and Change in German Expansion. In *Transcending the State-Global Divide: a Neostructuralist Agenda in International Relations*, edited by R. Palan and B. Gills. Boulder: Lynne Rienner.

Verheyen, Dirk, and Christian Soe, eds. 1993. *The Germans and Their Neighbors*. Boulder: Westview Press.

Vogt, Wolfgang R. 1994. Weltgesellschaft und Weltinnenpolitik: Begriffsklärungen und Modellbildungen. Paper read at Loccum Conference on Peace, at Loccum, Germany.

von Dirke, Sabine. 1996. Where were you 1933-1945? The Legacy of the Nazi Past Beyond the Zero Hour. In *Revisiting the Zero Hour 1945: The Emergence of Postwar German Culture*, edited by S. Brockmann and F. Trommler. Washington, D.C.: American Institute for Contemporary German Studies.

Walker, R.B.J. 1993. *Inside/Outside: International Relations as Political Theory*. New York: Cambridge University Press.

Wallerstein, Immanuel. 1995. *Historic Capitalism with Capitalist Civilization*. Seventh Impression. New York: Verso.

Warnke, Georgia. 1987. *Gadamer: Hermeneutics, Tradition and Reason*. Stanford: Stanford University Press.

Weber, Cynthia. 1995. *Simulating Sovereignty*. New York: Cambridge University Press.

Wertheimer, Mildred. 1971. *The Pan-German League 1890-1914*. New York: Octagon.

Wette, Wolfram. 1994. Neue Normalität. In *Extremismus der Mitte*, edited by H.-M. Lohmann. Frankfurt a.M.: Fischer Verlag.

White, Hayden. 1981. The Value of Narrativity in the Representation of Reality. In *On Narrative*, edited by W. J. T. Mitchell. Chicago: University of Chicago Press.

White, Stephen K. 1991. *Political Theory and Postmodernism*. Cambridge: Cambridge University Press.

Wickert, Ulrich, ed. 1990. *Angst vor Deutschland?* Hamburg.

Wilson, Woodrow. 1918. *Address of the President of the United States delivered at a joint session of the two houses of Congress, April 2, 1917.* Cambridge, MA: Riverside Press.

Wœver, Ole. 1997. Figures of international thought: introducing persons instead of paradigms. In *The Future of International Relations: Masters in the Making,* edited by I. B. Neumann. and O. Wœver. New York: Routledge.

Wolin, Richard. 1995. Review of Chomsky's World Orders, Old and New. *Dissent* (Summer).

Wood, Ellen Meiksins. 1995. *Democracy Against Capitalism.* New York: Cambridge University Press.

Wurm, Clemens, ed. 1995. *Western Europe and Germany: The Beginnings of European Integration.* Oxford: Oxford University Press.

Wyden, Peter. 1989. *Wall: The Inside Story of Divided Berlin.* New York: Simon and Schuster.

Zitelmann, Rainer. 1993. Wiedervereinigung und deutscher Selbsthass: Probleme mit dem eigenen Volk. In *Deutschland. Eine Nation–doppelte Geschichte,* edited by W. Weidenfeld. Cologne.

—. 1994. Position und Begriff. Über eine neue demokratische Rechte. In *Die Selbstbewusste Nation,* edited by H. Schwilk and U. Schacht. Berlin: Ullstein.

—, and et. al., eds. 1993. *Westbindung.* Berlin: Ullstein.

Zizek, Slavoj. 1993. *Tarrying with the Negative: Kant, Hegel, and the Critique of Ideology.* Durham: Duke University Press.

Zürn, Michael. 1987. *Gerechte internationale Regime.* Frankfurt a.M.

—. 1993. Bringin the Second Image (Back) In: About the Domestic Sources of Regime Formation. In *Regime Theory and International Relations,* edited by V. Rittberger and P. Mayer. Oxford: Oxford University Press.

OFFICIAL DOCUMENTS:

Aussenpolitik der Bundesrepublik Deutschland: Dokumente von 1949 bis 1994.

Auswärtiges Amt, Referat Öffentlichkeitsarbeit, Köln, Verlag für Wissenschaft und Politik, 1995.

Deutsche Aussenpolitik 1990/91: Eine Dokumentation, Auswärtiges Amt, München.

Bonn Aktuell.

Stenographic Reports of the German Parliament (Protocols of Parliamentary Debates).

Speeches, Declarations, and Announcements in *Bulletin*, Presse- und Informationsamt der Bundesregierung.

Official Party Documents (CDU/CSU, SPD, FDP, die Grünen).

Personal interviews with German policy-makers.

NEWSPAPERS AND MAGAZINES:

Franfurter Allgemeine Zeitung

Frankfurter Rundschau

The International Herald Tribune

The New York Times

Das Parlament

Der Spiegel

Süddeutsche Zeitung

Die Tageszeitung

Index